HIRING EXCELLENCE

PAT MacMILLAN

HIRING EXCELLENCE

SIX STEPS TO MAKING GOOD PEOPLE DECISIONS

NAVPRESS

BRINGING TRUTH TO LIFE
NavPress Publishing Group
P.O. Box 35001, Colorado Springs, Colorado 80935

The Navigators is an international Christian
organization. Jesus Christ gave His followers
the Great Commission to go and make disciples
(Matthew 28:19). The aim of The Navigators is
to help fulfill that commission by multiplying
laborers for Christ in every nation.

NavPress is the publishing ministry of The Navigators. NavPress publications are tools to help
Christians grow. Although publications alone cannot make disciples or change lives, they can help
believers learn biblical discipleship, and apply
what they learn to their lives and ministries.

© 1992 by Pat MacMillan
All rights reserved. No part of this publication
    may be reproduced in any form without
    written permission from NavPress, P.O. Box
    35001, Colorado Springs, CO 80935.
Library of Congress Catalog Card Number:
    92-61233
ISBN 08910-96914

Some of the anecdotal illustrations in this
book are true to life and are included with the
permission of the persons involved. All other
illustrations are composites of real situations,
and any resemblance to people living or dead is
coincidental.

Unless otherwise identified, all Scripture in this
publication is from the *Holy Bible: New International Version* (NIV). Copyright © 1973, 1978,
1984, International Bible Society. Used by permission of Zondervan Bible Publishers. Another
version used is the *New American Standard Bible*
(NASB), © The Lockman Foundation 1960, 1962,
1963, 1968, 1971, 1972, 1973, 1975, 1977.

Printed in the United States of America

FOR A FREE CATALOG OF
NAVPRESS BOOKS & BIBLE STUDIES,
CALL TOLL FREE 1-800-366-7788 (USA)
or 1-416-499-4615 (CANADA)

Contents

*To my wife, Jill,
for many years of prayer and
encouragement in all of the challenging areas
of life—raising godly children,
maintaining a healthy, growing marriage,
my Christian walk, building a business,
running, and writing. Marrying her was the best
people decision I ever made.*

Acknowledgments

The writing of this book has been, in the very truest sense, a team effort. The team members include my wife, Jill, who has been an unwavering source of encouragement and counsel. My kids, Becki, Jennifer, and Matthew, who have put up with my long hours at the keyboard in return for less time with them, taking that time to support their father in prayer. Gordon MacDonald, who for years has encouraged me to write, probably comes the closest to being a mentor to me in the area of communication. The staff of Team Resources who over the many years have taught me many of the principles that we have presented in this book. Terry Parker and Wendell Bird, two tremendously competent Christian attorneys who provided some technical guidance on the legal issues presented in this book. Dr. Timothy Irwin, a Christian industrial psychologist with whom I've worked for many years who helped me frame a number of the key ideas I present, particularly in the use of testing as an evaluation strategy. John Hoover, international vice president of Walk Thru the Bible Ministries, who took my many calls from phone booths all over the country to help me understand a scripture text. Dr. Os Guinness and John Seel who introduced me to the Puritan concept of calling and then tutored me to understanding. Charles Dunahoo and Dr. R. C. Sproul who helped me navigate some of the theological issues. And Pam McFee, my secretary who spent a good number of late nights and long weekends typing the manuscript. But more than just typing, she provided keen editorial insights and, most importantly, a bubbly, sparkling personality that pressed a lot of joy into what could have become a very onerous task.

Preface

THIS IS A BOOK about decision making. Its purpose is to provide executives with a practical, proven process for making people decisions—decisions about whom to place and promote as we staff the organizations we lead.

I'm writing particularly to Christian executives who make such decisions. Executives in both for-profit corporations and not-for-profit ministries. Executives who see the human side of their enterprise as a ministry and therefore take decisions involving this dimension very seriously.

As we attempt to match the people and the positions in our organizations, we need to become skilled in assessing both the demands of the job and the gifts and skills of the individuals we consider for it. I believe God is personally and vitally interested in the lives of Christians and in organizational endeavors committed to serving His purposes. Therefore, I believe He's interested and can be involved in the people decisions we make.

In Exodus we find God's involvement in both sides of the equation. Exodus 26 tells us that God gave Moses the plans for the Tabernacle—elaborate, detailed plans that, including implements and garments, take four chapters (Exodus 25–28) to describe.

11

These plans were, in some respects, position profiles for the crafts-men who were to undertake the job.

This was no small endeavor. To make things more difficult we might assume that the Israelites weren't skilled artisans, but rather manual laborers who made bricks of clay and built stor-age cities for the Egyptians (Exodus 1:8-11). In Exodus 35 God provides both the material and the people resources to imple-ment His plan. In Exodus 35:31-33, God set aside Bezalel and "filled him with the Spirit of God, with skill, ability and knowl-edge in all kinds of crafts . . . to engage in all kinds of artistic craftsmanship."

But God didn't stop there. He gave Bezalel a heart to teach others these skills as well. Moses summarizes God's human resource efforts in Exodus 36:1: "So Bezalel, Oholiab and every skilled person to whom the LORD has given skill and ability to know how to carry out all the work of constructing the sanctuary are to do the work just as the Lord has commanded."

God has equipped people to meet *your* organizational needs as well. Your task is to find and recognize them. That's what this book is all about.

One might wonder why I would write a book about hiring people in an era in which many organizations, corporations, and ministries are looking to downsize their structures rather than build them. Industry is confronted with a rapidly changing, tur-bulent global economy in which competitive intensity increases daily. New terms are beginning to penetrate the management lexicon—total quality, continuous improvement, and teamwork seem to be the most prevalent themes. These are not passing fads, but the first hints of a new management philosophy that must become sovereign in U.S. organizations.

In the corporate arena, increasing competition forces us to operate with leaner, more agile structures, and in the course of "delayering" the corporate behemoths of the late 1970s and 1980s, U.S. companies are pruning two to four entire layers of management from their structures. These leaner organizations have neither the time nor the resources to do things twice; thus, they must focus on getting it right the first time. They must learn to squeeze every ounce of synergy out of the few people who remain.

Christian ministries are confronted with the same economies and will follow suit as they, too, adapt structures and strategies better tailored to the 1990s. Both arenas will have fewer people. *This doesn't deemphasize the importance of people decisions, but rather increases it.* The fewer number of people we have, the more important each person becomes, and the more important the decisions made in selecting and placing those people become.

I am writing this book to executives in both corporate and Christian not-for-profit organizations because I want to communicate the biblical principles that we can apply in our people decisions in whatever arena such choices are made. However, there are some factors that complicate my effort. For example, the legal dimensions of people decisions in the corporate arena are much more constraining than those that confront executives in not-for-profit ministries. In such situations I attempt to explore the implications for people decisions in both environments.

To a large extent, this book is a combination of process and principles. Those of you who make numerous people decisions in the areas of selection, placement, and promotion may want to read it cover to cover. Others, who make such decisions less frequently, might want to refer to specific topics on an as-needed basis.

The book is organized into four sections: (1) "The Costs, Benefits, and Steps of the Hiring Process"; (2) "Finding the 'Fit' Between Job and Candidate"; (3) "Evaluating the Candidates and Making the Decision"; (4) "The Ongoing Process of Staffing and Recruiting." Within that structure you will learn six critical steps that can make your hiring decisions more effective. I hope this book will assist you in making great people decisions.

PAT MACMILLAN

PART ONE

THE COSTS, BENEFITS, AND STEPS OF THE HIRING PROCESS

CHAPTER ONE

Who Hired
This Person, Anyway?

BILL ATKINS STARED pensively out of his study window attempting to order his thoughts for his upcoming meeting with Steve. He
wasn't looking forward to the next hour. Deciding to let Steve go
had been one of the toughest decisions of his life.

First Church had grown dramatically during the first years
of Bill's tenure. Last year the elders had become convinced that,
if growth was to continue, it was time to bring on an associate
pastor.

Steve clearly stood out above the rest of the candidates. He
had graduated at the top of his seminary class and, prior to that,
had a short but successful career in business. He demonstrated
excellent platform skills and had impressed the search committee
with his knowledgeable answers, poise, and self-confidence during
the interview process. The decision to hire Steve was unanimous
and enthusiastic. Things were really going to take off now!

Three months later the problems began to surface. Sally, the
church secretary, was the first to complain. Not long after that
Andy, the youth pastor, dropped by for counsel on how he might
work better with Steve. Mrs. Phillips, head of the lay mission
council, resigned in frustration over things "not worth discussing."

The Christian education department was split in domestic warfare. The common thread running through all of these incidents was Steve. Over time the pattern became clear. Steve, despite all of his gifts, was not a team player. Although excellent on the platform relating to a group, he was an interpersonal disaster in a situation demanding cooperation. Bill had had numerous sessions with Steve over these past seven months, as had Bernie Johnson, the chairman of the elders. It was like trying to talk to a brick wall.

Instead of being the hoped-for catalyst for growth at First Church, Steve had just the opposite effect. A number of families even left because of the conflicts. "Where did I go wrong?" Bill pondered as he waited for Steve to arrive. "He seemed so qualified . . . so right for the job." There was a knock on the study door. Bill sighed as he rose from his chair and started across the room.

IT ALL STARTS WITH THE HIRING DECISION

Bill Atkins' story is not uncommon. During the past ten years I've spent many hundreds of hours working with leaders of both Christian and secular organizations as they have wrestled with how to handle their "Steves."

Over the years I have become convinced that a major—if not *the* major—ingredient to successful leadership is effective followers. Now, there are several ingredients for effectiveness—for example, motivation, skills, resources, strategy, etc. However, it all starts with the leader's decision to hire (or place from within the organization) an individual for a specific position. Your ability to choose effective people will not only determine your ultimate success as a leader but will greatly influence the amount of energy you expend to achieve that success.

People well suited for their individual tasks are invariably more positive in their attitude than those less suited. They are more motivated and productive, demonstrate higher levels of creativity and initiative, and make a more significant contribution to your overall objectives. Those not so well suited for their jobs contribute less and consume a disproportionate amount of management time and effort. Frequently there is little hope of remedy, short of relocation, for a bad placement decision.

"To make a decision," says well-known author Peter Drucker, "is the specific task of an executive . . . effective executives, therefore, make effective decisions."[1] I agree. Furthermore, I believe that people decisions are the most important and difficult decisions a leader will make. And that's what this book is about: making good people decisions.

WELLSPRINGS OF ORGANIZATIONAL SUCCESS

God's process is people, and as we study the Scriptures we must conclude that He wants us to team up to accomplish the tasks He has given us. Like Bill Atkins, many of us have found that in choosing our team, we often encounter both the promises and the problems of ministry or business.

People, not plans or products, are the wellspring of organizational success. And, although we bundle them together into various structural groupings from teams to corporations—from churches to conglomerates—individuals are the basic building blocks of any group or organizational effort. It invariably falls to an individual to enter data, to type a letter, to discover a new process, or to make a decision. Your success will ultimately be determined by the quality of the people you recruit.

Leroy Eims, former president of The Navigators, tells of a story he heard while attending a Christian conference that illustrates how vital Jesus' men were to His mission. The conference speaker shared that "When the Lord Jesus returned to heaven after His resurrection, one of the angels asked Him a question: 'What plan do You have to continue the work You began on earth?'

"Without hesitation Jesus answered, 'I left it in the hands of the apostles.'

"Another angel asked, 'What if they fail?'

"Again there was no hesitation, 'I have no other plan.'"

Eims says that the speaker was quick to note this was only a story, but it got the point across: Humanly speaking, the future of Christianity fell on the shoulders of these twelve men.[2]

People decisions are not only important, but also time-consuming and complex. However, there are processes and principles that can help us to be much more effective in our selection efforts. Many of these principles have their roots in God's Word. Have you ever noticed that some of the most memorable stories in the Bible are those describing the choosing of the men and women for God's assignments?

As we reflect on passages about Gideon, David, Moses, Esther, Paul, the apostles, and many other biblical characters, many of the details we remember most vividly center around God actually choosing them. We can derive a number of key principles for our people decisions from these incidents in which God selected His staff.

A PRACTICAL, TIMED-TESTED PROCESS
FOR MAKING GOOD PEOPLE DECISIONS

This book presents a practical, time-tested process that will greatly enhance your ability to recognize and select excellent people for your ministry team. The focus is on the selection process, which, if successful, can eliminate many of the more difficult, painful people decisions. We will also explore the subject of recruiting and performance problems as they relate to or touch the selection process.

In the chapters that follow, you will learn:

1. How to accurately define the demands and requirements of a given task or job.
2. How to develop an effective, exacting list of qualities and qualifications describing candidates who have the greatest potential to be a success in the position.
3. How to successfully screen candidates through the use of résumés, interviews, tests, and referencing.
4. How to apply key principles of selection and decision

making to each step of the process, thereby multiplying your effectiveness.

5. How to avoid common pitfalls to effective selection.
6. How to find, challenge, and recruit winners for your ministry team.

Let's start by identifying the costs and benefits associated with our people decisions. For it is a clear understanding of the pain or the promise each potential staff member can bring to our organization that motivates us to take such decisions seriously.

CHAPTER TWO

Counting the Cost

A FEW YEARS ago I met with the city coordinator for a client ministry's new strategy. He had been working for nearly a year trying to recruit participating churches to this effort. At the same time he was attempting to raise his personal support. He had made little progress in either area, and the ministry asked if I might get involved and try to help him. Minutes into my meeting with this young man I saw the problem. He was totally mismatched for the task of persuading pastors to get involved in this ministry program. He wasn't a communicator or an enthusiastic believer in this program. He would quietly and somewhat tentatively suggest this idea to a pastor and, in the face of any resistance, beat a hasty retreat. I was convinced no matter how much I or the ministry put into helping him succeed, he was doomed to failure. His gifts were definitely better suited for other tasks.

"He was the only one available." This was the ministry's response to my question about the reasons behind his assignment. "Atlanta was so vital to this new strategy, we didn't think we had a choice." Although this staff member had called on a lot of pastors during the past year, his ineffectiveness and poor presentations would make it much harder for his successor to establish a successful ministry. In some respects the ministry was further behind in achieving its goals than before he started.

The objective of any placement decision is to obtain the best possible fit between the person and the position. The greater the match, the greater the potential to succeed. To achieve the greatest match, the decision maker must know the demands of the task as well as the gifts, skills, and temperament of the people being considered for the position.

FIGURE 2.1

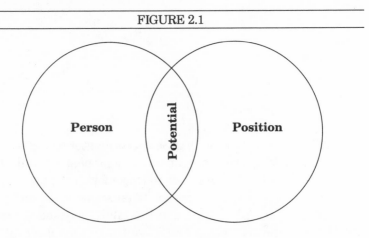

Although figure 2.1 depicts the objective of our decision, it fails to convey the complexity of the task. The selection process may appear to be straightforward, yet we tend to "blow it" quite often, primarily for three reasons.

First, the selection process involves many more unknowns than knowns. As we shall see, jobs are difficult to define, and the people who fill them are infinitely complex and their behavior somewhat inconsistent. People decisions are fraught with subjectivity, uncertainty, and risk. If we apply the principles outlined in this book, we can, at best, merely improve the odds. Judgment can be a fleeting, fragile attribute that, like all delicate mechanisms, sometimes breaks down under the load. Even the best people decision makers occasionally blow it.

Second, the selection process is hard work, the complexity of which prompts many leaders and search committees to make quick decisions, leaving the results to chance (often referred to as "the Lord" in their closing prayers). By being unwilling to invest the time and effort necessary to do the job right at the outset, they often find that to remedy the situation later is much more costly.

Finally, making good people decisions is a skill. It involves knowledge of human nature and proficient application of certain processes and principles. Not knowing the process or how to skillfully apply it causes us to fall back on the old standbys of intuition and gut feeling. The result is a decrease in odds of what already promises to be a high-risk game of chance.

There may be no such thing as perfect people decisions, but there can be better ones. Knowledge can be gained and skills learned, yet making good people decisions will always remain hard work. Drucker reminds us:

> People decisions are time-consuming, for the simple reason that the Lord did not create people as resources for the organization. They do not come in the proper size or shape for the tasks to be done in the organization—and they cannot be machined down or recast for these tasks. People are almost always "almost fits" at best. To get the job done with people (and no other resources available) therefore requires lots of time, thought, and judgment.[1]

The managers who invest time and energy to make good people decisions are those who have a clear understanding of the benefits and potential of a good decision, as well as the costs of a poor one. Let's start by exploring the downside in regards to cost.

Generally, mistakes in people decisions aren't immediately obvious. But when they do become apparent, we invariably go through a long, drawn-out, expensive process of analysis and attempted solutions. Instead of taking fast action to solve problems by transfer, training, or restructuring the task, we often delay, hoping the problems will solve themselves. And they seldom do.

When the basic fit between the person and the position is flawed, things usually become worse over time, not better. Often, another cause of delay is some feeling of guilt on the part of the hiring manager—"After all, I hired this person." So instead of moving against the problem quickly and objectively, we let things drift while we ponder possible causes—lack of management, inadequate training, more time for adjustment, and other possible issues that influence job performance. Although all of this is right and appropriate, it's important to remember that it takes time for the problem of a mismatch to surface and be resolved. In the meantime, you can't put the needs of your organization "on hold" until you get it worked out. And as you work through the process, several types of costs continue to mount.

DIRECT DOLLAR COSTS

The cost of a mismatch can be significant. We have estimated that the dollar cost of a mis-hire of a secretary in our firm is more than $17,000. Assuming that the secretary's annual salary was $22,000, that he or she was in the position for six months, and that during that time the person was 50 percent effective, our calculations looked something like this:

Interview time by staff other than the hiring manager	$500
Wasted salary (assume six months at 50 percent effectiveness)	$5,500
Wasted benefits	$2,200
Severance	$2,100
Training on our computer systems	$2,200
Wasted time, morale, etc., on the part of other staff	$4,000
Business loss, client problems, etc.	$1,000
TOTAL	$17,500

Imagine the cost in a similar situation of an associate pastor, a ministry head, a vice president of marketing, etc. These individuals have much higher salaries and more interaction with those they serve outside their organization. Using calculations similar to those above, a consulting psychologist estimated the costs of replacing a $20,000/year factory supervisor would be $36,500; replacing a $50,000/year salesperson would cost $171,500; replacing a $150,000/year technical manager would run about $380,000.[2] In February 1968, Henry Ford II hired Semon E. ("Bunkie") Knudsen from General Motors to become the new president of Ford. The chemistry between the two didn't work out, and nineteen months later Knudsen was terminated with a severance package estimated at $1.5 million! Pretty expensive chemistry lesson on Ford's part. Bunkie's replacement was Lee Iacocca.

Close Calls Dull Productivity

Blatantly obvious mistakes don't cause nearly as much organizational harm as close calls. Often, "borderline" employees create the biggest drain on our organizational resources. These employees live close to, but not within, acceptable boundaries of performance. These are the people who, although they seldom pull their own weight, always seem right on the verge of "making it." We're confident all they need is just a little more time, a little more training, a little more management help. It's these "borderline" employees who soak up most of our creative energies while we ponder how to tap into the potential we're so sure is there. Alas, they never reach that potential, and the process of working with them often drags into years of low performance, bearing heavily on the organization, manager, and the individual employee. Some experts believe that a single, exceptional employee can accomplish as much or more work as that of three marginal employees! Later in this book we'll explore how to quickly determine whether an employee's lack of performance is merely the product of untapped potential or a result of a mismatch that has little hope of remedy.

INDIRECT COSTS

As expensive as the above figures appear, the most significant costs are not easily calculated in terms of hard dollars. The indirect costs can be devastating—lost ministry opportunities and creative insights, lost sales, unsolved problems, and frustrated clients or donors. The time and emotional drain placed on us and our managers by poor people decisions steal the cutting edge of our creativity and energy.

Let's now explore a few of the more common indirect, but no less costly, consequences of a mismatch.

Mismatches Usually Lower Morale

A few years ago, I was retained to perform a management audit by a large evangelical ministry. While interviewing their field staff, it became apparent that many of their senior staff were experiencing a great deal of frustration. As I probed for the cause, I found for the most part it resided with the newer staff members. This organization was a faith ministry, requiring staff members to raise their own financial support. Many of the senior staff were products of this ministry—they had been discipled by the organization and had demonstrated Christian maturity, as well as a significant commitment to the organization.

Desiring to expand the ministry at a more rapid rate, my client had successfully applied for a foundation grant to subsidize salaries for new staff members. This influx of funds allowed hiring to push ahead at a rapid rate, but in its rush to establish beachheads in new cities, the organization chose some people who didn't fit the mold established over the years. Many of these new staff members didn't have the maturity or commitment levels of older staff members. Expediency and availability ruled the selection process of new recruits.

It was obvious that a number of the new staff members would develop into capable employees. However, it was just as obvious that some, although good people, didn't have the Christian maturity or the needed ministry skills to be effective in their new positions. The older staff were alarmed at this influx of unqualified staff members; the ministry's previous commitment to a quality ministry seemed to be crumbling. The result was a significant drop in morale, less cooperation among staff, and the beginnings of a "we-they" attitude by the older staff. Instead of a larger, more effective ministry, this organization was reaping just the opposite. Not only had leaders selected several unqualified and less effective new staff members, but the lower morale of the senior staff made the ministry less effective overall. It's now nearly seven years later, and the majority of staff hired during that incident have either left to new endeavors or have been integrated into the ministry. Things are back to normal, but normal for this ministry is about four or five years behind where they could have been had they been more careful in their people decisions.

Ministry Impact
We've all collected personal examples of how we've been "folded, mutilated, or spindled" by some employee of an organization with whom we are trying to transact business. One of my favorites happened a few years ago when I took my wife for a few days of Christmas shopping in New York. At a well-known department store a young, overly tired salesclerk approached us at the scarf counter and said with all of her New York directness, "Yah, whatd'ya want?" We decided we didn't want anything and have often found ourselves a little resistant to subsequent shopping at this store. I wonder how many other customers this one employee turned off, unknown to management?

There are also ministry equivalents, and the story at the beginning of this chapter is one. To cite another example, years ago I managed the donor services department for a large evangelical ministry. I learned the hard way that I needed responsive, people-oriented staff handling donor complaint letters about lost or incorrect receipts. Otherwise, wars would break out. A staff member who didn't have the ability to empathize with the donor's frustration could quickly turn a minor border skirmish into a nuclear holocaust. Often it wasn't our mistake at all but rather inattention or oversight on the part of the donor. I needed people who could identify with the challenge of interpreting one of our receipt forms; who could say, "I can sure appreciate how you missed that section, Mrs. Smith; I do it all the time." But some of our people took a more defensive posture—"Mrs. Smith, everything is on the form. You forgot to designate your gift in section 3A." You can imagine how giving might go down if that sort of response persisted!

Wasted Management Time

I spend many hours with leaders of Christian and corporate organizations every month, and invariably the topic turns to strategies for dealing with problem employees. Many of these leaders openly confess they feel more encumbered than empowered by some of their key employees. They are frustrated because they invest many hours working through the "urgent" issues of problem employees, rather than planning and laying the tracks for the future of the ministry.

It seems that much of the time these leaders have available for their managers is spent dealing with staff problems, rather than developing more effective employees and ensuring that the ministry is accomplishing its God-given goals. Their most earnest efforts are being poured into minimizing the losses rather than maximizing the profits! The key is to spend the effort on the front end hiring excellent people, rather than on the back end repairing the damage.

Alfred Sloan, former chairman of General Motors, knew the benefits of effective hiring practices, as we see in the following story, told by Peter Drucker.

> During the years in which I attended the meetings of GM's top committees, the company made basic decisions on postwar policies such as capital investments, overseas expansion, the balance between automotive businesses, accessory businesses, and non-automotive businesses, union relations and financial structure. The wartime operations, which had taken the bulk of top management's time before 1943, had become routine. Sloan and his associates were free to turn to GM's postwar future. Yet I soon real-

ized that a disproportionate amount of time was taken up with decisions on people rather than decisions on policy. Moreover, Mr. Sloan, while actively involved in the decisions on policy, left to others the chairmanship of whatever committee dealt with a specific policy area. But in any decision on people he was in the chair.

Once the committee spent hours discussing the work and assignment of a position way down the line—as I remember it, the position of master mechanic in a small accessory division. As we went out, I turned to him and said, "Mr. Sloan, how can you afford to spend four hours on a minor job like this?" "This corporation pays me a pretty good salary," he said, "for making the important decisions, and for making them right. You tell me what more important decision there is than about the management people who do the job. Some of us up here at the fourteenth floor may be very bright; but if that master mechanic in Dayton is the wrong man, our decisions might as well be written on water. He converts them into performance. And as for taking a lot of time, that's horse apples" (his strongest and favorite epithet). "How many divisions do we have, Mr. Drucker?" Before I could answer this rhetorical question, he had whipped out his famous "little black book" and said, "Forty-seven. And how many decisions on people did we have to make last year?" I didn't know. "It was one hundred forty-three," he said, consulting his book, "or three per division, despite all the people who went off to wartime service. If we didn't spend four hours on placing a man and placing him right, we'd spend four hundred hours on cleaning up after our mistake—and that time I wouldn't have."[3]

Bad Decisions Tend to Perpetuate Themselves

If a mismatched employee is in a managerial position, the consequences of the bad placement decision will likely ricochet throughout the entire organization as his or her poor decisions and plans

are developed and implemented. If the manager has hiring authority, the problems are likely to grow geometrically. Like tends to
beget like, and in this case weak or unqualified managers generally hire even weaker ones.

Charles Garfield, in his book *Peak Performers*, illustrates
this concept with a story about David Ogilvy, founder of the
large advertising firm Ogilvy & Mather. He sends every new
manager a Russian Matreshka doll. This is a very unique carved
and hollow wooden doll. There are five dolls in all, four of which
contain smaller ones inside of them. Ogilvy inserted a message
in the smallest doll, which read: "If each of us hires people who
are smaller than we are, we shall become a company of dwarfs,
but if each of us hires people who are bigger than we are, Ogilvy
& Mather will become a company of giants."[4]

Lost Opportunities

On Thursday, July 13, 1978, Henry Ford III fired Lee Iacocca. On
November 2 of the same year, the board of directors of the Chrysler
Corporation hired him. In the span of only 110 days Iacocca stood
at ground zero of two critically important people decisions—one
dismally poor; the other most providential. Iacocca had been with
Ford for thirty-two years; he had been president for eight. During
that time he had given birth to Ford's best sellers—the Mustang
and the more recent Fiesta. During the two years preceding his
departure, Ford Motor Company experienced record earnings.
Few people could understand the rationale of Henry Ford's decision. In his autobiography, Iacocca attributes it to impulse. Not
the stuff of effective people decisions.

On Iacocca's first day on the job at Chrysler, the worst deficit
in earnings in the history of the company was announced. He went
to work, and the story of his efforts over the next few years was
played out across the headlines—the bets of how long the company would last, the precedent-setting government-backed loans,
the loan paybacks nearly seven years early, the launching of the
"K-car," and record earnings of nearly one billion dollars within
five years of his coming on board. You have to wonder what he

could have done at Ford in the same time period with thirty-two years of momentum and Ford's vast resources.

As you can see from this story, poor people decisions don't just result in the problems of a mismatch but also in lost opportunities. There are two sides to a selection decision. Not only must we wrestle with the costs of having the wrong person in the job, but also with the benefits lost because we did not recognize the right person.

Stewardship Principles Are Violated

Each of us was created by God with a specific temperament, unique gifts, and a parcel of aptitudes, abilities, and interests. When the job doesn't fit we know it. More importantly, we feel it—the pain, fear, frustration, lack of a sense of fulfillment and achievement so necessary to our sense of purpose as children of God.

In their excellent book *Your Work Matters to God*, Doug Sherman and William Hendricks remind us our work is very important, for through this facet of our lives we

- Serve people.
- Meet our own needs.
- Meet the needs of our family.
- Earn money to give to others.
- Love God.[5]

Let me add one more to this list: It is through the process and context of work that we can experience significant growth in the Christian character traits that are so vital to our personal ministry and walk with God. For example, learning to stick with a task, to do what we say we will do, and to manage our time can encourage the qualities of perseverance, faithfulness, and self-control. Work, like all other areas of life, provides an anvil against which God can hammer to shape and strengthen the character of His children.

As leaders we are, to some extent, stewards of those who work under our supervision. It is the leader/manager who knows the most about the job—its demands, resources, and needs. It is the leader/manager who has the resources for the necessary "due-diligence" for making a good decision, matching the person to the position. The quality of our placement decision can help or hinder those under our supervision to experience the aspects of work just described in their day-to-day activities. As hiring managers, we're not doing a very good job. The Marketing and Research Corporation of Princeton, New Jersey, reported in 1976 that "fifty to eighty percent of Americans are in the wrong jobs."[6]

As leaders, we need to become more aware of the stewardship responsibilities that are placed on us, both in hiring and in managing our staff. What is our role and responsibility in helping those who entrusted themselves to our leadership to grow to their fullest spiritual and human potential? Will we be able to say, "Lord, You placed a young, inexperienced person in my stewardship; I saw the potential and now return to You a growing, skilled individual worth more now to our organization or any other than when he or she first arrived"? Does the parable of the talents apply to our staff as it does to our skills, money, time, and all of the other resources the Lord places into our stewardship for Him? Failing to recognize this aspect of our role as leader/manager and our role in God's overall plan for the lives of our staff may be the biggest cost of all in poor people decisions.

Although understanding the costs of poor decisions is important, a grasp of the benefits of good selection decisions rather than the costs of poor ones should provide the best motivation to develop excellence in our people decisions. In the next chapter I explore those benefits.

CHAPTER THREE

It's Worth the Walk

WHEN I WAS about five years old, my father took me on my first
fishing trip in the beautiful Cascade Mountains of Washington.
After a three-hour drive into the mountains, we pulled off on the
side of the road and began to prepare for our day of fishing. While
Dad rummaged in the car trunk for our equipment, I was busy
exploring the nearby landscape. I quickly found a small trickle
of water at the bottom of the graded decline on the side of the
road. To my five-year-old mind, liberally endowed with imagina-
tion, this seemed like the perfect place to fish. The pop cans and
other roadside debris that clogged this tiny leak in the earth did
little to dent my enthusiasm as I headed back to the car to grab
my rod.

"Son," my dad called over his shoulder as I headed back down
the hill, "not here. We have a ways to go." As my pace began to
slow and my shoulders dropped, he went on to explain there were
no fish this close to the road; anything worth having had been
taken by others years ago.

An hour into the foothills provided plenty more opportunities
for my father to curb my desire to drop my line into numerous
small streams we crossed on the way to richer waters above. Again

and again he patiently explained that the really big fish were found in much less accessible waters. My frustration increased as we passed others who had stopped to try their luck in streams my father deemed too small. There were even times I could actually see fish milling about in the quieter pools. Many fishermen, especially five-year-olds, would have certainly considered these fish to be "keepers," if not actually in the "whale" category. But not Dad.

As we trekked through some of the most beautiful scenery in the country, both my father's power of persuasion and my own limits of patience were sorely tested. "Be patient, son," he repeated over and over on that long walk. "Bigger ones lay ahead." By the time we finally reached our destination I was practically foaming at the mouth.

Dad had led us to a small, high mountain lake where we spent the afternoon, practically to ourselves, pulling in beautiful, large rainbow trout. It was clear these keepers fell into the whale category. "You don't find fish like these by the side of the road," my dad reminded me.

Our early evening hike back to the car was all downhill, but it didn't go any faster than our walk that morning. The pace wasn't slowed by the pitch of the hill but rather by my insistence that we stop and compare our fish with those caught by fishermen we had passed earlier in the day. There was no comparison, and with each "ooh" and "aah," a key principle was being pressed into my mind: The best fish were found farthest from the road.

Years of consulting with organizations in their selection and staffing efforts have brought back many reminders of that fishing trip and the lessons it contained. Three of these follow:

- Exceptional people are less accessible and are difficult to find.
- Finding exceptional people is hard work, but worth the effort.
- We are often too quick to settle for acceptable versus exceptional ones.

THE PAYOFF IS IN PEOPLE

Excellent companies and good leaders appreciate the difference between an acceptable employee and the exceptional, gifted one. As we have already discovered, this difference is significant. Staff who are well matched to their tasks invariably demonstrate higher levels of initiative and creativity, stay longer, and produce more.

Such benefits do not come cheap. Finding excellent people is hard work. Marriott Hotels and Resorts is an organization that believes good people are the key to continued success, and as a result, they invest tremendous effort in finding their kind of people. Several years ago they interviewed 40,000 applicants for 1,200 positions as they opened the Marriott Marquis in New York City.[1]

It takes strong convictions to hold the quality line under stress, and filling that many jobs in a short period of time would stress any organization. Many would have buckled under the pressure and approved anyone who even appeared to come close to meeting their criteria. Solomon reminds us that anyone who hires a fool or any passerby is like an archer who wounds at random (Proverbs 26:10). As we saw in the previous chapter, binding the wounds and burying the dead from such an approach will take more time and effort than doing it right the first time. The CEOs described below believed that and demonstrated they knew where to find the highest return on their investment of time and energy.

Several years ago *Harvard Business Review* interviewed John Smale, chairman and CEO of Procter & Gamble. If one area stands out at P&G, it is brand management. In describing his role in the brand-management process, Smale indicated he usually left these important decisions to his managers and focused his attention on "basic strategic issues." I wondered as I read the article, what could be more strategic to the CEO of P&G than making good brand decisions? The curiosity of the interviewer was aroused as well. "What do you mean, strategic issues?" she asked.

Smale's response was focused on the people side versus the

product side of the enterprise: "Where are we going? Are we organized properly, not just in a sense of having the right people in the right jobs, but in the sense of, Is the organization structured so that we can get as much as we ought to from the creativity of our employees? Are we hiring the right caliber of people we need? Are we hiring enough of them? Are our personnel policies encouraging the development of people and their participation in the business?"[2]

Another executive also emphasizes the importance of the selection decision. Shortly after Jack Welch was promoted to CEO of General Electric, he was invited to speak to a group of Harvard Business School students about his plans for the company. One of the students asked him what he considered to be his most important task as CEO. Welch answered without hesitation, "Choosing and developing good people."[3]

The selection of good people is so important that the CEOs of both P&G and GE consider it their primary task. Another "CEO" gives us an indication of the importance of people decisions. If Jesus was anything, He was a man of prayer. Over and over in the gospel accounts of His ministry on earth, we see Him retreating to be alone with God, His Father, in prayer. As we study the pace and pattern of His life, we are convinced He spent many whole nights in prayer. However, only one instance in the New Testament, Luke 6:12-13, categorically states that He spent the entire night in prayer. This was when He was confronted with a most important decision—choosing the twelve apostles. The Lord knew the importance of this decision. The success of His earthly ministry strategy depended on these key selection decisions.

COST-BENEFIT ANALYSIS

Although the costs and consequences of poor selection should prompt us to be more attentive to hiring decisions, research clearly shows it is the promise of benefits that motivate extra effort to produce good people decisions. Careful selection is worth it. You not only minimize your chances of incurring the costs described in the previous chapter, but there are definite benefits as well. Developing the skill of making good people decisions and expending the necessary effort will allow you to:

- Select people whose temperaments mesh more favorably with your work environment and the specific task for which you choose them.
- Select people whose needs and motivations blend most favorably with your organization.
- Reduce direct and indirect costs of poor placement and rechannel those dollars to assets and resources that contribute more directly to your organization.
- Channel scarce management resources away from people problems into areas of planning, decision making, and the development of your most promising employees.
- Watch as staff who are well matched to their tasks demonstrate higher levels of initiative, innovation, and creativity.
- Increase ministry and organizational impact as people operate out of areas of strength and giftedness.

These kinds of benefits aren't found lying around easily available to any casual passerby. Benefits of this magnitude are like those fish I caught with my dad. Their habitats were hard to find and difficult to get to. Most fishermen didn't have the motivation and energy to walk that far. But, as I discovered, they were worth the walk.

CHAPTER FOUR

Six Steps
to Staffing Excellence

I WAS TIRED. It was 7:00 p.m. on a Friday, and I was looking forward to a restful weekend. As I was packing my briefcase, I got a phone call from a young pastor in southern California.

"I hope it's not too late," he started—I could sense from the tenor and tone of his voice that I needed to stop and talk. "We need your help on some hiring decisions," he explained. "Yesterday, after nearly six months of agonizing, we let go an associate pastor."

This young man went on to recount that he was the pastor of a fifteen-hundred-person church that was only five years old. The church had grown rapidly, and this man and his staff frequently wondered what they were doing leading such a large group. He was concerned because his elders and congregation put so much faith in his leadership and expertise when, in fact, he knew he was sorely lacking in these critical areas. Now he was confronted with outright failure.

They had hired an associate pastor, and for the past year and a half had run into one major problem after another. Basically, the associate pastor's skills were not up to the job, and as a result, important tasks had dropped through the cracks, relationships were bruised, and ministry opportunities lost. It was very clear to the elders and congregation that they had the wrong man in the wrong spot. In trying to fix the problem, things had gone from bad to worse. It was obvious that this young man was agonizing over the decision, feeling poorly and somewhat guilty that he had been the primary decision maker. "We never want this to happen again," he explained. "From here on out we'd like to send every potential candidate to Atlanta for you to interview and test."

Although I'd love to have the business, I would have been going to extremes to advise a medium-sized church in southern California to incur such an expense and process to make basic hiring decisions. It was also clear that this young pastor/leader had lost confidence in his ability to make people decisions. He was still in pain from his previous decision and fearful of the next one.

All decisions are difficult, but few carry more stress than people decisions. Complex, difficult, risky people decisions make formidable adversaries, even to the most capable executives. The typical people decision is like a snowball at the top of the hill. It starts off small and manageable, but as it moves through the process it gathers momentum and grows in size and complexity.

Not long after we "start the ball rolling" a number of challenging questions begin to surface:

- Should we hire to meet current organizational needs or try to anticipate future ones?
- To what extent should we be willing to trade a candidate's present skills for promising potential?
- How do we know when we have enough data to make a decision?

As we interview more people, we discover there is no end to the information we can collect about them. We're not only buried under an avalanche of raw data, but we discover that virtually nothing we know about one candidate is comparable to another.

Finally, throughout the entire process we have carried a picture of the perfect candidate in our head, a picture that invariably fails to even come close to describing any of the people under consideration. But on what criteria do we compromise, and to what extent? By now our decision has "snowballed" into a cumbersome, complex, and confusing tangle of considerations.

With our decision-making circuits overloaded, the process has become bogged down. However, we can deploy several strategies to dig out—one is to delay, letting the dust clear until we can see better. Another is to finish it fast—make an impulsive decision and hope for the best. Some will rationalize, lower their standards, and compromise. In the face of a house-sized snowball rumbling down the mountain, many executives invest more energy and creativity in circumventing the decision than in confronting it. Here our intuition shouts to join the process. But instead of using it judiciously, we often default entirely to gut feelings, tossing the rational elements of our process aside for the sake of expediency. This doesn't sound like a decision, but more like throwing darts at a dartboard from twenty feet away, blindfolded!

Pretend for a moment that we can look into the future and examine all the hiring and placement decisions we'll ever make and contrast those decisions to actual performance. We might organize our thoughts on the matrix shown in figure 4.1.

FIGURE 4.1

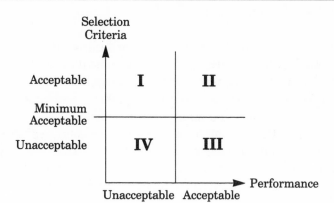

On the vertical axis we have our selection criteria—the qualities and qualifications necessary to do the job. The higher on this axis you move, the better qualified the candidate is. However, for simplicity, we'll separate this axis into acceptable (candidate appears qualified) and unacceptable. On the horizontal axis, we show performance, merely indicating acceptable versus unacceptable.

We can organize our matrix into four quadrants, which can be described as follows:

   I. Candidates appeared qualified and were therefore hired. However, they did not perform. *Poor decision.*

  II. Candidates appeared qualified, were hired, and performed acceptably. *Good decision.*

III. Candidates did not appear qualified, and were not hired. But had they been hired, they would have had acceptable performance. We lost out on good people. *Poor decision.*

IV. Candidates did not appear qualified and were not hired. Had they been hired, they would not have performed acceptably. *Good decision.*

Our goal should be to maximize the number of decisions that fall into quadrants II and IV. To do that we need a process of evaluation that will allow us to:

■ Integrate biblical principles into the decision process.
■ Mobilize our intuition at the appropriate place and in the appropriate manner.
■ Identify and prioritize essential qualities needed to succeed in the position we are trying to fill.
■ Surface the presence or absence of these qualities in the people under consideration.
■ Organize a large amount of subjective data into a logical, "usable" format to facilitate making a high-quality decision.

In the next chapters we will outline just such a process, including the following six steps:

1. *Defining the task*—This step will show you how to quickly and accurately profile the job you want done in such a way as to clearly see the match between the task and potential candidates.
2. *Developing selection criteria*—This is the heart of our selection process. Here we develop a list of qualities and qualifications that describe the person who has the greatest potential to succeed in the position we seek to fill.
3. *Outlining the selection strategy*—There are several sources of information, each varying in cost. Some are better at validating our selection criteria, and others are not so effective. Here we designate specific sources to use and who from our organization will be involved in the process.
4. *Evaluating the candidates*—Here we will explore how to effectively evaluate résumé information, conduct an interview, and reference candidates. We will also discuss the appropriate use and application of testing.
5. *Making the decision*—In this step we will outline a simple, efficient method of organizing the relevant information about each candidate, so that you will have an objective means of comparison.
6. *Recruiting*—We must learn to change our outlook on staffing our organizations. This chapter will focus on the need to be constantly on the lookout for people who "fit" with your organization. Recruiting is ongoing and the final step of the process we'll discuss.

Some people with certain temperaments will find any systematic process cumbersome and time-consuming. Intuition and gut feeling are much more appealing to these often overworked, bottomline executives or volunteers on a pastor-search committee. But as we discussed, many times the shortcuts lead to a dead end. Those that tend to "wing it" on the front end often "crash and burn" on the back end.

Having a systematic or structured process also provides the best solution to one of the biggest pitfalls in people decisions—bias. Inherent bias hinders the decision maker from recognizing the "best" alternative. Peter Drucker notes that an effective executive knows "that people don't start out with a search for facts. They start out with an opinion."[2] Other researchers have concluded that most of the time in an interview is devoted to confirming the hypothesis or impressions developed by the interviewer in the first few minutes. When the above selection-process steps are followed in sequence, your intuition will be properly integrated into the decision and the adverse effects of premature judgment and bias will be minimized.

Second, any management process such as planning, problem solving, or decision making resembles a complex football play or recipe—it takes skill to pull it off well, and that comes with practice and perseverance. When first attempted, the above selection process might seem a little cumbersome. But press on—it will soon become a natural part of your thinking.

INTUITION: A NECESSARY INGREDIENT IN SELECTION

Finally, what about intuition? How does that fit into such a "rational" process? Intuition, "the sixth sense," is the ability to perceive things or come to conclusions without appearing to work through a conscious reasoning process. All of us use intuition to some extent, but research teaches us that some are more intuitive than others. It is not so much the lack of reasoning that defines intuition, but rather the speed of it. Intuition is the ability to very rapidly process large amounts of information, integrating current data with past experiences and impressions stored in our subconscious mind. With proper stimulation, these pieces of information can surface as thoughts and judgments.

Often, intuition is challenged because we can't explain why

we feel one way or another—"I don't know why, I just don't feel comfortable about this guy." Peter Senge, in his best-selling book on learning, observes, "Numerous studies show that experienced managers and leaders rely heavily on intuition—that they do not figure out complex problems entirely rationally. They rely on hunches, recognize patterns, and draw intuitive analogies and parallels to other seemingly disparate situations."[3]

Some view intuition as a type of stepchild to be shunned in the face of logic, while others overemphasize its importance. Intuition is a valid, often significant part of making high-quality people decisions, but it must find its proper place and proportion in the overall process. The key is maintaining a sense of balance between reason and intuition.

Again, Senge provides some insight. "People with high levels of personal mastery do not set out to integrate reason and intuition. Rather, they achieve it naturally—as a by-product of their commitment to use all the resources at their disposal. They cannot afford to choose between reason and intuition, or head and heart, any more than they would choose to walk on one leg or see with one eye."[4]

I have found the key to integrating intuition and reason is to ensure that we attain agreement between the two. If the rational part of the process says person A is the best candidate but your intuition is screaming concern, stop. Revisit your rationale, reflect on the details and the nuances. What might be triggering this feeling of concern? Note that this influence can flow both directions. Many of us have experienced situations in which we really liked a candidate (that is, intuitively), but our reason was telling us that this person didn't fit. Continue to think and pray about this decision until the two elements (reason and intuition) are in congruence. I believe it is here that God's Spirit can interdict our process, working through our intuition to influence our conclusions.

The story at the beginning of this chapter is true, and the saddest part of it is that I can tell a lot of stories like that. We can grieve for all the people in this illustration, for the pain of this mistake is shared by all of them. I'm sure the associate pastor, who was recently terminated, experienced a miserable year and a half in the position. I observe that most people who are not performing well in a job know it, even if only at an intuitive level. They don't leave work in the evening with a sense of personal fulfillment and achievement. Instead, there is a gnawing gut ache of fear. Peter Drucker agrees, "Indeed, I have never seen anyone in a job for which he was inadequate who was not slowly being destroyed by the pressure and the strains, and who did not secretly pray for deliverance."[5] And in addition, the family suffers. I didn't ask, but this associate pastor probably had a family. They're feeling the pain as well.

The young pastor who hired the associate is hurting, too. He's not only confronted with a challenge to his self-esteem and leadership (after all, he hired this person), but I could sense he was feeling concern and even some guilt over the predicament of his former associate. What about the church staff and congregation members who experienced the pain of poor performance over the past year?

This book is for these people. The proper process can act as a magnifying glass, helping us structure and focus the myriad bits and pieces of information, as well as the diffuse and fleeting impressions we call intuition. Although every people decision contains a lot of guesswork and subjectivity, we do not have to rely on luck and happenstance for successful staff selection. There are principles that can greatly increase the probability we will choose the best person for a given position.

CHAPTER FIVE

Caution:
Handle with Prayer

IMAGINE FOR A moment a scene in a high desert village popu-
lated by shepherds and farmers. A man has just arrived and is
immediately surrounded by the dust of clamoring children and
their animal charges. Women whisper in small groups while men
suggest questions to the village elders hurrying past to welcome
this man—a man known throughout the territory as a messenger
of the most high God.

You could cut the tension in the air with a knife. The elders
are troubled over the presence of the seer; not only is he a prophet
of the Lord but also a confidant of their king. What could this
man possibly want in this small, out-of-the-way village that has
treasured its agrarian pace and peace so much?

Although outwardly appearing to be confident as he directs
the preparations for the sacrifice, the man of God is filled with
apprehension. This sacrifice is really a diversion allowing him to
assist God in choosing the next king. The nervous prophet is well
aware that if his current leader knew the real purpose of this visit,
the prophet's life would be quickly forfeited.

No stranger to the rigors and stress of people decisions, the
prophet had played a major role in the selection of the previous

king, a role he came to regret. Had he clearly known God's plans for this new king, the tension would have been even greater.

Why did this man feel so much tension? God's instructions had been very clear. Little was left to chance. The Lord had told him where to go, whom to see, and what to say. Surely nothing could go wrong. Even allowing for fear that the king would discover his present mission, some measure of stress was still left unaccounted for. The remaining fear must have resided in the pressure of the selection itself.

The risk of being wrong must have been uppermost in his mind, particularly in light of how the previous choice had turned out. That, of course, was God's decision, and the prophet had been only a messenger. But it must have crossed his mind that he was the most visible aspect of God's working among the people, and they (not known for their patience) were sure to hold him accountable for the results.

By now you have surely recognized our cast of characters. The king is Saul, Israel's first sovereign; the prophet is Samuel; the soon-to-be-anointed successor is David. "You are to anoint for me the one I indicate," the Lord had told Samuel. Now that seems pretty straightforward. But Samuel fell into a trap that entangles many of us as we attempt to make important people decisions under pressure. Just as Jesse's sons made their appearance, Samuel's emotions took over. Eliab, Jesse's oldest son, was tall and handsome. He looked the part of the leader, much as Saul had several years before. *Surely this is the Lord's anointed,* Samuel thought. But the Lord was quick to intervene: "Do not consider his appearance or his height, for I have rejected him. The LORD does not look at the things man looks at. Man looks at the outward appearance, but the LORD looks at the heart" (1 Samuel 16:7).

What saved Samuel was not his expertise as an executive search consultant, but rather his sensitivity and willingness to listen to God during the selection process. Regardless of our abilities in selecting people or the completeness of our decision process, our success in choosing people will be determined by the degree to which we involve God in the process. We saw this in the previous chapter as we described the foundation of prayer Jesus exhibited in choosing His apostles.

Good people decisions are the product of an effective decision process, one that must be founded on prayer and careful attention to the leading of God's Spirit each step of the way. This perspective must govern our process of making people decisions, which is why we'll come back to it again and again.

This is a book about people decisions. In it, I attempt to draw on biblical principles and examples that will allow us to make high-quality choices. I'm assuming that my audience consists primarily of Christian executives in churches, parachurch organizations, and in many cases, secular corporations.

Most of us would give intellectual assent to prayer and acknowledge its place as the foundation of any Christian endeavor. I'm sure many would agree that we don't pray enough. However, nothing should drive us to our knees more than a people decision. We've seen previously that the key to successful people choices is to get God involved in the process. A better perspective might be to get us involved in God's process.

If you are reading this book, you're most likely a leader in a ministry with the specific purpose of furthering God's purposes on earth. Or, you may have committed your life to this goal even though you work for "secular" organizations. All of us can agree that God has a plan for this earth and that He accomplishes that plan through people. E. M. Bounds notes that while the Church might be searching for better methods, "God is searching for better men."[1] And that's what we should be about, too.

In pursuit of God's goals, it is also clear that He intends for us to "team up." Ecclesiastes 4:9 tells us, "Two are better than one, because they have a good return for their work."

We desire the synergism that comes from cooperation. In fact, we desperately need it. From a human perspective, the key is finding and selecting the right people with whom we can team up. Synergism is not the product of a plan but of a unique union of gifts, skills, and personalities—every person in this mix will either help or hinder the effort. Every decision is critically important.

If we desire to get Him involved in our choices or find out His will, we must do it through prayer, based on His purposes and promises. Sometimes, when introducing a decision process, I have been tempted to say, "Let's pray and get down to work." In the case of making people decisions, I believe the real work is prayer itself. The Bible is replete with examples of the role of prayer in making people decisions. Let's look at a few.

Moses
In Numbers 27, we come upon a touching moment as the Lord tells His servant Moses to go to the top of a certain mountain to view the Promised Land—land toward which he's toiled for nearly eighty years—from a distance. However, God reminds Moses that he will not enter the land but be "gathered to his fathers," because of his role in the disobedience at Meribah (see Exodus 17:7). Moses doesn't plead for his life, but asks God to raise up a new leader for the Hebrew or Jewish people when he says: "May the LORD, the God of the spirits of all mankind, appoint a man over this community to go out and come in before them, one who will lead them out and bring them in, so the LORD's people will not be like sheep without a shepherd" (Numbers 27:16-17).

In response to Moses' prayer, God chose Joshua as the successor.

The Lord
We've already seen that the Lord Jesus Himself approached the task of selecting His apostles with prayer: "One of those days Jesus went out to a mountainside to pray, and spent the night praying to God. When morning came, he called his disciples to him and chose twelve of them, whom he also designated apostles" (Luke 6:12-13).

Let's look at the context of this decision. In Mark 3:7-19 we are told that tremendous crowds pressed in from every side. Within the multitude were a smaller group of disciples, learner-friends, who followed Jesus for more than entertainment, food, or healing. Although we're not sure of the exact number, Jesus called a group of disciples ("those he wanted") and went up on a mountainside (Mark 3:13). It is out of this group that He chose the twelve apostles, after He spent the entire night in prayer. It was a difficult, important decision—critically important—and He took it seriously.

The Apostles
In Acts 1, the apostles are confronted with the task of replacing Judas Iscariot, the one who betrayed Jesus. They propose two men—Joseph and Matthias. We read, "Then they prayed, 'Lord, you know everyone's heart. Show us which of these two you have chosen to take over this apostolic ministry'" (Acts 1:24-25).

God's Selection Strategies
In the Bible, we see God exercising several distinct strategies to staff His work. In some instances, He chose the person directly (Moses at the burning bush, Exodus 3; Gideon under the oak in Ophrah, Judges 6; and Paul on the Damascus Road, Acts 9). In other situations, although He sent men as the messengers, God still made the actual decision (Samuel with Saul, 1 Samuel 9:15-17; Samuel with David, 1 Samuel 16:6-13). We also find circumstances in which He sends people to choose others with no apparent guidance other than a list of qualities to look for. For example, the Apostle Paul writes to Titus, "The reason I left you in Crete was that you might straighten out what was left unfinished and appoint elders in every town, as I directed you" (Titus 1:5). He then goes on to list the qualities Titus is to look for in making his choices.

Imagine what was going through Titus's mind as he read Paul's letter. What an assignment! Do you think prayer played a part in his thinking? In most of our people decisions, we are in much the same situation as was Titus—having a desire to find God's person for the position, with nothing more to go on than a list of qualities that might help us recognize him or her. I've already noted that such a list is the heart of our selection process, but prayer provides the power. This list of selection criteria doesn't substitute for God's direct leading. Like Samuel and Titus, our success in selection will be determined by our perseverance in prayer and our sensitivity and responsiveness to God's leading.

WHAT DO WE PRAY FOR?

Each situation brings with it unique needs, but several common elements come to mind:

- Pray for wisdom and insight—the ability to discern God's mind, to probe for and understand the gifts and skills of those we evaluate (see 1 Corinthians 2:16, James 1:5).
- Pray for love and wisdom for those we evaluate—that our love will show through and they will feel our acceptance. Pray that they might have insight into God's will for them.
- Pray for courage—to make the right decision for the right reasons. Often the most qualified candidate may not be the most personable, or the person whose strengths most match our needs may have weaknesses that challenge our "comfort zone."

Prayer is not just the first step of a process, but rather an integral part of every step. Prayer must be a part of defining the task and developing the selection criteria, especially during the evaluation and decision process, when we must exercise great wisdom and discernment. For like Samuel, we look at the outward appearance—and the character traits that provide the greatest insight about a candidate's potential are found in the inner person. Prayer is one major way we involve God in the process, and without such involvement, regardless of the quality of our decision process, we will surely build an organization of Eliabs rather than of Davids.

CHAPTER SIX

Preliminary Caution: Those Loathsome Legal Issues

AT LEAST ONCE a month I get an inquiry from the owner of a corporation, usually small and privately owned, asking me to recommend or even make a formal search for a capable, Christian executive for that owner's firm. These owners' intentions are good. They are looking for someone who shares the same values. Someone with whom they can pray about business problems and who will apply biblical principles in decisions and in running the business. What an exciting possibility! Here are employers who are taking their faith into the work environment and looking for colleagues with the same heart attitude. However, caution is in order here. For there's a question we must ask: Is this request legal?

The legal aspects of recruiting have become increasingly more important over the past few years. Beginning in the 1960s the U.S. Government began to implement a variety of legal initiatives that influence, even govern, every aspect of how we staff our organizations.

This Is an Overview
In this chapter I'll provide a brief overview of the more important regulations and their implications in both a nonprofit and

corporate setting. This chapter is here because it influences how we apply various process steps in subsequent chapters. In those chapters I explore the various methods of evaluation (interviews, references, and testing) and provide additional detail concerning the legislation specific to that facet of selection.

Virtually every type of people decision is covered by some type of regulation. All of this is based on the conviction that all people, regardless of race, color, religion, ethnic origin, sex, or age, have the right to equal employment opportunities. The legal infrastructure that undergirds this commitment includes legislation (federal and state laws), regulations from various government agencies (for example, Equal Employment Opportunity Commission and state commissions), court decisions, and executive orders. Penalties for violating these regulations are vigorously enforced. They are, for the most part, financial and have proved costly to organizations convicted of infractions. As I write this chapter, newspapers report that a jury penalized American Airlines $7 million for discrimination against a female employee in a placement decision that, according to the judgment, violated statutes against sex, age, and disability discrimination.[1]

It's important to note that in many such violations, intent is not a concern. Only the actual effect of the oversight matters. Even if an organization violates a regulation through ignorance, the penalties are applied just as energetically. Therefore, it's important that the leaders of the organization understand both their rights and obligations under the law as they make their people decisions.

An Important Disclaimer

Before proceeding further, let me issue an important disclaimer. I'm not a lawyer. The legal aspects of recruiting, selecting, and placing people are highly technical, complex, and dynamic. Additionally, I merely brush the surface, with a brief overview of the primary legislation in this area. The objective of this summary is to alert you to the legal dimension of your people decisions, so that you don't blunder into a pitfall inadvertently. Even though many managers are aware of the basic legal aspects of selection, they generally do not appreciate the subtle nuances of application. For example, many of the violations of equal employment regulations brought to court are the result of well-meaning but illegal questions or comments made in the first few minutes of an interview as the interviewer tried to put the candidate at ease and build rapport.

Another reason I'm skimming over the legality issue is because I'm writing for decision makers in both the profit and nonprofit sectors and the law is applied differently depending on the size and type of organization. For-profit corporations are governed differently than are nonprofit organizations. The type of nonprofit organization also makes a difference. Secular nonprofit organizations (The American Red Cross, University of Chicago, etc.) have different restrictions than do religious nonprofit organizations (Campus Crusade for Christ, a denomination, or a church). Educational nonprofit organizations have different requirements than noneducational ones. As for profit-making organizations, many of the governing statutes do not apply to those with fewer than fifteen employees. Finally, just when you think you've got it, another court case establishes an entirely new set of interpretations and precedents.

For people and organizations confronted with such decisions, I highly recommend sitting down with your attorney and having him or her give you (and any staff making these decisions) an overview of the employment laws, highlighting areas that are particularly relevant to your situation.[2] The greatest protection against inadvertent violation of such regulations is an uncompromising commitment to impartiality and a broad understanding of the basic laws that govern people decisions.

LABOR LAW IN CORPORATE SETTINGS

Title VII, as amended by the Equal Employment Opportunity Act of 1972, is the primary legislation that regulates all aspects of employment for private employers of fifteen or more people (including part-time staff), public and private educational institutions, other nonprofit organizations, state and local governments, and labor unions. Employment agencies must adhere to this law in the same fashion as their clients. Title VII clearly prohibits any discrimination in recruiting, placement, promotion, or compensation of employees based on race, color, religion, sex, or national origin. An older law, the Age Discrimination in Employment Act of 1967 (amended in 1977), prohibits discrimination in employment against individuals between the ages of forty and seventy. The Rehabilitation Act of 1973 and the Americans with Disability Act of 1990 prohibit any discrimination because of disability or handicaps. Together these groups of people make up what your attorney would call a "protected class." The law looks at these groups with heightened attention and concern.

It was the Equal Employment Opportunity Act that established the Equal Employment Opportunity Commission (EEOC), a government agency established to not only respond to discrimination job complaints but to take any necessary initiatives on its own to prevent such discrimination.

Even though the U.S. Congress has been the primary initiator of labor regulations, even establishing the EEOC to give oversight, it has been the courts that have provided the deepest insight into the scope and influence of these laws and regulations. Over time, through a series of landmark cases, the courts have provided a broader understanding of how to apply these guidelines in real-life situations and, with few exceptions, they have taken the very broadest interpretations. For example, in a particularly significant employment case, the U.S. Supreme Court ruled that the results and consequences of the employer's actions, not his or her intentions, determine culpability. Even in the face of a sincere desire not to discriminate and a concerted attempt to follow the law, if there is any bias, even by accident or through innocence, the victims of such discrimination may seek legal remedy.[3]

NONPROFIT EXEMPT ORGANIZATIONS

Again, the application of Title VII and subsequent EEOC guidelines to exempt organizations is complex and highly dependent on the type of organization as well as the nature of the specific situation in which the question is asked. I can't overstress the importance of having your attorney brief you on the general guidelines as they apply to your specific situation.

In general, religious-exempt organizations can discriminate on religious or spiritual criteria,[4] while nonreligious nonprofit organizations such as the American Cancer Society or the March of Dimes cannot. Like decision makers in the for-profit sector, those in exempt organizations must be aware of the broad, overarching regulations that govern their hiring and personnel practices. Ask your attorney to keep you informed of new regulations or changes that will influence how you make people decisions.

TURNING PRINCIPLES INTO PRACTICE

With this background, let's revisit the request that began this chapter—"Find me a Christian executive who can help me run my company." The law is clear. In the case of a private company or corporation (even a secular nonprofit or government agency) with fifteen or more employees, this would be discrimination against those of another religious or even nonreligious persuasion. The Bible is also clear. We are told to be subject to governing authorities (Romans 13:1-3, Titus 3:1-2, 1 Peter 2:13-17). Some will argue that other verses apply here (for example, 2 Corinthians 6:14—"Do not be yoked together with unbelievers. For what do righteousness and wickedness have in common? Or what fellowship can light have with darkness?") and that when man's laws oppose those in the Bible then we must follow God, regardless of the consequences. But be prepared to face the consequences. This has been the basic tenet of many Christians in their fight against abortion. Though abortion is legal, they consider it immoral and unbiblical and willingly endure jail and financial penalties to express their belief.

I also want to make the observation that many fundamentalistic Christians see the admonition of 2 Corinthians 6:14 as being applicable primarily in situations concerning ownership and/or partnership where there is some *legal* type of "yoking." I believe any situation that promotes any constraint on our ability to live out our Christian value system is untenable and should be avoided. However, in situations where this is not the case, each individual must make his or her own decisions. Few attorneys would allow their clients to enter into any such situation without some stipulated, formal buy-out or dissolution agreement. In most such partnership agreements, many of these clauses emanate from value issues such as moral or ethical problems.

An Important People Lesson: Synergy from Diversity

An attorney friend of mine once shared a story of how God had dealt with the partners of his firm on this very issue. This was, at that time, a medium-sized law firm in which all the partners were Christians. In an effort to integrate biblical principles into their practice, they regularly held devotions and prayed over critical decisions.

A few years ago they were in the midst of interviewing young graduating attorneys. One in particular grabbed their attention. This individual had graduated at the top of her law class and displayed every indication of having the potential to be a top-flight attorney. There was one small problem. They knew that this young woman was Jewish. As the partners met to wrestle through their hiring choices, they were forced to face the fact that, whomever they hired, one day that individual would be eligible for partnership. With a Jewish partner, they feared their ability to have fellowship in their Christian faith could be compromised. They elected to make the offer to another young woman who had impressed them as well.

The last event in their selection process was a fancy dinner at a private club. Here the final candidates were exposed to the partners and their spouses in a social setting and at its conclusion were offered positions with the firm. During the course of the evening several partners shared with the second young woman about how they had become Christians and the impact this decision had on their lives. They explained the value system and culture of the firm that included attempting to integrate biblical principles into their treatment of clients and staff and their decision making. She appeared to be comfortable with such a climate and enthusiastically accepted the offer at the end of the evening. However, moments later, this ebullient young lady leaned over to my friend, the senior partner, and asked, "Will there be a problem if I don't have the same religion?"

She went on to explain that although she was committed to the priorities and values of the firm, she was Jewish. The next morning, somewhat chagrined, my friend announced to the other partners that God had solved their dilemma about hiring only Christians as they had just unknowingly hired a Jewish attorney. The young woman went on to become one of the top attorneys in the firm. And these partners, after deciding that God did not want them to discriminate on the basis of religion, recently awarded partnership to another individual of a different faith. They solved the problem of the devotions and prayer by making participation voluntary with attendance not being a factor in advancement in the firm.

This surfaces a critical point. In most instances, the driving motivation for seeking someone of the same religious persuasion is an attempt to find an individual with compatible values. Often when I probe the reasons behind seeking Christian candidates, I hear things like a concern for integrity and morality, for people who value people and treat others as they too would like to be treated. If these leaders could find someone who held and practiced those values, they'd be satisfied. Additionally, the hirer also wants the freedom to express his or her Christian values in the workplace and not be ridiculed. For instance, he or she would like to be able to say to a request for a decision, "Let me pray about that and get back to you early next week." Even if the other person doesn't believe in prayer but respects the desire of the other to do so, this is often sufficient. Many of us have learned the hard way that hiring a Christian is no guarantee that we get the values we tend to ascribe to "being a believer." In some instances we discover too late that this particular Christian's behavior wasn't tightly tied to his or her beliefs.

Articulating Your Corporate Values

It's not an organization's values that are at issue with our legal system, but rather the source of them. Having a clear sense of corporate culture (that is, "The way we do things around here"⁵) and a well-articulated set of nonreligious company values is legal. You can share these values with those you seek to hire and ask if such values are compatible with theirs—"Can you live and work within such guidelines?" If your values are strong, clear, and well expressed, individuals who don't hold to them will probably not purposely join your team. If they do, even inadvertently, the fact that they were briefed as to the role and importance of these values will give you some recourse. However, if you're unclear yourself or with others about your corporate value system, then you can expect to experience conflict as you attempt to exercise it.

One of my dearest friends is an Atlanta businessman named John Keeble. John has been a client for many years and a friend for a few minutes less than that. Although he is a client, there have been many instances in which I was confused about who should get the invoice, for I seldom left a meeting with John without learning something meaningful. John is well known for his excellent value system, personally and corporately, and if you asked him the source he would quickly reveal its biblical roots. As president of a large, national broker-dealer firm, John outlined the values and philosophies he felt were important for the organization. I show these on the next page, and you can see that he clearly articulates the biblical foundation of the company philosophy. Yet, many people of nonChristian religious persuasions (as well as those with no religious beliefs) worked enthusiastically and compatibly with these values. Additionally, John was very sensitive to those who came at life through a different paradigm and treated all employees with dignity and respect, regardless of the *source* of their value system. But they had to subscribe to the corporate value system (see figure 6.1).

In summary, I believe that the defendable ground is values and corporate culture rather than the core beliefs from which they emanate. A selection criterion for any job in a private secular corporation cannot, under any circumstances, be that an individual believes that the Bible is the true and inspired Word of God. However, the corporation can have a clearly stated value that says it wants its employees to treat each other the way they, themselves, would like to be treated.

Let me also observe that in most instances employment legislation applies only to private companies that have fifteen or more employees, including part-time staff. In a smaller firm, where lack of compatible values might be more visible and painful, there is more room for latitude. This allows you to frame your selection criteria in a tighter fashion. However, consider that, although the letter of the law might not apply in this case, the spirit of that law might.

FIGURE 6.1
EXAMPLE OF A STATEMENT OF CORPORATE VALUES

A BLUEPRINT FOR INVESTORS/FINANCIAL GROUP
by John B. Keeble

The kind of financial planning sales organization we want:
1. Full time and professional.
2. Financially successful.
3. Financial planning and client oriented.
4. Of the highest quality. This includes people who have high values and who cause us to be proud of each other and the company.

The kind of home office we want:
1. Fulfilled, well-trained, well-paid employees.
2. The finest possible attitude and performance, with a commitment to service at *all* all levels.
3. An attractive, productive, pleasant physical environment.
4. An environment conducive to growth and advancement.
5. An open, trusting environment where people are encouraged to communicate freely and take reasonable risks.

The kind of leadership we want:
1. People of very high intelligence who also have good sense. This includes good judgment and a sense of reality.
2. Strong vision and motivation toward high achievement and ideals.
3. Strength and firmness with flexibility and fairness. A willingness to make unpleasant, unpopular decisions when they are right.

4. Solid ability to communicate.
5. People who care about other people.
6. A sound sense of stewardship and fiscal responsibility, which includes careful attention to margin, sound use of resources, low debt, liquidity, and first class planning.
7. A high sense of regulatory responsibility. This includes acceptance of and a respect for the regulatory process and authorities. We want credibility with the regulatory people. We not only want to be legal, but we would like to avoid even being asked embarrassing questions.
8. An open environment of truthfulness, credibility, and mutual trust, where people can say what they think and treat each other like mature adults. We don't like "yes men" (or women). We want our bad news early and no negative surprises. We want leadership whose personal agendas are subordinated to the agenda and mission of the organization. We like candid, straightforward, on top of the table dealings. We don't want our achievements to be at the expense of people being hurt.
9. We want the leadership to remember always who the client is.

The kind of philosophy we want:
1. To be reaching for the highest spiritual values. This includes the primacy of relationships and, in my opinion, a commitment to and a reliance on God. It includes a high respect for the institution of the family and for human dignity.
2. To be committed to several key principles, "Love the Lord with all your heart and your neighbor as yourself" and to the concept of our business being a way of loving our neighbors.
3. To provide good service to our clients and their clients.
4. To have a repentant attitude when we fall and a forgiving attitude when the other person falls.
5. To always have a passion for the truth.

Summary: The Laws on Hiring Are Clear

The law is clear. Our people decisions should be made against objective, verifiable criteria. However, after interviewing a group of candidates, and all things being equal, if you choose a Christian because you "intuitively" felt he or she could do a better job or fit the corporate culture better, I would hope that such intuition would be based on the values, skills, and potential you sense in that person and not merely in his or her profession of faith.

No matter how objective or verifiable criteria can or ought to be, people decisions are largely subjective in nature. As I observed in an earlier chapter, many hiring managers, instead of attempting to narrow the gap of subjectivity by using a rational decision process, develop some type of intuitive process ("gut instinct") to shortcut the hard work of making decisions about hiring. Many Christian executives in a corporate setting wouldn't call it "gut instinct" but rather faith, and they often exercise a large measure of it as they hire a particular person only because that person is a Christian, delegating the issue of competence to God. It is as though they think that in hiring a Christian, regardless of the person's other qualifications, they are doing a favor for God and surely He won't let them down. I think they imagine God blessing the candidate with sufficient competence if He has not already done so. Remember Jesus' admonition "Do not put the Lord your God to the test" (Matthew 4:7). This would surely be one of those!

If you can find competent nonChristians who see a biblical value system as appealing, it might be that God has His own agenda for their presence. As a person sees Christian values lived out in the context of the work-a-day world, he or she may become more open to the source of that value system as well.

PART TWO

FINDING THE "FIT" BETWEEN JOB AND CANDIDATE

CHAPTER SEVEN

Defining the Task

EVERYONE WAS FRUSTRATED with the situation. In the past two years, the company had gone through two human resources directors and now was beginning a search for the third. They just hadn't been able to find the "right person." Oddly enough, both previous directors had been successful, seasoned human resources professionals with similar jobs in much larger organizations. During the selection process, experience had been stressed because of the need to "get on our feet fast."

With a growth rate of nearly 20 percent a year, the organization now totaled more than two hundred employees in three locations. The employees prided themselves on their "entrepreneurial spirit." This was one organization, the president boasted, that wouldn't get bogged down in procedures manuals and "bureaucratic claptrap." In fact, when the last human resources director asked for a job description during her interview, she was told that writing one would be her first task if she were chosen for the job! She was chosen, but she never got a chance to write that description.

Had the president thoughtfully analyzed the situation, he would have arrived at an important insight into this seeming "mankiller" of a job. First, the goals and expectations for the job were unrealistic, ambiguous, and too dynamic. The company's prejudice against anything that even hinted of routine or bureaucracy was a major barrier for putting any order into the human side of the enterprise. The result: Virtually no personnel policies had been developed, leaving a fire brigade to battle hot spots such as compensation problems, sick leave, promotions, transfers, and many other needs of the growing staff.

Bringing in an experienced person from a larger organization hadn't helped—these individuals had worked in more structured, well-resourced, corporate environments. They couldn't cope or perform effectively in the untamed, wind-tunnel atmosphere of this smaller organization, and had fallen victim to professional culture shock. Now the company was searching for its third victim.

GETTING THE LAY OF THE LAND

It is no wonder the president was frustrated—he had lost some troops. In a very real sense, these employees were casualties of inappropriate strategies by the commanding officer. The first step in any battle is to get the "lay of the land." Good leaders, whether generals or general managers, know that before you commit your people to the task at hand, you'd better have a handle on the task. You must know both the scope and the challenges of the task in order to effectively choose and deploy your human resources. Without such knowledge, you will certainly fall into traps and pitfalls, causing casualties—if not outright defeat. Sun Tzu, a famous Chinese general and trainer of generals in the art of war and leadership, wrote, "We are not fit to lead an army on the march unless we are familiar with the face of the country—its mountains and forests, its pitfalls and precipices, its marshes and swamps."[1]

Centuries before Tzu was instructing his generals in the art of war, the Lord was teaching His men the same lessons. Before sending the Israelites in to take the Promised Land, God told

Moses to send in twelve men to "explore the land" (Numbers 13:1-20). Notice the level of detail Moses presses into his request as he sends out his spies:

> See what the land is like and whether the people who live there are strong or weak, few or many. What kind of land do they live in? Is it good or bad? What kind of towns do they live in? Are they unwalled or fortified? How is the soil? Is it fertile or poor? Are there trees on it or not? (Numbers 13:18-20)

You'd think that Sun Tzu had read Moses! Joshua, one of those twelve spies and Moses' successor, learned this lesson well—before crossing the Jordan River, he too sent spies into the land to measure the task before them (Joshua 2:1-24).

Nehemiah, a highly effective general manager, carefully surveyed the broken walls of Jerusalem before calling the people to work (Nehemiah 2:11-16). He surveyed the situation, measured the ruined walls and rubble, and considered the mood of the people and magnitude of the task. Before he began, Nehemiah knew exactly what this job would require and what kind of people were needed to do it.

I don't find many Nehemiahs in the ranks of people decision makers. I'm continually amazed at the number of managers who are quick to throw employees into ill-defined jobs—jobs that are not challenging; jobs that are "mankillers"; jobs that contain conflicting goals; jobs that, even if done correctly, won't accomplish the desired goals. This chapter's opening illustration was clearly in this category.

Peter Drucker explains that effective executives "do not start out with the assumption that jobs are created by nature or by God. They know that they have been designed by highly fallible men. And they are therefore forever on guard against the 'impossible' job, the job that simply is not for normal human beings."

The rule is simple, concludes Drucker: "Any job that has defeated two or three men in succession, even though each has performed well in his previous assignments, must be assumed unfit for human beings. It must be redesigned."[2]

This is the time to stop and evaluate the scope of this job. Countless mismatches and casualties occur because the hiring executive was vague or confused about the job he or she wanted filled in the first place. In too many instances the "we'll figure it out as we go along" attitude prevails.

These managers are trading a little more work in the front part of the process for a lot more work fixing a bad match later. Robert Half, in his book *On Hiring*, notes, "The majority of hiring mistakes made each day could have been prevented if the people responsible for the hiring simply did a more effective job of determining exactly what they were looking for before they started to look."[3]

Remember, our goal is to achieve the best possible fit between the demands of the position and the capabilities of the person. Effective people decisions begin with the position, not the person. Defining the position is always the first step in making or evaluating matches between people and jobs.

YOU NEED MORE THAN A JOB DESCRIPTION

Often when we begin a search assignment for a client and have begun to ask about the job, we are quickly handed a job description with a smile that connotes "We're way ahead of you." But to find the "best" person for the job, more is needed than just the job description.

An accurate, well-written job description is indeed an important tool in the management of an organization. A good one generally includes the following:

- An overview or short summary of the major job responsibilities.
- A list of specific responsibilities to be accomplished.
- Reporting relationships.
- Levels of authority for the various responsibilities.

Job descriptions are used for salary administration and to communicate the task to the employees and others. They basically describe what the job is; however, in our selection process we really need a description of what it takes to do the job, not just what it is about.

Additionally, many job descriptions are incomplete or inaccurate. Usually, over time, the activities that were once relevant and of high priority in a job lose some of their "connectedness" to the real task we first wanted or needed to accomplish. Our selection process sounds the alarm when such drifts occur and helps to ensure that the "what is" and the "what should be" of a job are one and the same.

If our frustrated president in the opening illustration had first gotten a handle on the job, he would have been better able to find a person to handle the job!

PROFILING THE POSITION

There is no end of detail a manager can go into when defining a given job. Major corporations employ vast armies of technical specialists who measure every nuance of a specific task. Some of you may be wondering, even now, if it wouldn't be more profitable for you to skip ahead to the next chapter, as pictures may be coming to your mind of white-coated, bespectacled technicians, bearing stopwatches, measuring tapes, calculators, computer programs, and an endless supply of forms and files. The image conveys such themes as "technical," "complex," "time-consuming," or "difficult." The result, too often, is that we decide to "wing it"—to go with a more common-sense, cost-effective route. After all, it's just a job; anyone could do it, we say.

Well, most of us have learned the hard way that "anyone" can't do most jobs. Everyone can perform some tasks with excellence, but not all tasks. Our job as executives and hiring managers is to match people with positions. To do that with excellence, we must know both of them very well.

Every job has three major components:

1. Goals or results to be achieved.
2. Activities necessary to achieve these goals.
3. The climate in which these activities must be performed.

Let's explore these components in more detail.

What are the goals or results you want to achieve? The burning question in the hiring executive's mind should be, "What must this person accomplish in order to get an excellent evaluation from me?"

As an example, let's look back at First Church as they begin to profile the position for their new associate pastor of evangelism. For years the pastor and elders had sensed outreach efforts were fragmented and unskilled. They needed someone to orchestrate training for the congregation in the basics of evangelism, as well as lead development and implementation of a church-wide outreach strategy. The search committee gathered around the boardroom table, coffee in hand.

Let's notice how they begin to profile the associate pastor of evangelism's position using the flip chart:

FIGURE 7.1—FIRST YEAR'S GOALS

---

1. Develop (or find) and implement by January an outreach strategy for the church that incorporates our overall objectives and philosophy.
2. Develop and implement by March a program for helping new Christians to grow in their faith and for folding them into the church.
3. Train 30 percent of adult members in the principles and "how-to's" of evangelism by June.

Note that, for the most part, First Church followed the rule of good goal setting by making the goals specific, measurable, achievable, and datable. However, you can't "do a goal," you can only "do activities," so we must ask a second question:

What activities must be successfully completed to accomplish these goals? Each goal should be broken down into activities or steps that, if performed correctly, will accomplish the goal. The search committee at First Church used this approach, and their results were as follows:

FIGURE 7.2—ACTIVITIES

Goal 1. Outreach Strategy
  A. Research available outreach strategies that meet our criteria.
  B. Present recommended plan to elders.
  C. Develop implementation plan that will include goals, staff needs, promotion ideas, budget, and schedule.
  D. Recruit and train necessary lay leadership.

Goal 2. Discipleship Program
  A. Research effective discipleship strategies for new Christians.
  B. Evaluate our present program for folding new members into First Church.
  C. Present recommended strategies to the elders for approval.
  D. Develop an implementation plan that will include goals, staff needs, budget, and schedule.

Goal 3. Evangelism Training
  A. Procure or produce the approved program.
  B. Recruit trainers for the training program.
  C. Train the trainers.
  D. Develop and initiate a promotional strategy that will communicate the program to the congregation in a motivational manner.
  E. Schedule and implement training sessions.

Such an activities list helps us to see more clearly what must be done in order to accomplish our goals. However, we must not neglect the third component found in any job:

In what type of environment will these activities be exercised? Earlier in this chapter, we described an all-too-typical instance where employees who had demonstrated high levels of competence in one job environment failed to apply these same skills successfully in a different environment. To type seventy-five words per minute without error in an environment characterized by one boss, a measured pace, predictable workloads, and a quiet, stable work atmosphere is one thing. It's quite another in a situation of multiple bosses, little predictability of workloads, entrepreneurial chaos, and changing priorities.

Different types of people work better in different environments; thus, defining the task must include surveying the "climate" of your workplace. Some of the more influential climate dimensions include:

- *Leadership style*—The most immediate consideration is the general style of the leader himself or herself (autocratic, democratic, laissez faire, etc.). However, also consider issues concerning the use of authority and delegation. Leadership style can be reflected in a single manager, pattern, or value permeating the entire organization.
- *Support/resources*—Have you allowed for the necessary help, training, and time to get the job done? Many situations, due to lack of resources, demand individuals who take the initiative to roll up their sleeves and figure it out.
- *Philosophy*—What's important around the workplace? People? Results? Growth? Loyalty? Someone who is people-oriented may feel too much pressure in a highly task-oriented environment and, therefore, not be productive.

As you can imagine, any of the above factors, as well as many others, have a significant impact on an individual's ability to perform in a given task. We often try to fool ourselves by thinking our work climate is better than it really is. Who likes to admit their workplace might be described as having high pressure, less than competitive compensation, weak leadership, or ineffective systems?

It's better to acknowledge the reality of your work environment and fix what you can (or find someone else to do the job), than it is to incur the terribly high cost of finding, training, and then replacing a long line of uninformed and newly hired employees who could never function effectively in that climate.

While climate is not an entirely tangible entity, you can oftentimes get a general feeling for what your work environment is like by contrasting word pairs such as those shown below:

structured and orderly. . . . . changing and confusing
well resourced with   under resourced with
  needed materials,   needed materials,
  assistance, etc. . . . .   assistance, etc.
relaxed . . . . tense
united . . . . divided
people-oriented . . . . task-oriented
measured pace. . . . . fast-paced
highly directive   highly laid-back,
  leadership style. . . . . . .   delegative leadership style
high morale . . . . low morale
affirming . . . . critical

The list could also include risk-seeking versus risk-avoidant, growth-oriented versus status quo, etc. All of these factors affect, to some extent, the way people can work. Some employees like to focus on one task at a time in a quiet, uninterrupted environment. Others thrive in the hustle and bustle of people, phones, and pressure. The basic tasks and skills remain the same, but the types of people who exercise them are radically different.

BACK TO THE DRAWING BOARD

The search committee at First Church refilled their coffee cups, turned to a new page in the flip chart, and began to brainstorm on climate factors that might affect the task of the new associate pastor. They came up with the following list:

FIGURE 7.3—CLIMATE ISSUES

---

1. Bill, the senior pastor, is not an effective manager. He's a superb preacher, loves studying and teaching the Word, is a people person, but is untrained in management basics, and does not have the aptitude for them.
2. The church has only one secretary, who is almost to capacity

in her work. After hiring the new associate pastor, it's unlikely we can afford to hire an additional secretary for some time. The new man will have to make do—find volunteers, etc.—until additional help can be budgeted.

3. In the past, the church has tried to implement church-wide evangelism strategies—with poor results. Inappropriate programs, poor training, lack of commitment, and weak leadership all played a role in the demise of these efforts. Therefore, there may be built-in preconceptions: "Here they come again, with plan number five." This may hinder the acceptance of any new initiatives.

4. This new associate pastor will be the second full-time professional staff member under the head pastor. Therefore, he or she must anticipate assisting in other pastoral and staff duties, in addition to managing the outreach strategy.

5. Many of the First Church congregation are business and professional people. This is reflected in the makeup of the board of elders. Results orientation is an important part of their makeup and expectations.

These climate descriptions will influence the type of person who can perform effectively in this position. For example, since the head pastor is not a manager, the elders will want to look for a self-starter, someone who is mature enough to take the initiative, but also wise enough to seek direction when needed.

A QUICK REVIEW

I've said the key in making good people decisions is to make a good match between the position and the person, and to accomplish this we must know both very well. The first step is to define the task. We noted that the most accurate way to profile a given job is to break it down into three component parts:

1. *Goals/results*—These are the outcomes or standards of performance we desire.

2. *Activities*—Specific steps or actions that, when done properly, will accomplish the goal. Many of these are reflected in the job description. However, job descriptions are often inaccurate and should be reevaluated

periodically to ensure that they will accomplish what we really want done.

3. *Climate*—The same activities performed in different climates require different kinds of people. Every climate contains forces, constraints, and resources to make a given task easier or more difficult. Climate issues include dynamic factors such as attitudes, philosophies, and style, as well as more concrete items such as salary, support, office setting, etc. The list of possible climate factors is limited only by our creativity; however, we want to identify only those that significantly impact the task.

For the purpose of illustration, we chose a task of moderate complexity. The level of effort and detail you would put into defining a task must reflect the complexity of the task and the consequences and costs of a poor selection decision. The chief executive position of a medium-sized corporation or parachurch organization might require more detail and analysis. The task of an executive secretary or of a telemarketer might be worked through on a single sheet of paper.

Would this type of exercise have helped the company described at the beginning of this chapter? Probably so. The answers to three simple, straightforward questions—goals, activities, and climate—may help the third incumbent to be a lot more productive and long lasting than his or her predecessors.

We've defined the position, now let's move on to the task of describing the type of person who can best fill it.

CHAPTER EIGHT

Describing the Person

THE PEOPLE'S PROGRESS in the wilderness bogged down as more and more time was spent working through bureaucratic tangles and resolving issues of dispute (this particular group had a lot of them!).

Moses was starting to burn out under the load of leadership when his father-in-law, Jethro, arrived for a short visit. Jethro provided some much-needed counsel to his overly tired son-in-law. "Select capable men to help you," he suggested. As we piece this event together from Exodus 18 and the first chapter of Deuteronomy, we see what Jethro had in mind when he used the word *capable*:

- Men who fear God
- Trustworthy men who hate dishonest gain
- Wise men
- Understanding men
- Men respected by others

Why would Jethro include these particular qualities and qualifications? How did he develop this specific list of selection criteria?

I believe they came out of a clear understanding of the task. Before advising Moses on the types of men he needed, Jethro spent a day "profiling the position," watching Moses exercise his office, and asking a series of probing questions. Once he got a handle on the task, he knew what kind of men were needed to perform it. When Moses implemented this strategy in making his people decisions, he held the selection criteria up as his guide.

The pattern is repeated in Acts 6 as the early Church began to outgrow its administrative systems. Luke writes, "In those days when the number of disciples was increasing, the Grecian Jews among them complained against the Hebraic Jews because their widows were being overlooked in the daily distribution of food" (Acts 6:1). The apostles were quick to respond and asked the disciples to choose seven men to carry this burden. Like Jethro, they provided the selection criteria to guide the decision—"men of good reputation, full of the Spirit and wisdom."

The Apostle Paul gives a detailed list of criteria to guide the selection of elders and deacons in 1 Timothy 3:2-13 and Titus 1:6-9. Again, the level of detail reflects a thorough understanding of the task.

THE HEART OF OUR PROCESS

A pattern emerges from these biblical examples. Selection criteria that help decision makers recognize qualified candidates are critical to successful people decisions. These criteria are the heart of our process. Such a list includes: gifts, skills, knowledge, aptitudes, interests, personality traits, character traits, and spiritual qualities that would ensure a good match between the person and position.

So how do we develop such a list of selection criteria? The answer is found in how we define the task. In the previous chapter we profiled the position, identifying the goals to be achieved, the activities necessary to achieve them, and the climate in which these activities will be conducted. Using this position profile, we begin to develop a description of the individual who could successfully perform in it. The list of activities will point us toward the needed skills; the climate factors will give insight into certain personality traits needed by a qualified candidate.

As was the case in defining the task, the level of detail will be determined by the complexity of the task you are attempting to fill. The selection criteria for a receptionist or any other entry-level position might be quickly listed on a yellow pad:

FIGURE 8.1—SELECTION CRITERIA
FOR THE NEW RECEPTIONIST

- Able to type 60 words per minute with less than three errors
- Likes to type
- Demonstrates warmth, friendliness, and courtesy on phone
- Organized/orderly
- Attentive to detail
- Maintains composure in face of distractions and interruptions

---

The list of criteria for a fund-raising/development officer, vice president of administration, or an associate pastor may be more involved. For every position, your list of criteria must be both complete and accurate—complete in that all important criteria are included, and accurate in that the qualities listed really do determine success in the position.

In order to ensure that the list of selection criteria for a given position is complete, we generally break it down into several broad categories. Then we attempt to identify several specific requirements for each category. For years I've used seven such categories when I profile a job for a client. This isn't an exhaustive roster, nor are all of these pertinent in every instance, but the following seven categories will serve well as a framework for our discussion here.

- *Competency*—the necessary gifts, skills, and knowledge to accomplish the required activities.
- *Compatibility*—the interests, aptitudes, and personality qualities necessary to "fit" the job.
- *Chemistry*—the "fit" with the organization, its strategies, philosophies, etc.

- *Character*—emotional and heart toughness; character drives conduct.
- *Christian walk*—the spiritual qualities required by the position and organization.
- *Compensation*—the needed and desired salary and benefits.
- *Call*—the "pull" to the organization and position.

Throughout this book, I try to position both the process and the principles for making good people decisions so that they would be applicable in both a corporate and a religious, nonprofit environment. In most cases, this works well. However, tension often emanates from the legal dimension of our decisions. The principles are the same, but the law creates some very distinct differences in how these principles are put into practice. As I pointed out in chapter 6, legislation concerning job discrimination is applied differently to the profit and not-for-profit sectors.

We see this distinction in how we specify our selection criteria. For example, in a for-profit corporate setting, overall criteria must be job related—even more specifically, it must be tied to job performance. For example, a criteron that the candidate believes that the Bible is the inspired Word of God would be legally acceptable for most nonprofit Christian ministries (churches, denominations, parachurch organizations, seminaries, etc.), but would definitely be out of bounds for a corporation owned by a Christian layman who wants to hire an executive with a similar value system. You will remember that in chapter 6 I pointed out that the corporation can legally specify the values it would hope to see in an applicant, if they are job related, but designating the basic source of these beliefs (race, religion, etc.) is off limits.

Make sure your criteria do not exclude protected groups of people (women, minorities, elderly, etc.), either directly or indirectly. For example, women could not be excluded from consideration of a position merely because the organization (which has been male only since its inception) does not have restroom facilities for women. Again, I encourage you to sit down with your attorney and have him or her explain the regulations that are applicable to your particular situation.

Because the case study used in this chapter to show the development of criteria for a given position is drawn in a church setting, I ask those of you from a corporate setting to adapt the process to your particular situation. Now, let's explore the above categories in more detail.

COMPETENCY

This category includes the spiritual gifts, skills, and knowledge necessary to perform well in the position. We have already identified the goals of the position and the activities necessary to accomplish them. Now we ask, "What gifts, skills, and knowledge are needed in order to successfully perform these activities in this type of climate?" Do you see the progression of our questions as we move from goals to activities to competencies? This approach helps ensure a good connection between our criteria and the job needs.

Let's look in again at First Church as the search committee continued to develop the list of criteria for the new associate pastor of evangelism. They already developed a comprehensive list of goals and activities required in the position, as well as some climate issues that would impact how the job is done. For purposes of illustration, we have shown the results for one of the goals below. You may review the entire list on page 74.

Goal 1—Develop (or find) and implement by January an outreach strategy for the church that incorporates our overall objectives and our goals and philosophy.

Activities
  A. Research available outreach strategies that meet our criteria.
  B. Present recommended plan to elders for approval.
  C. Develop implementation plan that will include goals, staff needs, promotion, ideas, budget, and schedule.
  D. Recruit and train necessary lay leadership.

In discussing what it would take to perform these particular activities, the committee came up with the following list of competencies:

■ Technical knowledge and experience in the principles and strategies of evangelism. (For example, understanding the distinctives, real and perceived, between lifestyle and proclamation evangelism; knowledge of the various programs used by churches; etc.)
■ Ability to facilitate meetings, lead task forces, etc.
■ Communication skills.
■ Planning skills.
■ Ability to select and recruit capable people.
■ Ability to organize.

Why don't you try it? Review the complete list of activities developed in the previous chapter and develop a list of gifts, skills, and knowledge you believe are needed in order to perform these activities.

Write your list on a tablet, then compare it to the search committee's complete list shown in figure 8.2 below.

FIGURE 8.2

■ Judgment/discernment.
■ Technical knowledge and experience in evangelism principles and strategies.
■ Ability to facilitate meetings, lead task forces, etc.
■ Communication skills.
■ The gift of evangelism.
■ The gift of leadership/administration (hopefully).
■ Planning skills.
■ Ability to select and recruit capable people.
■ Ability to organize.
■ Ability to persuade and motivate.
■ Seminary degree.
■ Training skills.

How did you do with your list? Notice that the committee included a seminary degree but didn't specify three to five years of experience in some type of outreach or organizational endeavor. In discussion, they decided that seminary or some other specific experience was an important means of obtaining skills and knowledge but not sure evidence of its existence. The focus must be on competencies and specific areas of expertise. They were right. Required experience may lead to wrong assumptions of what that means in the way of acquired competencies.

There are, however, instances where the degree or particular experience is a valid criterion. Examples include jobs where formal certification is required (CPA, Ph.D., pilot's license, etc.). In other instances, an individual's credibility is important to ensure successful performance in the position. For the position of associate pastor this would hold true.

In this category of criteria we specify the desired gifts. In any ministry position, spiritual gifts are a critical criterion, and the search committee at First Church felt that the needed gift in this position was that of evangelism. Although the topic of spiritual gifts would seem indispensable to any book on people decisions, I have elected only to mention their importance and role in the process. The subject of spiritual gifts is both complex and, to some extent, controversial.

The importance of spiritual gifts is evidenced by the number of citings in the New Testament (Romans 12:6-8; 1 Corinthians 12:4-11,28-30; Ephesians 4:7-13; 1 Peter 4:10). Spiritual gifts have proven controversial in that some believe not all of the gifts mentioned in the New Testament are valid today. The proponents of such a position would assert that some or all of the gifts ceased to exist with the death of the original apostles.

The manner in which Paul lists the actual gifts leads many to conclude that he did not intend to provide an exhaustive inventory, but that it is "only suggestive of the various ways that God enables the church to fulfill His calling."[1]

I believe that the subject of spiritual gifts is vitally important when making people decisions in a ministry setting. But because of both the complexity and the controversy of the issue, doing justice to the subject is beyond the scope of this book. Additionally, a number of excellent books dedicated to the topic of spiritual gifts are readily available.[2]

COMPATIBILITY

Not long ago the workload in our firm grew to the point where we needed another secretary. The major responsibility of this individual would be typing with a capital *T*. After interviewing several candidates I found a woman (let's call her Susan) who really impressed me with her personality. She was bright, energetic, articulate—she just bubbled over with personality. Soon I was caught up in a web of possibilities as she described how she was looking for a place where she could grow to her fullest potential. This sounded great to me, and I agreed to hire her.

Susan had the right background and certainly could type fast. After all, I'm supposed to be an expert selector of people, and I had my criteria. What I overlooked was the issue of personality. Susan had a people-oriented, highly expressive type of personality. She had very low "sit-ability" and an even lower tolerance for detail. After I spent an hour proofreading the first letter she typed, I knew we were in trouble. Upon returning from a business trip, I was informed Susan had quit, having been on the job only three weeks.

A few days later she came to see me. Susan said she really hadn't expected that much typing, and this experience had helped her decide she didn't like typing at all. In fact, she was now determined to find a job that didn't require secretarial skills, a job where her people skills could be used more effectively. Both of us had gotten caught up in the wrong things during our interview. She had warmed up to my description of the firm's ministry and growth. I had been taken in by her vivacious personality and promotion potential. What I really needed was someone who loved to type.

"Fit" with the Job

Compatibility refers to the fit with the job as it relates to a person's temperament or personality, interests, and aptitudes.

For example, if the job requires precision and high attention to detail, you certainly don't want someone (like Susan) who has little interest in detail, and would thus be ineffective in such a position.

Many aspects of a job fit best with specific personality characteristics. For example, does the job you are filling require:

- Long hours sitting at a keyboard?
- The ability to knock on "closed" doors and hear lots of no's without taking it personally?
- The ability to follow a systematic, repetitive process with a high degree of accuracy?
- The ability to think quickly on one's feet and handle difficult questions with diplomacy?
- The ability to juggle several tasks at once and change direction at the drop of a hat?
- Careful attention to detail?
- The ability to make decisions with little precedent and even less help from the manager?

Certain personality types suit these needs better than others. Much of our behavior can be accounted for by our personality type. In large measure, personality influences our preference for specific types of tasks and the nature of the work climates in which they are performed. I don't want to oversimplify this very important issue. People are highly complex. They can't be labeled, stereotyped, or pigeonholed—they are versatile and multidimensional. Our purpose here is to merely sensitize you to the need to take personality and the issue of compatibility into account when you are making people decisions.

This is particularly true of younger people. Most people tend to select vocations compatible with their personality, even if it's on an intuitive level. But the younger employee may not have enough work experience to have developed those intuitive safeguards. Another area of caution is people who "really need the job" for one reason or another. The pressing need for the work may stifle their natural caution about taking jobs that "don't fit."

I've often found that a yellow flag in this type of situation is when someone is making a major change in direction. Someone with twelve years of accounting and bookkeeping experience who applies for a sales job that requires a lot of people skills, mobility, and high energy should get some second glances. It's important for you, the hiring manager, not to rely only on whether the candidate believes he or she fits the position, but also to develop your own sense of how well the job matches that candidate's temperament.

The scope and complexity of temperament and personality merit an entire book, and more than enough has already been written on that. Licensed psychologists use a number of very reliable and valid testing instruments that provide comprehensive insight into an individual's personality. For the most part these personality inventories are not available to the general public. However, there are several very credible test instruments that are available to nonprofessionals. They do not provide the breadth and detail of those used by psychologists but they do offer easy-to-understand, straightforward insight into our unique personalities. These are educational instruments designed specifically to teach people about themselves and others. They are particularly effective in team settings in which understanding the different work, communication, and social styles of individual members can increase interpersonal effectiveness.

The most popular of these personality instruments fall into one of two different categories, depending on the model of personality on which its based. One of these models is popularly known as DISC. The other instrument is the MBTI (Myers-Briggs Type Indicator). I provide some further explanation of these two models and references for additional resources beginning on page 263.

Interests and Aptitudes

Interests are another important personality consideration when matching people to positions. To a large extent, your interests determine your level of motivation. Therefore, it is unwise to place a person in a job that lacks the types of activities the individual would find interesting. The greater the correlation between the interests of the person and the activities of the position, the greater the levels of energy, creativity, and initiative that will be displayed by the worker.

The cousin of interests is aptitude. The word *aptitude* comes from a Latin root meaning "tendency." It's a natural talent or inclination. Some people have an aptitude for languages, others for math or mechanics, still others for music or certain types of physical prowess. Often these aptitudes can be greatly enhanced and developed with training. Whenever possible, match people with appropriate aptitudes in a given position. Compensating strategies can be developed in situations where a certain aptitude is important but not available, or where the candidate's other positive qualities override the missing one.

In regards to job compatibility, the search committee of First Church observed that the several "false starts" with outreach strategies may have caused the congregation to become somewhat cynical. Furthermore, people need to be recruited into the program both as leaders and as participants. Therefore, the committee decided, "We need a people-oriented person." They also agreed that they needed someone with a positive outlook and the ability to persevere in the face of opposition.

In further discussion, the elders made it clear that they wanted to see measurable results: "What we really need is someone who has demonstrated the ability to show balance between both people and the task."

Recognizing that Bill, the pastor, wasn't skilled as a manager, the group agreed they needed a self-starter, someone who naturally takes the initiative and yells for help when necessary.

Finally, they concluded this individual must be able to juggle a number of tasks and change priorities quickly due to an inadequate number of staff for this fast-growing church.

When they had finished this portion of the job profile, their compatibility criteria looked something like figure 8.3.

FIGURE 8.3

- Able to maintain a balance between a people-orientation and a commitment to the task and results
- A self-starter, someone with initiative
- Able to juggle several tasks at one time with the need to change priorities

CHEMISTRY

Whereas compatibility concerns a person's fit with the job itself, "chemistry" is the fit between the person and the culture of your organization. In a Christian organization, church or parachurch, this would include the candidate's ability to embrace your particular strategy in achieving goals (your philosophy of ministry), your doctrine, and your organizational ethos. Many ministries have a statement of faith to which a staff person must adhere.

We must be alert to a number of subtle concerns as to this chemistry. For example, individuals of a more liberal theological persuasion may be uncomfortable in a conservative climate and vice versa. Often, strategy itself is the issue, regardless of the theology undergirding it. For instance, someone committed to a more relational evangelism approach might have difficulty in an evangelical organization whose strategy was more direct, aggressive, and proclaiming in nature.

Besides the doctrinal or theological issues, chemistry affects an organization's philosophy about growth, debt, promotion from within, risk, quality versus quantity, and many other facets of policy that contribute to the overall mix we call "culture."

I have found that older employees or individuals higher in the structure notice and react more quickly to the lack of fit between themselves and an organization. I suspect experience has taught them to recognize the source of discomforting messages, appreciate their importance, and be willing to act on them. Alas, there's not much you can do to adjust the culture of the organization, at least not in the short run, and therefore the lack of fit is almost always terminal for the relationship.

Amazingly, few organizations understand the importance of chemistry and rarely take it into account when making people decisions. This is particularly true of organizations led by highly focused, entrepreneurial individuals. For example, the president of a large Christian ministry we work with is one of the most effective recruiters I've ever met. He has recruited many top corporate executives into the administrative ranks of his ministry, only to see them leave within the year, critical of the constant change in direction and shifting priorities of the organization. "It's not corporate," they stated in their exit interviews. Unfortunately, they were right, and this should have been taken into account when looking for a "corporate" executive to help in administration. Being able to help an organization become better organized is a skill; the willingness and ability to work effectively in an environment that values flexibility and rapid change is a matter of chemistry.

In the case of First Church, the search committee identified the following chemistry criteria:

FIGURE 8.4

- The ability to embrace the doctrinal statement of First Church
- A healthy balance between the use of both proclamation and lifestyle evangelism
- A commitment to a small-group strategy

CHARACTER

Character resides in both the head and the heart. Those elements of character found in the head deal with the traditional issues of morality, ethics, and integrity. I include them because I sense that too often in the Christian community we assume these elements are present. Even when our intuition is almost shouting for attention, we sometimes hesitate to be too direct, for fear of affronting a qualified candidate. Over the past several years, I've become extremely direct in listing such criteria for a given position as I interview and take candidate references. To date, I've never had someone take offense.

Another dimension of character lives in the heart. Here it might be better termed courage, and it's the ability to make the tough decisions (to rebuke, discipline, fire someone, etc.), or to uphold the quality line in the face of lack of resources, time, or pressure to do otherwise.

Earlier, I mentioned the numerous places in the Bible where we find lists of selection criteria. As you study these lists, you will find that they deal primarily with issues of character, such as the following:

- Trustworthiness (hating dishonest gain—Exodus 18:21)
- Temperateness
- Self-control
- Respectability
- Hospitableness
- Not loving money (Timothy 3:2-3)
- Not indulging in much wine
- Not pursuing dishonest gain (1 Timothy 3:8)

By stressing the criteria necessary to be a part of His management team, God gives us insight on where to put our emphasis as well. Character is the foundation on which all of the other qualities are laid. It's the safety net, the fall-back position if something goes wrong, and possibly the criteria on which you would be least willing to compromise.

Conduct is the best indicator of character, and although we don't specifically list behavior or conduct in our criteria, we'll attempt to validate its presence as we interview and reference our candidates.

The search committee at First Church continued its deliberations and agreed the new associate pastor needed to have the following character qualities:

FIGURE 8.5

- A positive outlook; a sense of optimism
- The ability to persevere in the face of opposition
- Emotionally mature—the ability to take criticism without becoming defensive

CHRISTIAN WALK

This category is critical, particularly for those decisions involving church or ministry positions. These criteria must specifically reflect the type of position, especially if it involves leadership responsibilities. Generally, if an individual is to have leadership responsibility in a ministry setting, I recommend that the hiring manager apply many of the qualities the Apostle Paul lists as requisites for elders and deacons in 1 Timothy and Titus. As you can see from the examples used above, criteria can be placed in any of several categories. Placement and precision are not as important as completeness.

The search committee at First Church felt that the following criteria summarized the needs of this area:

FIGURE 8.6

- Maturity and growth as a Christian. This individual will evidence the characteristics that are described for elders in 1 Timothy 3 and Titus 1.
- Evangelistic—committed to personal evangelism with a track record of personal outreach.
- Strongly committed to the authority of Scripture.

Note that the first criterion is summary in nature. Therefore, it's important to be familiar with these biblical passages, where fifteen to eighteen additional criteria for leadership are listed. The list covers family, personal, and spiritual issues that should be part of the overall evaluation of potential candidates. If some qualities are particularly important in a given job, list them separately so as not to overlook them. The First Church committee did this in the third criterion (figure 8.6) regarding commitment to Scripture, which closely parallels Titus 1:9, "He must hold firmly to the trustworthy message as it has been taught, so that he can encourage others by sound doctrine and refute those who oppose it."

I can't stress the importance of the category of Christian walk enough. I find that some ministries (parachurch organizations) are either presumptuous in their evaluation process, or they gloss over these points because of their tremendous staff needs. These qualities are not only needed to perform the task itself, but like the character traits discussed above, they often form a type of safety net when performance is lacking. If a person is mature and growing spiritually, there is practically no people or performance problem that can't be resolved.

The qualities I find most important in regard to the Christian walk are an understanding of the basic "how-to's" of the Christian life—how to walk in the power of God's Spirit, how to deal with sin, how to have a consistent prayer life and time in the Word, and how to handle interpersonal relationships from a biblical perspective (giving preference to our brethren, forgiveness, love, etc.). These qualities, coupled with a teachable spirit, are vital in dealing effectively with any number of tensions or problems that might arise in a work setting.

I have worked with managers in various corporate and ministry settings in dealing with personnel conflicts, motivational questions, and other performance problems. Often, these issues occurred with staff who, although in positions of leadership, were not mature in their Christian faith and didn't have a handle on the qualities outlined above. Thus, the resources and strategies at our disposal to develop solutions to these problems were severely limited. Invariably, the manager had assumed they were there when the original placement decision had been made.

Many of the readers of this book are Christian laypeople who hope to apply these principles and practices in their companies. I want to encourage this to the greatest possible extent. However, in the corporate arena, significant legal constraints as to selection criteria and the selection process as a whole can limit the use of the criteria outlined here. As you will remember from chapter 6, this limitation can be overcome to some extent by focusing on the values you desire in a candidate.

COMPENSATION

I include this particular category because in many organizations, particularly ministries, compensation is a very significant boundary line and will invariably help define or limit the pool of available candidates. At this point it's best to be "up front" with your desires, needs, and limits in the area of salary and benefits. Your alternative is to dodge the issue and hope, by some miracle, that the needs and desires of your first-choice candidate and your ministry pocketbook will match. The dilemma is that the two often don't match, and in the end the process becomes very expensive, financially and emotionally.

Generally, the salary range is not actually written down on your list of criteria but has been decided on and can be readily communicated. Often, compensation is stated as a range so that you can be flexible, depending on how some of the other criteria are met.

Continuing with our example at First Church, the search committee agreed that their salary range for the new associate pastor would be $30,000–35,000. Obviously, an appropriate "fit" between the church and the candidate would depend on the candidate's willingness to be compensated in that range.

CALL

The subject of call merits its own chapter, so we will deal with it here only briefly. I don't believe I've ever done a search for a Christian ministry where one of the criteria wasn't "a sense of call to this ministry." Like any good consultant, I dutifully wrote it down and included it in our final list. It seems so right and needed when talking about ministry positions.

The concept of call protects us if we have misread the presence of our other criteria. It's a catch-all that often overrides other considerations in the decision, including intuition. Like many aspects of our Christian walk, the term and concept of "call" are so often used (and with such confidence) that we assume we have a handle on its true meaning. However, we'll discover in a later chapter that such confidence might be ill-deserved. In its most general form, call is an important concept in people decisions, but many of us tend to define it in the narrow sense and, as a result, miss the point entirely.

However, there are instances in which call can be misused. I have seen some situations in which call and compensation are packaged together. In this case, ministries trade compensation for call. They are severely limited in their ability to pay what many would consider an acceptable level of compensation, and therefore they attempt to force candidates to "prove" their sense of call by being willing to work for the lesser amount. Even when they can negotiate such an agreement, the relationship seldom lasts.

The search committee at First Church discussed the issue of call and concluded that their ideal candidate must "have a sense of call to the purpose and ministry at First Church."

PUTTING IT ALL TOGETHER

It had been a productive evening for the search committee. They had defined the task of their new associate pastor of evangelism and had developed a list of selection criteria that accurately described the ideal candidate. As they reviewed their work on the flip chart (figure 8.7), Bob Jenkins, chairman of the committee, was the first to comment. "The key to success in this job will be the ability to lead," he said.

Mary Leta was quick to respond, "Bob, that's important, but not nearly so much as the gift of evangelism and an understanding of the principles."

"Leadership, Mary, that's what . . . ," Bob began, but was cut off in midsentence by Steve.

"You're both wrong," Steve said. "The top priority must be spiritual maturity."

(As tired as they were, the committee hadn't lost their heart for debate as each began to argue for their pet criteria.)

"Remember a few years ago when we made the decision on where to build the church?" All eyes turned toward Susan Thomas, who had been listening to the debate intently and now spoke. "The consultant told us we needed to prioritize our criteria—to put them in order of importance. Do you think that's what we need to do here?"

The expressions on her companions' faces gave quick assent. "He had us divide them between the 'must-haves' and the 'want-to-haves,'" someone else remarked. "Then we ranked the 'want-to-haves' in order of importance, with ten being very important and one being relatively unimportant."

"Okay," Bob concluded, "we're tired now. Everyone take a copy home with you and, on an individual basis, prioritize it just like we discussed. We'll meet for a few minutes after the morning worship service on Sunday to compare notes and agree on a final weight for each criterion."

"Can two different criteria have the same priority?" someone asked.

"Sure," Susan responded. "I remember the consultant said it was all right, but to try not to make them all tens."

When the group met again the following Sunday, they had all completed their assignment, arriving with their prioritized lists of criteria. However, they discovered that consolidating their lists in an agreed-upon sequence took much longer than a few minutes—more like a few hours. Slowly, they worked through the desire to make all the criteria "must-haves," and they hammered out their individual differences as to the relative importance of each of the criteria. Finally they agreed on a single, prioritized list of qualities and qualifications they believed accurately described the ideal candidate. Their list is shown as figure 8.7.

FIGURE 8.7—ASSOCIATE PASTOR OF EVANGELISM
SELECTION CRITERIA

Must-Haves
- The ability to embrace the doctrinal statement of First Church.
- Mature and growing Christian. This individual will evidence the characteristics described for elders in 1 Timothy 3 and Titus 1.
- Evangelistic—committed to evangelism with a track record of personal outreach. Hopefully has the gift of evangelism.
- Strongly committed to the authority of Scripture.
- Must have a sense of call to the purpose and ministry of First Church.

Want-to-Haves	**Priority**
Judgment/discernment	9
Technical knowledge and experience in the principles of evangelism	10
Ability to facilitate meetings, lead task forces, etc.	5
Communication skills	7
The gift of leadership	9
Planning skills	4
Ability to select and recruit capable people	6
Ability to organize	3
Training skills	8
Ability to persuade and motivate	5
Seminary degree	7
Positive outlook; a sense of optimism	6
Ability to persevere in the face of opposition	5
Ability to maintain balance between a people-orientation and commitment to the task	6
Emotionally mature—able to take criticism without being defensive	6
A self-starter; someone with initiative	8
Ability to juggle several tasks at one time	7
A healthy balance between proclamation and lifestyle evangelism	7
A commitment to a small-group strategy	8
Able to come for $30,000–35,000/year	7

The committee was now ready to begin their search. With this list, they knew what they were looking for and would be able to recognize qualified candidates. Certainly this list of qualities represents an ideal, and it's very unlikely that anyone will meet all of these criteria. But such a list is a plumb line against which they can compare alternative candidates. Not only will it provide a means to assess the degree of necessary compromise, but it will highlight the specific areas in which the "best" candidate is lacking and facilitate the development of compensating strategies.

Remember, the principle is the process of systematically identifying the key success factors of a given position and writing them down for reference as you begin your search and selection process. Some positions can be quickly profiled on a yellow pad, others require more detail and discussion. Such a discipline is the heart of effective people decisions.

CHAPTER NINE

Call: Conviction, Confusion, and Controversy

IN THE PREVIOUS chapter I identified seven broad categories of selection criteria describing the qualities and qualifications we should look for in people when filling a position. One of these criteria, "call," warrants further discussion. Not only does it play a critical role in making people decisions from a biblical perspective, but in the years I've spent assisting Christian leaders in making such decisions both in corporate and ministry settings, I've seen few subjects discussed with as much conviction, confusion, and controversy. Let me illustrate with some real-life instances.

Case Study 1—The Complacent Candidate
It was about 11:00 p.m. West Coast time, and I was in the midst of an intense phone discussion with the chairman of a large and growing Christian ministry. His concern was whether or not a key candidate for the president's post was, in fact, "called" to this position and ministry. I don't remember the conversation word for word, but it went something like this: "I don't sense the passion and conviction I wanted to see," complained my friend. "This job's too tough if a person isn't really called by God to stand in the gap. . . . There's no energy!" He went on to explain that a sense

of call was the most important selection criterion on his list. The candidate about whom we were talking was exceptionally qualified for this position in every way. He had been very involved with this ministry as a layman in his community, volunteering both time and money in a sacrificial way; he was a high-level leader in a secular corporation with management responsibilities much greater than those required for this position; and he was a mature and growing Christian leader in his own right. The only concern was his sense of call. When the chairman asked him if he felt called to this ministry, his response was, "What do you mean by call? If you're asking if I've had some supernatural insight, then no. But I love this ministry, and I want to serve God to the best of my abilities. If you need me, then I'm willing to leave my career to come here and serve." Although his response was clear, it was also calm and seemed to lack the level of enthusiasm and conviction the chairman felt was so important. Did this man have a call to this ministry?

Case Study 2—The Off-Again, On-Again Call

Bob and Carol are a couple in their early forties. Both were successful professionals, although Carol had long since left her career to focus full time on the raising of their five small children. They were mature and growing Christians with a strong commitment to evangelism and discipleship. They were vitally involved in their church as well as in a parachurch ministry whose primary focus was professional people. They had come to Christ and had been discipled through this ministry.

Because of Bob's active involvement in this ministry and his demonstrated leadership ability, he was suggested by several people as a candidate for president as the ministry began to implement its succession strategy. When I first approached them, they expressed a willingness to pray about it but explained that they didn't feel "called" in this direction, at least not now.

Not long after this, the search committee decided that, although Bob and Carol were open to exploring the possibility, the demands of the position were not compatible to a young family with five small children. They put their interest in this young couple on the back burner, news of which Bob and Carol greeted with relief as they went on with their lives.

Several months later I got a call from Bob asking for an appointment to see me as soon as possible. Later that week as he sat in my office, he energetically explained that recently God had really begun to work in his and Carol's hearts, and that they were feeling a strong sense of call to full-time ministry. "I know that the other position is probably already filled," he explained, "and our call isn't to any one organization or position. It's just that we really believe that, to be the best possible stewards of our talents, we should become involved with a ministry of evangelism and discipleship on a full-time basis. I'm here for counsel on how to proceed." As we continued to discuss the issue, it was evident that his sense of call was clear and full of passion. He went on to explain that when we had first talked months ago a seed had been planted and, as they continued to pray about it over time (even after the search committee had turned a different direction), the idea took root and began to grow with increasing energy. How can this couple feel not called one moment and called the next?

Case Study 3—A Number of Calls to One Position
Several years ago a large Christian membership organization began the search for a new executive director. The first place they went was to their own constituents, announcing the opening and qualifications for the job in their membership newsletter. The response was overwhelming. Several people sent résumés with letters expressing a clear sense of "call" to the job. As the search progressed, the committee evaluated a large number of people and finally decided on a person who has since proven to be very successful in the position. What about the other people who were so clear God was calling them to this situation?

Case Study 4—The Corporate Call
As I sat in the office of a Christian business executive, he was expressing a fair amount of frustration. We were meeting to profile

the qualities needed to fill the recently vacated senior vice president's slot in his company. "My greatest desire would be to have someone with a sense of call for what we do and why we do it," he explained. "Since I started this company almost twenty years ago, God has shown me how it can be a vehicle for ministry and not just for making widgets. It's been hard finding top executives who can see this as an opportunity for ministry as well as a business. I guess," he concluded somewhat reflectively, "that 'call' is really only for full-time ministry." Is this right? Is call only applicable to full-time ministry?

These case studies surface only a few of the questions surrounding this vital topic, like the following:

- What is a call and how do I tell if I have one (or for that matter if the person I'm interviewing for a position in my organization has one)?
- How do we find our call and what do we do with it once we have it?
- Is a call to a specific organization, place, and task, or merely to a general direction?
- Can one be called only into full-time ministry or into other vocations as well?
- What if there is disagreement as to the call of a person?

In light of the subject of this book and the importance of call in making people decisions of any type, it merits special attention. The relevance of call is not a matter of debate. My own experience and the evidence of Scripture speak too clearly of this. The debate begins, however, when we attempt to apply the concept of call to specific, real-time circumstances.

WHAT IS CALL?

Like many words in the English language, the word *call* has come to mean different things to different people, depending on the context of its use and the perspectives of its users. In most instances when we refer to the will of God in the areas of vocation, career, or job we tend to use the word *call*. The typical person would define call as a conviction or inner leading, a sense of confidence and conviction that God is designating a particular direction.

However, this definition is not true to its original, biblical meaning, nor is it precise enough to assist us in understanding and using this key concept in an effective manner as we make people decisions. Many define call as being guidance—the same type of guidance we seek from God over any specific decision confronting us. But, as we will see in a minute, that was not how the term call was originally construed.

Over the years, the terms *call, calling, purpose,* and *guidance* have slowly lost their distinctive meanings and, as a result, are often used interchangeably. This adds to the confusion that already exists with this very important facet of the Christian life.

Let's explore the meaning of these words in more detail to better understand how they fit into key people decisions—not only about others but about ourselves as well.

Biblically, call comes at several levels. First and foremost, the call is not to a place or a task. Rather, at the highest level, a call is by God, to God, for God. In this sense call, as used in the New Testament, is a synonym for salvation. Such a call is to repentance, salvation, and sanctification and is often referred to as our "primary" or "effectual" call (Matthew 9:13, Romans 8:28-30).

How, then, did call get applied to specific areas of our lives such as jobs? Since people who felt called by God wanted to place every element of their lives under God's sovereignty (including their jobs), they were quick to apply the concept of call to many key life areas, particularly to specific tasks or places. This has a vital consequence. Specific calls in the Bible to a place (such as Macedonia) or to a task (such as the priestly office) are rare and exceptional. Such calls are not the norm.

Gary Friesen explores this dimension of call in detail in his book *Decision Making and the Will of God.* He observes that the call to a specific task or office occurs only three times in the New Testament (Romans 1:1; 1 Corinthians 1:1; Acts 13:2, 16:9-10).

All of these instances deal with the Apostle Paul and reveal the exception rather than the rule when it comes to understanding the principles governing call. Friesen notes that in each case communication came in some form of supernatural revelation; it was issued only to certain people at certain times; and, in these instances, the call was unsought and unexpected.[1] He concludes, "While the concept of the call of God is a prominent one in the New Testament, the vocational sense of the term occupies only a minor place. And when it occurs, it is never presented as pertaining to all believers. . . . The rest of the time, He accomplished His purposes through saints obeying the moral will of God."[2]

I can sense some of you moving up to the edge of your chairs. Wait a minute. Does not the God of the universe speak to selected individuals in special ways? Cannot God, by His choice, call people to specific tasks and places? The answer in both instances is yes, God's power and sovereignty are just that, but many writers who have studied this subject would say that such leading is more the exception than the rule.

A better question would be, why doesn't God speak more directly to specific points of guidance? It's because He has created us with a unique faculty for reasoning and made us to be responsible and enterprising. God has left us with many areas of life in which He expects us to apply our reasoning using guiding principles from His Word.

The issue here is not the principle but the process. God has a will; Scripture describes Him as a God of both purpose and planning (Isaiah 46:10-11). He is the Master Designer not only of the universe but of man. Job 10:8-12, Psalm 139, Jeremiah 1:5, Galatians 1:15, and many other passages throughout the Bible speak to the fact that the creative craftsmanship of the Lord is exercised on a person-by-person basis. God does not oversee a mass production operation. That God has a will, a purpose, and a plan to achieve that purpose, and that He has handcrafted us to play a special role in that plan combine to support the concept that knowing God's will for our individual lives is of immeasurable importance to each of us (Ephesians 5:17).

When we discuss the issue of God's will in other areas of our lives, most Christians can support the idea that through prayer, the study of His Word, the counsel of godly men and women, circumstances, and the leading of the Holy Spirit we can discover God's will for us. However, when it comes to a career or a job, many of us look for a Damascus Road experience—an immediate flash of insight—that allows us to circumvent the more arduous process and move through uncharted waters with confidence. When people decisions are made, particularly in a ministry setting, we so expect such a leading that our first question is often, "Why do you feel 'called' to this position?"

At this point, we have forced the concept of call into a milieu for which it was not designed. There are many different types or levels of decisions in our lives. Some are broad, general issues of direction and destination; others are of a more immediate or specific nature, concerning a particular path or fork in the road to this destination. As originally used, the term *call* applied to these broader types of decisions. Friesen is alerting us to the problem when he tells us that we are applying the concept of call to a level of detail in our lives for which it was not intended.

Martin Clark defines call as being "God's personal guidance through which He enlightens us in regard to His plan for our lives."[3] The emphasis in this definition is "plan for our lives"—the broader issues of direction and destination I mentioned earlier, not the specific, everyday decisions about which we often seek God's guidance.

THE DIMENSIONS OF CALL

Part of the confusion with the concept of call is that we spread its meaning too thinly, forcing it to do the work of several words. The Puritans—who more than any other group have helped us make meaningful, practical application of this concept and its principle—defined call or calling in a much more precise fashion. It will help our understanding to review this term from their perspective.

The seeds of calling as it relates to our profession or work were planted in the New Testament. But the concept pushed into the spotlight during the Reformation when Luther challenged the division between the sacred and the secular, defining "good works" as those chosen by God and "comprehended within the bounds of a particular calling."[4] Later, Calvin would expand the concept and give it greater definition. He used the term *call* (*vocation* in French and *vocatio* in Latin) in two senses: the "primary call" is from God to God; the "secondary calling" is to a particular work, occupation, or station in life. The purpose of work, in Calvin's view, regardless of what kind of work it was, was to glorify God, to be a service to Him through service to men.[5] Calvin exalted the common and refused to give preference to a particular religious vocation, which might be esteemed above others.[6] All work, whether preaching a sermon or digging a ditch, was to be done as a service to God and not for personal gain or pleasure. It was a calling.

The Puritans really gave the concept of calling its momentum, turning the principles of Calvin and Luther into practice. William Perkins, a Puritan preacher and writer in Elizabethan England, refined the concept further by distinguishing between the general call and a particular call.[7] The general call was common to all Christians as Christians (to be holy, to be peacemakers, to be salt and light, etc.). The particular call was to a specific person because of his or her character and gifts.

Let me clarify one important point. I believe that if Perkins were here today, he would distinguish between "work" and a "job." Work would be defined as vocation or career, a life task or general direction. Within this "vocation," even numerous "jobs" should form a pattern, a continuity that contributes to our broader vocation—or, as Perkins would say, our *particular* calling. Perkins even outlined a series of rules to govern our choice of a vocation, declaring that in our personal calling we must

1. Have a particular calling.
2. Choose an honest and lawful calling.
3. Base our call on public need rather than the desire for personal gain.

4. Stay in it once chosen.
5. Avoid covetousness in our calling.
6. Be diligent in our calling.
7. Fit it into the framework of the general calling.[8]

The Puritan concept of calling was one of the first things our forebears unpacked as they landed on the shores of America, and it played a very crucial role in establishment of the culture and values of this country. Dr. Os Guinness believes the concept of calling, as it was imported by the Puritans, was the preeminent biblical truth that harnessed and shaped the restlessness and dynamic of our young, ambitious country. "It's at the very heart of the American existence," observes Guinness.[9]

By calling, Guinness would agree with Perkins. It means much more than something exclusively spiritual, like guidance, but rather that "the expression of our personalities, the exercise of our gifts, all that we are, everywhere we go, and everything that we do is seen as a response to the Lord and is done as part of our calling to Him." "In scripture," Guinness notes, "calling is primarily to Someone (God). It is not to somewhere (a place); it is not to something (a task). Where we go and what we do is the secondary part to calling, merely the outworking of our primary calling, which is to God."[10]

Oswald Chambers echoes this same thought in his book *So Send I You*: "The call of God is the call according to the nature of God; where we go in obedience to that call depends entirely on the providential circumstance which God engineers. The call of God is not to any particular service, although my interpretation of the call may be; the call to service is the echo of my identification with God."[11]

Over time, like so many concepts or values, the vitality of the notion of calling began to fray and weaken around the edges. In later Puritan times general calling became a matter of particular acts rather than an attitude of over-arching devotion to God.[12] To a great extent, the boundaries between the two dimensions of general and particular call have weakened. Today, Christians see little connection between their walk and their work. In large measure the wall between work in the marketplace (the secular) and the ministry (the sacred) has been reinstated. Many lay people and ministry people alike have become convinced that the work of the church must be done by "professionals"—people with special call, training, or gifts for ministry.

There is another dimension of call, another level, that people begin to confuse with the broader definition. To this point I have noted that calling comes at several levels. First, in our primary or effectual calling to salvation and sanctification; second, our secondary or general calling to all things Christian. The next level of call is what William Perkins termed "particular calling," reflecting the gifts, character, personality, and skills with which God gifted us. This is often reflected in our vocation.

There is still a fourth level of call. My own experience provides a good example. To this point in my life, my wife and I can recount several instances in which we felt certain God was leading us to a specific place and situation. Although I would casually note that we felt "called" in these situations, I would be referring to God's guidance. This guidance in each of these specific instances fell within what William Perkins would term "particular" calling. That we can be "led" by God's Spirit to very specific situations is of no doubt. There have been even more cases where I have been just as constrained to set my direction or deploy the resources in my stewardship on the basis of God's Word, the counsel of godly people, and my own thinking process influenced by God's Spirit.[13] And, very importantly, this guidance falls within the boundaries of my calling. It is this type of guidance, this "specific" call, to which earlier in this chapter I said Gary Friesen was referring.

I firmly believe that people will seldom, if at all, receive specific guidance from God outside of their calling. That is, we must first choose to place our lives and all that they contain under the sovereign will of God. It is within this circle that God may, at His discretion, from time to time issue a clear, specific call. The accompanying diagram might better illustrate this relationship.

Particular call resides inside the broader circle of general calling and specific guidance within that. Again, I believe it is unlikely that God would issue a specific call to any person who had not first come to grips with his or her "calling" in the broader sense.

Oswald Chambers speaks to the issue: "Profoundly speaking, there is no call to service for God; it is my own actual bit', the overflow of super abounding devotion to God. . . . When people say they have had a call to foreign service, or any particular sphere of work, they mean that their relationship to God has enabled them to realize what they can do for God. Their natural fitting for service and the call of God is identified as one in them."[14]

With this foundation, let's build some answers to the questions in the beginning of this chapter.

HOW DO WE FIND OUR CALLING?

In many respects a synonymous term for calling might be purpose.[15] What is the purpose of your life? Purpose deals with the question *why?* Why do I exist? (Or more accurately, "For whom do I exist?") Pat Morley, in his excellent book *The Man in the Mirror*, notes that there are two aspects to finding significance: "The first answers the fundamental question, 'Who am I?'. The other answers life's second big question, 'Why do I exist?' We derive meaning and identity from understanding who we are in Christ. It's a position we occupy. On the other hand, God has a purpose for our lives—a mission, a destiny—which is why we exist. It is the direction in which God wants us to be moving."[16]

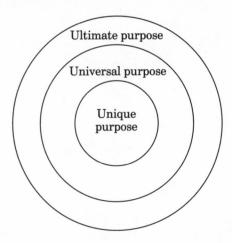

As Christians, our primary purpose is to glorify God (Isaiah 43:7). The first statement in The Westminster Shorter Catechism sums it up in an eloquent, straightforward manner: "Man's chief end is to glorify God and enjoy him forever." Actually, this really isn't our purpose, but rather God's over-arching purpose for us. We can find the purposes of God for men on three levels. Picture these levels as three concentric circles. We'll label the outermost circle God's ultimate purpose—ultimate in that it encompasses the entire scope of history—past, present, and future (Isaiah 46:10). It's played out from Genesis 1:1 to Revelation 22:21, and every person, Christian and nonChristian alike, will play his or her part on the stage of God's ultimate purpose.

The middle circle is God's universal purpose—universal because it applies to all Christians. His Word makes it clear that all followers of Christ are to devote themselves to prayer, to love one another, to study and apply God's Word to their lives, to share the gospel, to be salt and light, as well as the other spiritual disciplines the Lord admonishes us to pursue. They do this so that they might "walk in a manner worthy of the Lord, to please Him in all respects, bearing fruit in every good work and increasing in the knowledge of God." Universal purpose is equivalent to what the Puritans termed general calling.

In the innermost circle we find God's unique purpose for each individual Christian. Unique, in that each of us is handcrafted by the Creator for some special purpose. In Galatians 1:15, the Apostle Paul notes that the story of the Gentile church didn't start on the Damascus Road, but rather many years earlier when God set him apart in his mother's womb to be the apostle to the Gentiles. God told Jeremiah that He knew and consecrated Jeremiah in the womb of his mother to be a prophet to the nations (Jeremiah 1:5). David acknowledges as much in Psalm 139:

> Thou didst form my inward parts;
> Thou didst weave me in my mother's womb. . . .
> Thine eyes have seen my unformed substance;
> And in Thy book they were written,
> The days that were ordained for me,
> When as yet there was not one of them. (verses 13,16;
>   NASB)

We could write the same message in our journals. One of the most fulfilling challenges for Christians is discovering God's unique purpose for our lives.

Finding our unique purpose is, to a great extent, a pilgrimage—a journey of exploration rather than an immediate "ah ha" experience. It comes in little bits as God, over time, reveals insights into why you (as a unique individual) are here. It comes as we pray asking God to reveal His purpose for us (Matthew 6:7-8), study His Word, and reflect on the influences and forces He has brought to bear in and on our lives. When it comes to a unique purpose, we must take into special account the way God crafted us, that is, the gifts, interests, aptitudes, and temperament He designed into our lives just as He did into the lives of David, Jeremiah, and Paul. Doug Sherman and William Hendricks observe in *Your Work Matters to God*, "You will make your greatest contribution when you work in a career that corresponds to the way God has designed you."[17]

Have you gone through the exercise of defining your personal purpose? Do you have a clear understanding of your own purpose and calling in life? Do you have a written statement of purpose for your life? These are questions not only for you but for the people with whom you will staff your organization as well.[18]

With our more precise definitions in hand, let's return to a few of our opening case studies to develop a clearer understanding of the issues.

CALLING IN SECULAR (CORPORATE) VERSUS SACRED (MINISTRY) SETTINGS

You'll recall that the Christian business executive in case study 4 was looking for top executives who shared his sense of call—that the company could be a vehicle for ministry. In this case, my counsel would be as follows:

As we saw above, both Luther and Calvin challenged the concept that a sacred occupation was of greater value than one in the secular realm. In discussing how to choose a career, Sherman and Hendricks plead, "Just make sure that you don't base your decision on the idea that going into ministry (i.e. full-time, vocational ministry) will bring you greater significance. . . . The ministry is not a 'higher calling,' but rather an important calling for which God has designed some people. Those in ministry are not of higher value to God than other professionals, although they can make an outstanding contribution to the glory of God and to the lives of people."[19]

What this executive should be seeking are not necessarily people who feel "called" to his particular business, but rather people who are clear about their "calling," their purpose—people who see their lives and all that they contain to be at God's disposal, that is, to be salt and light wherever God would place them. I would look for people who were secure in their identity in Christ and their mission; people who were clear about their doctrine of work and see how their work fits into furthering God's purposes (Matthew 5:16); people who are in touch with themselves and have thought through why this position is the best stewardship of their strengths, gifts, skills, and knowledge; and finally, people who have approached this decision through prayer, counsel, and wisdom, using the sound mind that God has given them.

The underlying issue here is that of alignment between the larger purpose of the business (that is, is it viewed primarily as a means to make money or rather as a vehicle for ministry to staff, customers, and vendors?) and the purposes of individual executives. When the company and individual purposes are in alignment, then the individual staff person has everything to gain from the company's success. For when the company succeeds, the individual succeeds. If I, as an individual, agree with the purpose, philosophy, and strategy of the organization, we're in alignment.

PURPOSE, PASSION, AND PERSONALITY

Let's return to case study 1 for a moment, for it contains a critical insight. You'll remember that the chairman of a large Christian parachurch organization was uncomfortable with the key candidate for the position of president over the question of call. The chairman of this ministry came to faith late in life and embraced it with great passion. This was, I suspect, due in part to circumstances of his conversion experience, but to a much greater degree it was influenced by his own temperament or personality. He approaches everything in life with tremendous energy and enthusiasm. He speaks with great conviction and forcefulness. When he was confronted with a candidate whose temperament expressed itself in a calmer, more controlled, and subdued manner, he began to doubt this person's sense of call.

The issue wasn't calling as I've defined it, but rather that of specific guidance. Here the real issue was one of personality rather than God's specific leading. Providentially, both men ultimately decided that this was a good match. But there's more to the story. About a year later, the candidate's former company approached him with a substantial offer—a top position with a salary many times greater than his current one. "No," he said. "I'm right where God wants me to be." His particular leading to this ministry, wrapped tightly in a greater sense of the calling God had on his life, was not in doubt.

Personality, faith, motives, and many other aspects of our makeup all combine to influence how people will respond to a specific call (i.e., guidance), whether issued by God through human messengers as with Samuel and David, or directly from God in some Damascus Road experience. Isaiah was positive and proactive in finding his call into God's service. It would appear from the biblical record that Noah accepted God's call to build the ark with no argument (Genesis 6). The same could be said for Abraham when God sent him out from Haran to Canaan (Genesis 13:1-7). Moses wasn't so positive in his response. When God confronted him from the midst of the burning bush with the challenge to bring the people out of Egypt, Moses brought up argument after argument about his lack of qualifications and the difficulty of the assignment (Exodus 3). Gideon reacted in a similar fashion (Judges 6), as did Saul with Samuel (1 Samuel 10). At the far extreme we find Jonah, who fled outright from his call.

All of these people and others were called out of their comfort zone into something that appeared to be significantly less safe than their current situation. In most instances there were few specifics as to the details of the task to be accomplished. Outside of certain positions (for example, the Levites), the Lord has never been into job descriptions in a big way. He expects obedience based on faith and has shown great patience with the various responses His servants initially displayed when they wrestled with their sense of call.

CALL CAN BE A TWO-SIDED AFFAIR

In case study 3, a membership association advertised for a new executive director. A number of people who responded did so with the observation that they believed God was guiding them to this position. The candidate who was ultimately chosen was not one of these people, and after some time on the job, the board is giving him high marks. God certainly didn't direct all of these people to the same position, and the board (godly people who sought God's will in the matter) obviously thought God hadn't called any of those candidates.

On an individual level, it can be a challenge to discern God's guidance or leading. Often our own desires, needs, or even interpretation of circumstances can spark our powers of rationalization, and the results seem "so right" that we believe this *must be* the will of a loving God. Gary Friesen points out that, in his opinion, "it is often forgotten that many, if not most, such inward impressions lead nowhere. Promptings are followed to deadends as often as to avenues of service."[20] Such inward promptings, which may or may not be the inner witness of God's Spirit, need the support and reinforcement of the Bible, circumstances, mature counsel, and probably a good dose of common sense and reasoning.

Second, as in marriage, there's more than one party involved in this transaction. In this instance, if God had specifically called a particular person to the position, He would likely have led the decision makers in the same direction.

It is clear that God can, has, and will continue to guide or lead His servants to specific tasks in special places. However, there is also strong and consistent evidence that in many, if not most, instances He expects that we work out many of the critical occupational decisions ourselves, using His Word, the advice of mature counselors, and the inner leading of the Holy Spirit. The nonnegotiable element is the issue of "calling," the more general concept of a person's proactive subordination of his or her gifts, skills, time, and resources to the will of God in all circumstances. Within this boundary we sometimes find the more specific leading to a particular situation when and if God issues one.

The question here is not one of calling but of guidance: "How do you know that God wants you in this job?" A perfectly acceptable answer is, "I don't, but as I've prayed, sought counsel of godly friends, and examined my gifts, skills, and desires, it appears to be an excellent match from my perspective. I'm confident that God will use you and this evaluation process to either confirm this impression or redirect me to a better path."

Each person will respond to a sense of call in a manner consistent with his or her temperament. I can't use my energy level as the only indicator of God's will. And, in an occupational setting, when God does guide in a specific direction, it must include all the parties involved in the decision process. Whether a person is responding out of a general sense of calling or to a specific, well-defined leading; whether the call is to full-time vocational ministry or to a profession in a secular setting; we must look for individuals who, like David, are people after God's own heart because they are willing to do all of His will (Acts 13:22). If this is the case, the details will fall into place.

CHAPTER TEN

What I Look For in a Candidate

I'M OFTEN ASKED, What do you look for in a candidate? Do you have a short list of qualities that you look for in general, regardless of the position? The answer to the last question is yes. I believe that almost every manager has such a list, those few core characteristics that we've learned, over time, generally predict success on the job. Although mine is a dynamic list, changing as I learn and am exposed to new situations, most of the time it contains about ten to twelve characteristics. Although they apply primarily to management positions, these qualities can be adapted to a much broader range of jobs. Admittedly, there's a lot of overlap between one item and the next, but forcing myself to categorize my criteria in some fashion is a great help to me when I am evaluating people.

Spiritually Mature and Growing

This is a critical ingredient in any leadership position, particularly in a Christian ministry, and as far as I'm concerned, a nonnegotiable. If an individual is mature spiritually, then I know I can work through almost any problem down the road. Defining spiritual maturity would require a book in itself, and I don't approach the question with a detailed checklist in mind. But spiritual maturity would definitely include a clear sense of calling and personal purpose, as I defined them in the previous chapter. It would also include a love and knowledge of God's Word, a growing understanding of our identity in Christ, prayer, and faith. J. Oswald Sanders observes in his classic book *Spiritual Leadership* that spiritual leadership is a matter of superior spiritual power. "The spiritual leader influences others not by the power of his own personality alone but by that personality irradiated and interpenetrated and empowered by the Holy Spirit."[1]

In any ministry position in which being a Christian was a criterion, I'd want to see a heart for God and a demonstrated commitment to growth as criteria for selection.

Emotionally Mature

An emotionally mature person would be able and willing to take responsibility and to handle a reasonable amount of stress and ambiguity on the job without becoming dysfunctional. The ability to maintain a sense of perspective and the use of judgment, particularly under pressure, would also mark the emotionally mature.

Teachable Spirit

The cornerstone of this quality is accurate self-knowledge. One who is teachable will ask for help and admit and learn from failure. Such individuals generally have much intellectual curiosity as well. They're always into something new.

Self-knowledge is a critical ingredient of teachability. In a classic *Harvard Business Review* article, Paul Brouwer observes that "growth implies changes within people—in how they use their knowledge, in the ends to which they applied their skills, and, in short, in their view of themselves. The point is clear that growing people examine themselves; and as they do, they emerge with new depths of motivation, a sharper sense of direction, and a more vital awareness of how they want to live on the job. Growth in this sense is personalized and vital. And such growth in self-concept is at the heart of a real manager development effort."[2]

Although it's an important trait, individuals with an accurate self-knowledge are few and far between. Brouwer notes, "Unrealistic self-appraisal has cost many a manager his or her job. Think of the people you know who have been fired, eased out, or moved laterally because they no longer seemed to be 'up to the job.' Has there not been, in many such cases, the subtle flavor of unadaptability, of rigid inability in a manager to adjust his or her sights to a new role as times have changed?"[3] In reality, self-examination and the insights about ourselves that it brings are a matter of personal stewardship of the gifts and skills God has given us. J. Oswald Sanders draws the same conclusions: "Most people have latent and undeveloped traits which, through lack of self-analysis and consequent self-knowledge, may long remain undiscovered."[4] As you can imagine, this quality becomes a rich and important part of my interview and reference efforts. I look for people who can give me an accurate, balanced list of personal strengths and weaknesses, and I'm very interested in how they came to this insight.

Character

I've covered this in detail in chapter 8. This quality includes more than being honest and trustworthy. It includes the character and courage to hold the line under fire, to make the tough decisions, and to do the right things for the right reasons, even when confronted with the pressure not to do so.

Team Player

I always look for people who have a cooperative, unselfish spirit. Someone who is willing to subordinate individual interests and job-related goals to those of the group when and if appropriate. Such an individual demonstrates the initiative to maintain good working relationships and to support the efforts and goals of others. Such a person understands and practices the admonition of the Apostle Paul in Philippians 2:3-4: "Do nothing out of selfish ambition or vain conceit, but in humility consider others better than yourselves. Each of you should look not only to your own interests, but also to the interests of others."

Unremitting Commitment to Excellence
This attitude might be characterized by a mind-set that believes that everything can always be a little bit better, that details are important, that the judge of my results must be the people I serve.

Interested in This Job
Interest in the actual work involved with the position is one of the most important ingredients in motivation. It's not the title of the position but rather the actual, day-to-day activities that tap into motivational energy. This is what engenders a sense of ownership and excitement about the position and keeps it from becoming "just another job."

I've found three primary causes for mismatches between the job and the interests of the person. First, people who badly need the work often don't work out. Abraham Maslow alerted us to this principle when he explained the hierarchy of personal needs. Interest in the work is desirable, but when I am out of work and need the job I'm often willing to do anything. The problem is that no matter how badly I need the job, if I'm not interested in it, I won't employ all of my creative energies in getting it done. A second reason some people take a position that doesn't match their interests is that they are interested in the next job up or over. The current position is seen merely as a steppingstone to the more desirable one. It's difficult to perform today's tasks with excellence when your mind is on the task for tomorrow. Finally, there's the young worker who does not have enough life experience to be in touch with his or her interests in the work setting. As I point out in a later chapter, discovering and confirming interests is an excellent use of testing.

This criteria reminds me of something I don't look for: someone who is overly concerned with managing his career. The key word is *overly*. A moderate amount of ambition and sense of direction are healthy and needed, particularly in individuals aspiring to leadership. I get concerned when the career becomes the predominant focus. In this case, people see each position as merely a rung on the ladder, which needs to be climbed as quickly as possible. Their focus is not on the task at hand but on the ultimate goal. The motives of such people often deal more with prestige and titles than challenges and contribution. One indicator of this is a pattern of quick moves from one organization to another based on perceived opportunity rather than completion of the task at hand.

Of course, an argument can be made that one can't be successful in a career without good performance in each incremental position. And, when we see an individual moving quickly through a series of positions in the same organization we often find good performance. In the best case, a strong performer was placed too low, and the organization is big and wise enough to allow that person to find a more challenging position. In the worst case, those allowing such rapid progression are either too easily persuaded or they are evaluating the person on activity and perceived potential rather than actual results.

I remember one client who promoted a very promising staff member four times in only nine months. During this time the individual never even changed offices, but the company kept increasing his responsibilities by putting additional departments under his supervision. Every time he was given a new department he dazzled management with his initial observations of how poorly the department had been run and how fast he was moving to develop action plans. Nine months into the year it became apparent that for all the talk, nothing was happening. Not only that, their all-star manager was spread so thin trying to manage seven departments that you could almost see light through him.

This was a sad event for both parties, for in spite of the poor performance this man was very capable. Had he been forced to prove himself before additional responsibilities were added, he probably would have done so. He would have been promoted but at a much more measured pace. He got caught up in his "career" and how he appeared rather than what he accomplished.

Cares About People

This is a person who values other people. I'm not talking about a "people person," but rather an individual who respects others, appreciates the differences and diversity of other people and the unique contribution they bring to the team.

Demonstrated Need to Achieve

Many human resource experts believe that the need for achievement is the single best predictor of success in business.[5] One of the key principles in this book is that the best indicator of what a person will do is what he or she has already done. The biggest indicator of a person's need to achieve is past achievement. Is this a person who has demonstrated a consistent ability to set and achieve goals?

Initiative

Is the candidate a self-starter? Will he or she look for things to do if I'm not around with the next assignment? If a person with initiative sees a problem, he or she tries to figure out what caused it and how to fix it. Others, observing the same difficulty, think, *Here's a problem. I wonder when someone is going to fix it?*

Intelligence

Intelligence plays an important role in performance in most job settings, particularly in management positions. In general, most successful managers will score above average in intelligence tests. I include a lot of things under this characteristic: common sense, judgment, analytical and problem-solving ability, and conceptual ability. It is the ability to conceptualize that allows us to see and build patterns, to draw inferences from data, and to look into the future with strategic insight.

Balance

One thing I always want to know about everyone is, What is this person's core competency? What can he or she do exceptionally well? The age of the Renaissance man is over, at least in the typical organizational setting. Our organizations, by necessity, have become vast armies of specialists. Where does this person fit into that army?

However, I'm not looking for a narrow, one-dimensional person either. Many successful people have achieved in one area of life by subordinating everything else to that one endeavor. This approach has been particularly prevalent with business executives. In fact, I'm feeling a little guilty myself as I write this. Such success is seldom long lasting because, at some point, the areas not receiving adequate attention will collapse, and often the resulting consequences wash over into the area of success. The really successful people that I admire most have a sense of balance in their priorities. Although they have significant success in a given area, it has not been at the expense of another important life area. Look for people who show a total life pattern of success consistently, over time.

Well, that's my list. How does it compare with yours? Others have drawn up similar lists. Charles Garfield, author of *Peak Performers*, thinks successful top managers exhibit the following behaviors:[6]

- They strive to transcend previous behavior.
- They avoid getting too comfortable in their jobs.
- They enjoy the artistic part of their work.
- They vividly rehearse coming events in their minds.
- They do not place the blame for mistakes on others or on themselves.
- They examine the worst consequences before taking action.

You'll notice that none of the above qualities deals with skills but rather with matters of personality and heart. In an earlier chapter, I noted that the biblical requirements for leadership also focused on character rather than on competencies. Skills can be taught in a relatively short time; character doesn't come so quickly or easily.

Such a list is just as important in recruiting as in evaluation, if not more so. We'll see in a later chapter that good recruiters are always recruiting, always on the lookout for people. They have a general idea of what they're looking for even if they don't carry the list around in their pockets. Dr. John Kotter, a professor at the Harvard Business School, has studied and written about leadership for many years. Several years ago he studied firms that did a particularly good job at recruiting good people. They were aggressive recruiters who had identified sources of people and were always on the lookout for the best people. Kotter observes that

> Most of these firms did not have a clear written profile
> of what they were seeking in these recruiting efforts;
> nevertheless, if one talks to the senior officials involved, a
> common profile emerges. They look for people who are reasonably smart; grades, test scores, and an ability to think
> in an interview are all seen as indices. They look for people
> who are motivated; grades, extracurricular activities in
> school, and any kind of achievement against difficult odds
> are seen as relevant. They want people with integrity; anything in a person's record that might indicate a lack of this
> trait is seen as potentially important. Finally, they seek
> people who can relate well to others; this is labeled in many
> different ways, but the underlying issue is the absence of a
> history of interpersonal problems and seem to be caused by
> emotional difficulties.[7]

I use my list of criteria when looking for and evaluating people whether the client has included them or not. Hopefully they will be of help to you as you develop your lists for particular positions. Keep these qualities in mind as you read the forthcoming chapters on evaluation. How would you identify the presence of such characteristics in the interview or references of your candidates?

PART THREE

EVALUATING THE CANDIDATES AND MAKING THE DECISION

CHAPTER ELEVEN

Evaluating the Candidates— The Process Overview

WE HAVE PROFILED the task and developed a detailed list of selection criteria that describe the ideal candidate. Let us assume for a moment that we have, through some process, identified a number of candidates who appear to be qualified and have expressed an interest in the position.[1]

How do we evaluate these candidates and identify the very best one? Our list of selection criteria was reassuring in its seeming completeness and objectivity, but now we are confronted with the task of discerning which candidate has the best communication skills, or relates in an effective manner with top management, and demonstrates poise under pressure. How do we find these sorts of things out, and even more to the point, how do we measure the relative presence of such criteria among several candidates?

The goal of our evaluation process is to gain accurate insight into the strengths, weaknesses, and qualities of an individual that would impact his or her ability to successfully perform in a given position. Some criteria are "hard" and thus easily verifiable (for example, a master of divinity degree); others are "softer" and more subjective and, as a result, much harder to discern.

What are the sources of information (tools of evaluation) that will allow us to discover this information, and what are the principles and pitfalls associated with their use? In making people decisions, be they for in-house promotions or transfers or for selecting an outside candidate, we have only four sources of information about our candidates. It is from the proper use of these four sources—the résumé, interview, reference, and testing—that we must draw our insights and make the final decision.

Although we would seldom use all four sources for any given decision, too often decision makers use too few and even the wrong sources to verify a specific criterion. As it takes three separate readings to triangulate the source of a radio signal, I recommend that you use at least three of the four sources in gathering the information about a person and his or her potential to perform successfully on the job. As to which three, the odd man out will usually be testing, a source best suited for special criteria. It is used in situations where this type of criteria play an important role in the overall job and where the risks of being wrong are high.

Without a doubt the interview receives the most attention and often carries a disproportionately heavy load in the decision-making process. Although always present, the résumé or application form is a passive instrument and doesn't provide the interaction and dynamic offered by the other sources of information. It appears so straightforward that we tend to take it at face value. Many decision makers have written the reference off as being too time consuming for the benefits received. Over the years those who provide references have accrued the reputation as being "too soft" in their assessments and more than willing to export their problems to the purview of others.

Although it's too often overworked, the interview is a primary source of information and critically important in the evaluation process. One analyst estimates that in 1987 American business spent approximately $26 billion in managerial time preparing for and conducting selection interviews.[2] Additionally, some evidence shows that much of this investment was wasted. Some researchers have found that the typical untrained interviewer has only about a 22 percent chance of predicting job success for a candidate. With training that percentage doubles to about 44 percent but still presents less than a fifty-fifty success ratio in choosing a qualified person.[3] Although the possibility of doubling our interviewing effectiveness through training and study makes such an effort worth it, it is also clear that this one source of candidate information cannot carry the entire load. This calls for a more balanced approach to our evaluation.

Finally there is testing, a source of information veiled in mystery. So few of us as laypeople understand the underlying principles, and often the results of the tests must be interpreted by trained specialists—*very expensive* trained specialists. When this is coupled with the challenge of explaining to a highly qualified candidate that we want to "test" them, well, it just seems easier to bypass this source of information.

TOOLS OF THE TRADE

Think of each of these four sources as a different tool or diagnostic instrument for evaluating the qualifications of the candidates. The more skilled we become in the use of these tools, the better our evaluation will be. We must not only learn to master each tool individually, we must be able to blend them properly into an integrated evaluation strategy. We greatly increase the effectiveness of our evaluation if we know the strengths and weaknesses of each tool and how one can augment or enhance the information of another. Additionally, if used in the right sequence, we can not only increase the speed and efficiency of our evaluations but decrease the overall cost as well.

View the evaluation/screening process as a funnel. We need a process that is both effective and efficient: effective in that we want to ensure that the very best candidate both applies and is identified; efficient in both time and cost. Consider the graphic on the following page.

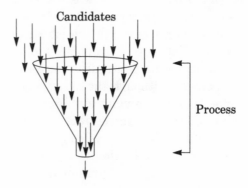

All of the candidates enter the top of the funnel and, optimally, only the very best one will emerge. As we proceed through the funnel, fewer and fewer candidates make it to the next step in our evaluation process. At the same time, the costs of evaluation in time and money are rising. Therefore, we will want to sequence our strategy and evaluation tools in a fashion that knocks out unqualified people early in the process.

In chapter 8, I suggested that you break your selection criteria into two groups: must-haves and want-to-haves. The must-have criteria are the knockout factors. You want to make sure they are visible and identifiable up close to the top of the funnel.

For example, the résumé or application form is invariably the first piece of information we have about a candidate. In fact, it is often the ticket for admission to our funnel. Because the résumé is up front in our process and very inexpensive, it would be great if we could identify knockout factors here. Often, the typical résumé doesn't have a key piece of information that might signal the presence or lack of must-have factors. Therefore, many companies and nonprofit organizations require an application form, in addition to the résumé, that highlights this information.

Which information source (i.e., evaluation tool) you use and when in the process you use it depends on several things:

- *Cost factors*—testing is generally costly and therefore, in most instances, is left until the end of the evaluation.
- *Critical criteria*—each source has particular strengths in helping us evaluate the presence of certain qualities or qualifications. For example, references are certainly the best source of character. Tests deal effectively with criteria that are influenced by personality or IQ.
- *Importance or risk in the position*—the more important or risky the decision, the more emphasis should be placed on certainty rather than costs.

Note that we don't always use these tools in any certain sequence, and that we often use them several times in the overall process. For example, a typical screening process for a midlevel executive in either a ministry or company might look like this.

1. Collect and screen résumés.
2. Initial phone interview.
3. Preliminary reference (by phone) if travel is involved for interview. Purpose here is to be certain cost of travel is merited.
4. In-person interviews.
5. Referencing.
6. Testing.
7. Final interviews.

Remember the funnel; as candidates proceed through the process, some are eliminated at each step. Because of costs, many organizations test only the final candidate. When possible, I recommend that we test the final two or three candidates, assuming they appear to be closely bunched as to their qualifications. Generally, we arrive at the final interview with one candidate. It's in this session that we can clarify any reference or testing data that may be of concern.

In many situations we could shorten the process. For in-town candidates it's unlikely you'd conduct preliminary references. You probably would do an initial phone interview. It only takes five to ten minutes and can save you forty-five to sixty minutes if the candidate is not qualified. For important or risky decisions you might add steps to the process. The principle is to balance the effort and cost with the benefits and risk of the decision.

With this overview in mind, let's jump into the next few chapters and learn how and how not to use these four key tools of evaluation.

CHAPTER TWELVE

The Résumé:
Sizing Up and Sifting Out

SEVERAL YEARS AGO I was reviewing a résumé for a ministry position at the end of which the candidate included the following summary of strengths:

- Training others
- Computing quantitative data
- Organizing people
- Meeting the public
- Inventing new ideas
- Managing people— negotiating
- Implementing plans and objectives
- Helping others
- Selling products

- Coaching for performance
- Coordinating events
- Analyzing quantitative data
- Synthesizing technical data
- Writing instructions
- Cost analysis
- Selling ideas
- Solving problems
- Making decisions
- Processing ideas
- Planning programs

I knew this man personally. He wasn't trying to present himself as a superman. But few of us have the breadth of skill shown in this list. A fleeting acquaintance with such skills maybe, but not in-depth competencies across the board. Generally those gifted in the people side of life (communication, selling, negotiating, etc.) are not as gifted in the quantitative dimensions (analysis, problem solving, cost analysis, etc.), and vice versa.

The first question that comes to my mind when I see such a résumé is whether or not this person understands what we mean by skills, and if so, is the person in touch with his or hers? Plato observed that an unexamined life is not worth living. Additionally, I often see elements of murky communication. In the case above, what does he mean, "meeting the public, inventing new ideas, processing ideas, etc."? In summary, this person is casting his net too wide, trying to appear qualified for almost anything, and as a result, when I compare this résumé to others in my stack, I cannot discriminate. I know that no one is good at everything, but I can't tell what this person is good at. I go on to the next résumé.

The first information about any candidate usually comes from the résumé. This document often determines whether or not we'll interview this person. However, it's a challenge to glean necessary and relevant information from the typical résumé.

Reviewing résumés may be tedious, mundane work, and the signals of "real" qualifications are generally faint. Therefore, we tend to want to delegate this task. However, since the résumé is the key screen for choosing whom you will interview, the hiring manager must stay close to the process. The higher the level of the position, the less this task should be delegated to "screeners." However, in some situations too many résumés demand that we get assistance. In these instances, give the task to someone thoroughly knowledgeable about the position and ask to see a sample of the rejects in order to verify his or her understanding of the criteria as well as his or her judgment.

TYPES OF RÉSUMÉS

We usually find two basic types of résumés: chronological and functional. Chronological résumés present job history, focusing on the time frame and the specific position or job title. Generally, the most commonly accepted format starts with the most recent position and works backward. Although there is usually more information included than merely date and title, nevertheless these two items normally form the basic organizational structure of this résumé document.

FIGURE 12.1—CHRONOLOGICAL RÉSUMÉ

Bill Jones
123 Sample Avenue
Anywhere, USA 37698

Experience
1987 to Present   Acme Electronics Corp., Albany, New York
Vice President of Consumer Affairs

Provide direction for thirty-two-person department through the supervision of five managers. Responsible for the development and implementation of all warranty policies, product update information, and field service contracts.

1983 to 1987   General Manufacturing, Inc., Dallas, Texas
Director of Clearing Operations

Managed the Field Service and Service Contract Departments of this medium-sized industrial electronics firm. Responsible for department budget development and implementation, staffing, policy recommendations, all operations, and annual customer satisfaction survey. Through the implementation of several pivotal customer service strategies we saw a 23 percent reduction in customer complaints from 1984 through 1987.

The second type of résumé stresses experiences, achievements, and skills rather than the position itself. This is often referred to as a functional résumé, and in it the candidate assumes that relevant experience, knowledge, and expertise are more important and make a better impression than the specific positions or employment chronology.

FIGURE 12.2—FUNCTIONAL RÉSUMÉ

Bill Jones
123 Sample Avenue
Anywhere, USA 37698

Management—Seventeen years of comprehensive management experience including all staffing functions (hiring, appraisal, and staff development), decision making, planning, and problem solving. Skilled in creating a motivational environment that encourages teamwork, creativity, and innovation. Have developed and implemented several highly rated on-the-job training programs that became corporate standards.

Customer Service—Experienced customer service specialist who works well with top management of client organizations. Thirteen years of customer service management in complex, customized electronic manufacturing robotics. Have demonstrated the ability to satisfy tough customer demands creatively, while at the same time maintaining corporate policy and profit guidelines. Have consistently lowered the number of customer service complaints and raised customer satisfaction levels.

Project Management—Have provided leadership for numerous special project task forces both corporately and for joint company-customer projects. Have published several papers for the Association of Electronics Manufacturers on the management of design and implementation of complex customer service system programs. Am familiar with PERT, CPM, and Gantt project management/control systems.

Most professional search consultants prefer the chronological format. They are generally familiar with the various jobs in a given industry and, therefore, have a pretty good grasp on the typical skills and expertise needed to perform in a given position. They are more interested in a short, straightforward chronological listing of the various positions held over time.

Additionally, the list of experiences, achievements, and skills shown on the functional résumé are best brought out in the interview process. I might also note that even a functional résumé should include a short listing of the positions held in chronological order. When I receive only a list of functional skills, I'm quick to discard, or at least discount, the résumé. Why? Because it doesn't give me enough information for evaluation, and time doesn't allow for going back for more information. In most instances I have too many other seemingly better alternatives available in the remaining résumés.

WHAT TO LOOK FOR IN A RÉSUMÉ

Achievement—Look for specific instances of goal accomplishment, the ability to bring a project from concept to completion, to make a profit, to solve a problem, to implement a plan. In summary, I look for anything that would show that the candidate actually knows how to get something done.

Unless this is the major focus of the position, be cautious of "process" jobs. In a previous chapter I mentioned some of the yellow-flag words such as *coordinate* and *facilitate*. Be wary about qualifiers like "assisted with," "exposure to," "knowledge of," and like terms that indicate this person was at the game but not necessarily on the playing field. Also, don't confuse credentials with achievement. Certifications, association memberships and awards, and even formal educational degrees do not necessarily confirm competence or accomplishment.

Look for specific achievements. If the candidate managed the "fastest-growing territory," ask: Out of how many territories? How fast was this territory growing before you came? If these statistics aren't in the résumé, list them for follow-up in your initial phone interview or for when you meet in person.

Growth and progress—Look for growth in skill and responsibilities. Some personnel experts insist that successful candidates will show a steady, clear series of promotions. However, the trend toward flattening organizations by cutting middle management and staff roles that began in the last half of the 1980s will continue well into the twenty-first century. As a result, we'll see people spend more time in a given position. There may be added challenge and responsibilities, but the basic position and titles will be more static. Good people will still progress, but it will become more difficult to see this movement in the résumés alone.

Clear thinking and communication—You can glean a lot of insight about a person's thinking and communication ability through a résumé. Is it wordy, stuffed full of descriptive adjectives and superlatives, and disorganized? Or is it realistic and clear? Do you get the sense the candidate is trying to bluff or con his or her way into an interview?

Some candidates know they're not qualified for the position but feel that if they can just get an in-person interview they can talk themselves into the job. Glib language and broad generalizations pepper their résumés. Others are also unqualified but neither appreciate the demands of the position nor are connected with their own strengths and weaknesses. Finally, there are those who may be qualified but have done such a poor job in writing their résumé that it's nearly impossible to determine if they merit further consideration.

Stability—Conventional wisdom says to reject people who have changed jobs frequently, and in many instances this is probably right. However, don't be too quick to discount these people. There are excellent candidates out there who, if given the opportunity, may have reasonable explanations for such moves. If I see a résumé with a lot of changes but excellent experience that's relevant to the position, I'll probably have a brief phone conversation with this person and give him or her a chance to explain the moves before I make a decision about an in-person interview. This person could be a star on your team even though other coaches weren't able to get the person to play up to his or her potential.

With such a résumé look to see if there wasn't at least one job of significant duration (five years or more) even if it was some time ago. I've seen many résumés of individuals who spent ten to fifteen years with major corporations like IBM, General Electric, and Procter & Gamble—they leave for one reason or another and then go through three jobs in three to five years. I've discovered that many people coming out of big organizations didn't understand how much support, resources, and assistance these situations provided and didn't appreciate the contribution of the culture and environment of these organizations to their own personal success. They don't find this kind of support in a smaller company, and without even understanding what's missing or different, they begin switching from one job to another to find the missing ingredient. Often, it takes some time and a few changes for them to get their "sea legs."

While we're on this topic, let's talk about dates. Look for gaps, and if changes between jobs show less than two years in a position, get the month as well as the year for start/stop dates. I frequently see instances in which a person was in job A from 1987 to 1990 and job B from 1990 to 1991. With a little probing I find that job B was actually from November 1990 to April 1991. Different picture, isn't it?

Education—First, be clear about the extent that education is a requirement for the position, then look for that particular information.

Be cautious about lengthy, detailed lists of every seminar and workshop the applicant has ever attended, too many degrees, and long lists of papers published (unless relevant to the position).

Be alert to vague references to lack of education. One red flag would be showing the college attended, even the dates, but not listing the degree. Without careful reading, many reviewers would fill in the blanks and assume there was a degree. It's not the lack of the degree that is the issue but rather the attempt to detract from or cover up its lack. This alerts me to be particularly attentive to character issues.

Personal data—This is a helpful section in that it often contains nice-to-know information that, in a secular or corporate setting, is illegal to ask. For example, marriage and family information. However, be alert to too much irrelevant detail in this section. It may indicate lack of focus, an attempt to pad the résumé here to make up for weakness elsewhere, or poor judgment as to the appropriate topics and amount of information to include in the résumé.

Graphics—I've often thought there might be an inverse relationship between the quality of the candidate and the glitz or slickness of the résumé. Odd typefaces, overdone graphics, and textured or colored paper tend to challenge my inclination to follow through with an interview. In defense of the candidate, such an approach is an effort to get his or her résumé to stand out in a sea of paper, but it also says a lot about the person's judgment or taste as to what's appropriate in this situation. This person would not arrive at the interview dressed in a flamboyant outfit in order to stand out from the other interviewees. Neither should he or she take such an approach with the résumé.

I've also found in some instances that very qualified candidates don't put a lot of work into their résumés. The résumé of one of the best people I've ever found for a client (a head of data processing) was a copy of a copy of a résumé typed on a typewriter with a poor ribbon and at least two broken letters. There was no pizzazz, just a series of code words and jargon. Not very impressive to a search executive or hiring manager who didn't know a lot about data processing. Being the expert selector of people that I am, I discarded the résumé and went on to others of less substance but better graphics. Good graphics I can understand! Somehow there was a mixup, and the résumé ended up in a stack that I was having reviewed by a more technically minded friend. The following morning I got the call: "MacMillan, you've found your man! Although for the life of me I don't know how you got him, he has one of the best reputations in the industry." I didn't share this story with my client, but he did hire this candidate, and I have examined résumés with a more careful attitude ever since.

APPLICATION FORMS

In many respects the application form serves the same purpose as the résumé. It provides a written summary of the candidate's work history and qualifications. Unlike the résumé, the application form is standardized, thus making it easier to compare candidates. It also provides an opportunity to gather crucial information that normally requires a preliminary phone conversation, for example, why he or she left previous positions and his or her salary history. I believe that broader issues like significant accomplishments, objectives, etc., are best left to the interview.

In some respects I'm ambivalent about application forms. In my experience at higher-level corporate recruiting, I often find the better candidates resistant to filling them out. In many instances I have approached, on behalf of my client, potential candidates who were not looking for a job and often did not even have a current résumé. These people feel that filling out an application form conveyed too much interest on their part; after all, we were the ones trying to recruit them.

For mid- or lower-level positions, particularly when you must process a lot of candidates over time, there is a need for a more standardized approach. An application form not only minimizes the screening cost to the employer but allows for easier comparison against predefined standards (e.g., must-have criteria) as well.

SCREENING RÉSUMÉS

Like any detailed, tedious task, we need to develop strategies for screening résumés that allow us to remain alert and attentive to the pertinent details. A number of experts in this field suggest limiting your screening sessions to twenty to thirty minutes (and five to ten résumés) to minimize fatigue and maintain your ability to discriminate between résumés.

In the process of screening, sort the résumés into three piles: yes, no, and maybe. The yeses are those you definitely want to interview; the nos are clearly unqualified. You're going to think about the maybes; you may even give some of these applicants a brief phone interview to clarify an issue. However, at some point, all of the résumés in this pile must be sorted into one of the other two groups, yeses or nos. The résumés in the yes pile represent tickets of admission to your evaluation process, the funnel I described in the previous chapter. As you screened these résumés you marked or highlighted any significant points, good, bad, or "of concern," for easy reference later.

The next step in the screening process is a brief phone call to clear up any questions or concerns, before committing to an in-person interview. "Mr. Jones, I found your résumé very interesting, but I do have a couple of details I need to clarify. . . . You moved to organization B in 1990. Can you give me the specific month you left organization A and the month you started at B?"

If the answers satisfy you, schedule an interview. That's the subject of the next two chapters.

CHAPTER THIRTEEN

"Inter" Viewing:
The Art of Inner Viewing

IT WAS LATE morning in San Diego. I was midway through my second pot of coffee and the third and final interview. I was interviewing candidates for a southwestern sales manager position for a Swedish computer firm. Although all three candidates had looked promising on paper and in phone interviews, I was sure I had found the person in candidate number three. He was head and shoulders above the others. His experience was ideal, he was very familiar with the territory, and in a previous sales position he had called on my client's target market, architects. He even had an undergraduate degree in construction management, so he knew the industry. As to manner, I found him articulate, bright, poised, and very energetic. He was a little jumpy and squirmed around in his chair a lot, but I put that off to high energy and the natural tension resident in any interview situation.

With sales candidates, I focus on performance against goals (quota) and on the salesperson's ability to realize sustained performance improvement from year to year. His responses to my questions in this area bolstered my belief that he would be the ideal candidate. He was a self-employed distributor of computer equipment, the number one or two performer among all of his

147

firm's distributors for four consecutive years. I frequently use compensation to validate performance data. In a sales setting, sales performance and compensation are generally tightly linked. If the salesperson is contributing at an outstanding level, compensation generally follows close behind. "What'd your W-2 say last year?" I asked.

"Oh, that depends," he responded with a grin that was halfway between sly and sheepish.

"On what?" I asked, my heart beginning to sink. My intuition and naturally skeptical spirit were having a field day with the hopes I'd entertained only moments before.

"Oh, nothing much," he said. "Do you want to know how much I earned or how much I declared?"

"Both figures would be interesting to me." I was beginning to wonder if I should switch to decaf.

He went on to explain that many of his current customers had small businesses and often paid in cash. He didn't feel obligated to report all of it on his tax return.

"Hmm," I responded nonchalantly. "Kind of like having a bonus on Uncle Sam." He smiled back; we were just two "street smart" businessmen talking business.

I went on with the interview, and because of the tax issue, I probed several other areas that lent themselves to flexible ethics. On some he did well, but on others he was soft, communicating that the situation would determine his response.

He was out. In spite of extraordinary sales skills, his character disqualified him from further consideration. He was open with me and revealed this dimension of his character because of the rapport we established during the front part of the interview. I had not conveyed my philosophy either in my questions or in response to his answers. As a result, I caught a glimpse of the truth in the inner man, an insight masked from our other evaluation tools. As we closed our time together, I couldn't resist asking one more question: "Jim, regarding the issue about declaring full compensation for taxes, how could we be sure you'd accurately declare your expenses for reimbursement if you went to work for my client? After all, you'd be managed from Sweden, and your supervisor would be here only occasionally."

"Oh," he shot back quickly, "that would be different."

The goal of our evaluation process is to gain insight into the relative qualifications of our candidates. An interview, in the ideal sense, is a time for asking a series of carefully crafted questions that allow us to capture this insight.

Each question plays its respective role in broadening our understanding of the candidate. In some respects this activity might be better termed "inner" viewing, for our questions, if properly designed and asked and coupled with keen observation and careful analysis, will allow us to see past the surface and at least catch a glimpse of the inner person. King Solomon wrote, "The purposes of a man's heart are deep waters, but a man of understanding draws them out" (Proverbs 20:5).

The interview can be an excellent tool for evaluating a candidate's qualifications, *if*:

- The questions are tied to relevant selection criteria.
- The questions are properly designed to elicit the right information.
- The questions are asked in the suitable manner.
- The climate is conducive to open, candid, nondefensive communication.
- You maintain an attentive, open, nonbiased attitude that allows you to really hear what the candidate is saying.
- You correctly interpret and evaluate the results.

No other selection tool receives as much attention and emphasis as does the interview. As only one of our four sources of information about a candidate, the interview often carries a disproportionately heavy part of the load in the decision-making process.

Many, if not most, of the books written on people selection focus entirely on the interview. I don't provide that much detail, but because the interview is our primary evaluation tool and source of information about the candidate, I have expanded my observations into two chapters. In this chapter, I identify the ten primary pitfalls that hinder interviewing effectiveness, as well as the compensating principles and disciplines that, if applied correctly, will allow you to avoid such traps.

In the following chapter, I'll explore barriers to effective interviewing that arise not so much because of lack of skill but from the basic thinking processes and perspectives we bring to the interview. Additionally, I'll discuss how many interviews you should schedule and who should do the interviewing. I've included an annotated bibliography for those who want to dig deeper into this topic (page 287).

TEN COMMON PITFALLS

The following ten pitfalls chip away at interviewing effectiveness, all of which are the product of lack of training and skills.

Pitfall 1: Lack of Preparation

Communication—talking and listening—appears to be deceptively easy, at least on the surface. This perception, coupled with lack of training and overly busy schedules, prompts many hiring managers to "wing it," depending on their intuition and ability to think on their feet to get them through the interview. An interview is not something to "get through," but rather a critically important fact-finding expedition with a clear objective and significant consequences hanging on the outcome. Research findings are very clear in this area. Interviewers sitting down with candidates in an unstructured interview merely to "discuss" job requirements produce consistently poor results.[1]

As we'll see in a moment, good questions are the currency of an effective interview. At a minimum, preparation should include the development of relevant questions tied to specific selection criteria. Additionally, any paperwork or information on the candidate should be reviewed to identify areas of focus and issues needing further detail. Even a small amount of preparation not only increases the productiveness of the interview but also communicates both competence and organizational interest to the candidate.

Pitfall 2: Poorly Constructed Questions

All of us have experienced the power of a thoughtful question. How interesting we find pithy, provocative questions and the people who asked them. Jesus skillfully used questions to provoke the Pharisees and stimulate the thought and insight of His disciples: "Can you drink the cup I am going to drink?" (Matthew 20:22); "John's baptism—where did it come from? Was it from heaven, or from men?" (Matthew 21:25); "What do you think about the Christ? Whose son is he?" (Matthew 22:42); "Who do people say I am? . . . Who do you say I am?" (Mark 8:27,29).

Like a building, an interview is no better than the raw materials used in its construction. Questions are that raw material, the building blocks of the interview. Good questions are not the product of spontaneous mental combustion during the interview, but rather the result of hard work and thought during our preparation. Questions that are not tied to our selection criteria or that are illegal, unclear, leading, loaded, or closed all generate piles of irrelevant information. Questions are the currency in the interview, and therefore, each must be "handcrafted" with your criteria and overall purpose clearly in mind.

A good interview question has five qualities:

Purposeful/relevant—Each question must be tied to a specific selection criterion. In an earlier chapter we observed that varying from our criteria produces not only the wrong information but too much of it. This is where the art of actually designing the question comes into play. We must construct the question in such a way that the response really does relate to the criteria under evaluation.

Focused on recent past behavior—One of the most important principles in making good people decisions is that the best indicator of what a person will do is what he or she has already done. Past behavior is the key to understanding future behavior—"Well done, good and faithful servant! You have been faithful with a few things; I will put you in charge of many things" (Matthew 25:21). This principle should be the cornerstone for all of our questions—always emphasize job-relevant behaviors, under what circumstances, with what results.

For example, I might ask, "Mary, was there an instance in your previous work where you had to juggle too many balls in too little time and still maintain extremely high quality? Tell me how you managed to do that?" Such a question will give you a lot more insight into Mary's ability to operate effectively in a hectic environment than a question like, "Mary, can you juggle a lot of projects at one time and still maintain high quality?"

Focused and clear—At some point you will have to interpret the results of this interview by comparing the responses to specific criteria and, ultimately, even to the responses of other candidates. To ensure that you will be able to clearly understand the responses long after the interview, maintain sharp focus as you structure your questions. For example, don't combine two questions into one—"John, how did you feel when your boss gave you such an unrealistic deadline, and what did you do about it?" Breaking that question down would help John give both issues equal attention. Also, consider asking several questions about larger, more important, and complex criteria as well. For a recent corporate management position, we had five or six questions alone for a single criterion dealing with strategic planning.

Comparable—A good question can be used with all candidates so as to ensure comparison of responses.

Open-ended—*What, why*, and *how* are excellent words with which to begin a question. They will invariably motivate a deeper, wider response than launching a question with words like *did, can, are, do, would, could, were*, or *have*. There are few questions for which a yes or no answer will suffice, and when such responses are put forth, they are often wrapped in other words and thus escape our notice.

Even with such a strategy you will often get a shallow or

abbreviated answer. Merely ask for more detail—"Can you elaborate on how you . . . ?" "How did you . . . ?" I would have turned down many a well-qualified candidate had I based my decision on his or her response to a question. Pushing the point to ensure that the candidate really understood what I was asking, or that I really understood what the candidate was saying back to me, has saved the day for both of us innumerable times.

Pitfall 3: Not Taking Effective Notes

Many interviewers feel that taking notes in an interview not only interferes with their ability to listen but can be distracting, even threatening, to the candidate as well. As we'll see, it isn't so much a matter of *if* but rather of *how* the notes are taken that determines their contribution to the evaluation process. Research clearly shows that good notes are critical for effective evaluation. Notetakers not only remember more after the interview, but they remember it more accurately.[2]

During a typical interview, candidates give out a tremendous amount of information. It comes at you rather quickly and lacks a structure with which you can control the direction and pace of the interview and thus capture and organize the information. It is possible, even, that you will leave the experience more confused than when you arrived. A well-reasoned set of notes provides such a structure and ensures that you will be able to effectively use this data for later reference and comparison.

As to how to take notes, I usually write out the questions in advance in a logical sequence, leaving space to record the candidate's answers. I also leave space for important observations and conclusions that have more to do with the overall interview experience than with a specific question—for example, eye contact, apparent energy level, poise, confidence, etc. Having the questions written in advance saves precious time during the interview itself.

I don't always follow the order of my questions, because oftentimes the interview takes on a life of its own and it's sometimes better to go with the natural flow and pick up the other items later. Frequently, an answer to a question that has not yet been asked will come up in the course of the interview, and having the form in front of me, I have a place to put that information so it will be accessible.

I've placed a generic version of an interview form we have used at Team Resources on pages 273-277. If you think it would be helpful in your interviewing, please feel free to adapt it for your use.

After we've had a chance to chat and get to know one another a bit, I use my notetaking as a lead-in to my questioning—"Barbara, do you mind if I take notes during our time together? God didn't bless me with a photographic memory, and I need all the help I can get to ensure that I remember our time accurately." I've never had anyone object.

During the interview, without making a big deal out of it, try to keep your note pad and notetaking as unobtrusive as possible. I always make sure that the candidate can't see what I'm writing.

Be consistent in your notetaking. Nothing is more disconcerting to a candidate than to see you go for a long time without taking a note and then suddenly start writing furiously when he or she mentions a past mistake or area of weakness. In fact, I often delay writing down a negative comment for a few minutes so as not to alarm the interviewee.

Learn to keep notes short and allow time after the interview to amplify the candidate's comments and your observations while your memory is still intact. Tie in illustrations and examples to your observations. For example, on a recent job one of the criteria was "a demonstrated ability to train and develop subordinate staff." During the interview this was brought out by asking for specific examples in the candidate's past that would show this ability. One fellow shared that a number of years back he inherited a department in which virtually all of the staff were young and very inexperienced technically. He needed a way to train twelve employees fast and instituted a two-hour training class every Tuesday afternoon called "Tuesday's Topics." It was an excellent example, and I merely wrote "Tuesday's Topics" in my notes during the interview. However, after our time together, that was enough to help me recall and write out the illustration in more detail.

I'm really making two points here. The first is to use a personal shorthand during the interview and allow time afterward to amplify while the thoughts are fresh. Second, link observations about your selection criteria to specific examples. For instance, if you believe the candidate is assertive, provide a specific example as to why you can draw this conclusion—"Mary demonstrated a lot of assertiveness by pressing her supervisor until he saw the financial potential in the widgets."

Pitfall 4: Talking Too Much, Listening Too Little

I have participated in many joint interviews with client managers and have seen too many of those managers dominate the interview with their own comments. Consequently, they arrive at the end of the interview having found out very few relevant facts about the candidate.

Obviously, the interviewer needs to communicate—to build rapport, to explain the position, and to describe the organization. What I'm referring to here are situations where such communication goes to the extreme and hinders rather than helps the interview. Such overcommunication may result from several factors—the desire to be polite, lack of preparation, lack of training/skill, or high ego strength. Regardless of the motivation, when you become the "featured speaker," you not only learn less about the candidate but you are likely telegraphing desired responses as well. Don't feel the need to editorialize on every answer. Smiles, nods, and an occasional "that's interesting" will convey the needed warmth and the fact that you are listening.

Learn how to view each message as having two tracks, music and words. Words alone account for only for 7 percent of the message. Ninety-three percent of any communication is accounted for by tone, body language, inflection, emphasis, gestures, and facial expression.[3] Attention to these other areas is a critical ingredient of the effective interview.

So what is the correct ratio of talking to listening? It must be determined on a situation-by-situation basis. Which interview you're in (assuming a series of meetings), the level of the position, and the length of the interview all influence how much you, as the interviewer, talk. However, as a general rule of thumb, most experts would agree that the interviewer should be actively listening 80 to 85 percent of the time.

Pitfall 5: Not Establishing and Maintaining Rapport with the Candidate

Critical to any interview is a nonthreatening climate that encourages open discussion of both strengths and weaknesses. Creating such a climate requires a creative blending of both tone and setting, and this is seldom achieved without some forethought and skill.

Another term for climate would be rapport. The lack of rapport can endanger the decision process at several levels. First, if rapport is low or absent during the interview, the interviewee's willingness to be open and candid will be, at best, muted. Second, should you ever penetrate the "air defenses" such an atmosphere engenders and discover a person you want to choose, that person, in turn, may conclude that, if this is how things are in the "recruiting mode," he or she will probably be worse-off after the chase.

A clear understanding of what rapport really is will go a long way in helping to create it. Webster defines rapport as a state of mutual trust and emotional affinity. In the context of an interview, this definition may prove to be a little soft, even misleading. One author observes that too many interviewers go into the interview expecting to "click" with the right candidate—that is, they expect immediately to feel a positive chemistry, mutual interest, or friendly feeling toward the interviewee.[4] This is an unrealistic expectation and, in some respects, an unhealthy one. The diversity of an organization's personnel makes such chemistry unlikely, particularly with strangers on the first meeting.

Rapport comes from a French word that means "to bring back." The essence of the meaning is "alignment," which is to be in a proper relationship to some point of reference. When we can bring the expectations of both parties into alignment regarding the purpose and the process of the interview and wrap such an alignment in a tone and setting that engenders openness and candor, we will have rapport.

As for setting the tone, let me ask this: What kind of climate would encourage you, in an interview situation, to be open and candid, even about possible shortcomings? Typical responses to this question in our training seminars describe climates that are warm, sincere, relaxed; climates where interviewers are clear about the objectives and the process of achieving them.

Small talk at the front end is a good way to give the candidate a chance to ease into the interview situation. However, you must be careful. Certain topics are legally off limits in job evaluation, and a good number of EEOC suits arise out of inappropriate "small talk" at the front or back end of the interview when the interviewer has let down his or her guard ("Where does your spouse work?" "How old are your kids?" etc.).[5] The key to preventing discrimination claims is to assure that an interview question is directly related to the hiring decision and relevant to the job. Politics, weather, traffic, the economy, and the impressionistic art in the lobby are all acceptable small-talk subjects.

Next, spell out the purpose and the process of the interview so the candidate has a frame of reference—"Barbara, our goal today is to give both of us an opportunity to evaluate your qualifications for this position. Let me explain the position and then, over the next hour, I'd like to ask you a number of questions that will help me get to know you better, both your strengths and weaknesses as they relate to the task. We'll conclude our time by answering any of your questions about the job or the organization and outlining next steps."

Which brings us to the interview setting. In 1987 an independent survey found that 78 percent of the interviewees exiting an interview listed some aspect of the physical setting among their top three impressions.[6] Setting is a matter of courtesy and common sense. Eliminate the intervening desk (physical barriers create psychological barriers), ensure privacy and no interruptions. These and the many other common-sense points of meeting courtesy all contribute to the setting and reinforce the rapport between you and the candidate.

Pitfall 6: Telegraphing the Desired Answer

Giving too much feedback the wrong way can, over the course of the interview, "give the answer away." Although we must constantly challenge interviewers to be alert, active listeners, no such encouragement is needed for typical candidates. A potential job is on the line, and their listening radar is highly attuned to every word and nuance. They pick up any verbal or nonverbal clues that might help them assess how they're doing. They are extremely attentive to our responses to their answers—a smile, a nod or shake of the head, a verbal "uh-huh," energetic notetaking—each of which may connote, to them, either our approval or disappointment. If not managed carefully, our responses to their answers can create forces that will crack our lens of insight into the true nature of the candidate.

Often the signals sent out by the interviewer are unconscious, a matter of habit. Most of the telegraphing I've encountered with Christian interviewers is of a positive nature, often the result of an inappropriate attempt to develop rapport or to be polite. While we want to provide a warm, positive climate that promotes openness and candor, we don't want to inadvertently contaminate the objectivity and accuracy of the candidate's responses in the process.

When an interviewer signals his or her displeasure with a particular answer, it's often communicated with an attempt to debate the issue or to get the interviewee to recant. "Don't you think . . . ?" or "Don't you mean . . . ?" are clear giveaways. To avoid this tendency you should establish acceptable answers to your interview questions beforehand. Don't use the interviewee as a sounding board for your own thoughts or ideas still under construction. If the candidate gives the wrong response and you're sure he or she understood the question, note it and move on. You've just captured an important piece of data. Your objective is not to correct or change his or her mind on the matter.

In the process of attempting not to signal the desired responses, it's important not to go too far in the other direction and lose your rapport with the candidate. As we discuss below, selling is just as important as screening, and a cold, unresponsive facade doesn't send the right signals either. The key words are balance and consistency.

Pitfall 7: Taking Things at Face Value
Research has shown that candidates tend to distort their interview responses more than they do the information on résumés or application forms. Additionally, they generally upgrade rather than downgrade such information.[7] Although one practitioner estimates that only 7 percent of the thousands of people he's interviewed for corporate clients were totally honest in their responses,[8] I've found that most of the Christians I interview are candid in how they portray themselves to prospective employers. As a result, I tend to approach the interview with the anticipation that the interviewee will be honest and open in responses. Additionally, thorough referencing and multiple interviews provide a safety net with which to catch inconsistencies and allow me to concentrate on catching the meaning of the responses rather than uncovering a fib or exaggeration.

However, we shouldn't be naive about people. Someone once observed that "success has a thousand fathers but failure dies an orphan." Much interview information is of a very subjective nature, and all of us can honestly overestimate our contribution to the results, particularly as we reach too many years into the past.

There are two instances when I stop along the way and probe more deeply than I might normally. The first is when I find it difficult to get specific answers or an acceptable level of detail in response to questions about responsibilities or job results. The *ate* words (*coordinate, orchestrate, facilitate, initiate, generate*, etc.) alert me to dig a little deeper. Other yellow-flag words might include *contributed, developed, maintained, organized, provided,* and *supported.*

One thing I really want to leave the first interview with is a crystal clear understanding of what this person did in his or her day-to-day responsibilities and how the person performed against goals or standards. Generally, I have reviewed the résumé before the interview (that's the natural habitat of these types of words) and if I find some, then I adjust the emphasis of my questions accordingly. If under repeated questioning I still can't gather the specifics, then I'm open to classifying this candidate as either lacking integrity or very confused. Either way, it will probably be his or her last interview with me.

The second instance where I prod a little more than normal is when the terminology might carry different meanings to the respective parties. Words like *strategic, conceptual,* and *successful* are but a few examples.

Recently I interviewed a young woman who had left a marketing position with a Fortune 100 company to join a fast-growing ad agency. After only four months it was obvious that this was not a match in any sense of the word. She was devastated; and the company was concerned over her distress, taking full blame for the mismatch. Returning to her former position was not an option, and she was confronted with having to find another position and establishing her credentials in a new corporate environment. How did this happen?

During our interview she explained that the ad agency was looking for someone with a "strategic background." Now, who among us wouldn't think that our background wasn't "strategic"? However, when the company said it, they meant "big picture," or high-level strategy. When she said it, she meant "targeted goals and effective use of data and analysis." The word *strategy* has a broad spectrum of meaning, and to the surprise of both parties (after the decision!) they lived on different ends of that spectrum!

What about confronting a candidate? There are instances when, in your probing, you must take the risk of losing rapport in order to capture a critical piece of information or maintain control of the interview. Dr. Tim Irwin, an industrial psychologist and a good friend, has taught me a lot about people decisions over the years. He has always stressed the need to move toward the resistance. Here are a few of the instances in which such counsel is particularly relevant.

Inconsistencies—Sometimes I find inconsistencies in the answers given to different questions. Usually with some probing, I find it's just a matter of clarification, but it needs to be addressed. "Bill, let me see if I have this right. A few minutes ago you noted that you quit, but now you're implying that your boss was intending to let you go for some time. Clear this up for me, will you?"

Dodging the question—"Bob, that's not what I'm looking for. Specifically, why did you . . . ?"

Vague answers—This is the first cousin to the above item. "Joan, I need specifics. Out of the fifteen telemarketing people, how did you rank, even allowing for the fact that you didn't start until two months into the fiscal year?"

One author suggests threatening to check the records as one means to motivate a truthful response.[9] Basically, this is a subtle but clear message that you are going to perform a thorough check of records and references. "Bill, although I'm sure we'll answer this in references, how would the elders at First Church describe your ability to lead the church staff?"

Each of the above circumstances, as well as others like them, puts us in risk of losing rapport and, with it, the ability to obtain a clear, accurate picture of the interviewee. Therefore, we recommend that, even when you pick up inconsistencies or even an unequivocal sidestep, you wait until at least three quarters through the interview before you push the rapport to a possible breaking point. Patience will give you a greater data base on which to draw your conclusions regardless of the response to your more direct inquiries.

Pitfall 8: Too Much Screening, Not Enough Selling

I've talked to too many candidates who described their interviews with Christian organizations or with professing Christians in secular corporations more along the lines of the Spanish Inquisition than those of a purposeful evaluation. Selling is as important as screening. Too frequently, after intense screening, the hiring manager decides, at last, that the company has found the ideal candidate, only to discover that the candidate felt so "mauled" in the interview process that he or she elected to look elsewhere.

Remember, there are really two interviews going on at the same time. There are two sides to the table. By selling I don't mean hyping, but rather being clear and energetic about the job and your organization. Why is this organization worth working for? What is the significance of its purpose? Why is this position important to the accomplishment of this purpose? In a later chapter we'll explore in more detail how to communicate the challenge and the benefits of a position. At this point I merely want to emphasize the importance of not allowing the interview to become an inquisition. In studying survey notes of why people accepted one job over another, it has become very clear to me that money alone doesn't attract good people. Over and over individuals comment on how impressed (or conversely, unimpressed) they were with the interviewing manager.

Recently I was getting feedback from a top candidate I had submitted to a corporate client. I was uncertain of our prospects in recruiting this individual because we were basically asking him to make a lateral transfer in salary and responsibility. However, the client organization was growing rapidly, and the future offered plenty of professional challenge. "I can't believe the vision and enthusiasm they have for their company and products," responded my candidate. "Rick (the hiring manager) is very exciting. He really gives his department heads a lot of leeway and support." Although the candidate was willing to make the lateral move, Rick elected to go with another person who was even more qualified. It was obvious that he was able to maintain a healthy balance between screening and selling.

Courtesy, consideration, sensitivity, treating others as we would be treated (Matthew 7:12), and common sense are the prescription for success in this area.

Pitfall 9: Jumping to Conclusions

The typical interviewer makes hire/no-hire decisions way too fast and with too little information. One of the most extensive research projects on the selection process confirmed that the typical interviewer reaches his or her conclusion within the first four minutes of the interview.[10] The pace of the decision seems to be the same regardless of the conclusion, positive or negative. But, as we saw above, in the process of jumping to our conclusions, the driving force seems to be negative information. Unfavorable information appears to carry more weight than positive information.

In summarizing the findings of interview research, Michael Nash observes that, in jumping to our conclusions, we tend to be influenced on the positive side by appearance, approach, and the ability to make conversation. The lack of negative information and a positive fit with our stereotype of the perfect candidate buttress our quick conclusions. This stereotype is based, to a large extent, on our own personality and our perception of the demands of the position. Nash sums up his remarks by observing that "the successful employment candidate is one who makes a quick, positive impression and then avoids contaminating that impression during the rest of the interview."[11]

Pitfall 10: Stepping Over the Legal Line

The law clearly states that you cannot discriminate (and therefore ask direct or indirect questions) in the areas of:

- religious background, beliefs, or practices;
- race;
- national origin;
- age—particularly those between the ages of forty and seventy;
- gender;

- marital or family status;
- handicaps; and, in most instances,
- financial affairs.

Religious questions are particularly dangerous in a corporate setting. Any questions dealing with religious background, beliefs, or practices are clearly illegal. Any good attorney will tell you not to address this issue even when the candidate puts it on the table. That same attorney would advise you to remind the candidate that religion doesn't play a part in your criteria or selection process, and that legally you're not allowed to discuss it.

Your attorney will tell you not to ask questions about the origin of a candidate's last name or where the candidate or his or her parents were born. You *can* ask if the candidate is a U.S. citizen.

Be careful about family questions. And be direct. If a lot of overtime is needed on short notice, ask the candidate if he or she can handle that. That's legal. Asking if he or she has young children at home or if a spouse would mind about overtime is not. Focus on what the candidate can do in reference to job requirements, not why he or she may or may not be able to do it.

Often, it's a matter of approach. For example, you can't ask if the candidate has been arrested, but you can ask if he or she has been convicted. Although in most instances questions about the candidate's financial affairs are off limits, in most states you can run a credit check.

The key is to focus on work experience pertinent to your selection criteria. Ultimately, you are not constrained so much by the law as by your creativity in developing information-rich questions tied to the criteria that predict job success.

Sometimes the greatest hindrance to effective interviews is not the lack of skill but rather the lack of objectivity. The next chapter explores the paradigms and prejudgments we, as interviewers, bring to the meeting.

CHAPTER FOURTEEN

No One from New York Could Do This Job

SEVERAL YEARS AGO a man in his late middle age requested an appointment and asked me to help him identify ministry opportunities. He was an extremely well qualified chief financial officer with an international corporation. In his younger years he had received excellent training in accounting from one of the largest accounting firms in the world. "I've approached several ministries," he explained with a disconsolate shrug. He was discouraged, as his hope of taking early retirement from his corporate position and spending his last years in ministry seemed at risk.

This man's experience, financial knowledge, and executive skills were absolutely outstanding. As a mature Christian, the quality and consistency of his walk with the Lord more than met the standards of the ministries he had approached. As far as he knew, these ministries were looking for strong, experienced management but had expressed little or no interest in taking a hard look at him. After some exploration, which included talking to a number of the people who had met with this person, I concluded that they were blinded by their own biases. He was in his late fifties (but looked older) and, although his English was excellent, he spoke with a pronounced accent. They had a different "picture" of what they were looking for. None of these organizations had gotten below the surface, and as a result, they had missed a rich vein of talent and commitment.

I contacted another mission organization whose executive director had asked me to keep my eyes open for strong managers and made the introduction. It was a perfect match, and to the loss of the other ministries, this man is still serving very effectively as that ministry's head of finance and accounting eight years later.

BLINDED BY OUR OWN BIAS

Bias, stereotypes, and prejudice can be very dangerous pitfalls in making effective people decisions. All three spring from the same psychological foundations. They are, for all practical purposes, judgments made in advance and, as such, are a very normal (even necessary) part of our efforts to make sense of our fast-changing, complex world.

Although these terms carry negative connotations, they are, in themselves, not wrong unless they are unfounded or invalid. Few of us would consciously hold prejudices we knew to be wrong; but when they become internalized and therefore unexamined assumptions, they are most dangerous. Then they distort and twist our thinking without the slightest alarm. Feelings based on inaccurate information become facts, and such facts seldom allow us to construct high-quality people decisions.

Groundless, false generalizations about groups of people, be they ethnic, gender-based, regional, or socioeconomic in origin, are not the sole purview of the uninformed. Only this past month, a very bright vice president of a large consumer products company refused to see one of our top candidates because of his last name. "Sounds too New York to me," he observed. "I don't think he would fit in around here." Actually the candidate was from Alabama, but that seemed like a long shot, too!

Few of us are totally free of unhealthy biases and are often subtly, even unconsciously, negatively or positively influenced by looks, accent, pedigree, or some other aspect of the interviewee.

Many of these unhealthy generalizations flow out of childhood influences, unmet personal needs, or emotional problems. Still others are products of poor logic or thinking processes. Two of the more common pitfalls are as follows:

Halo-or-horns effect—The halo-or-horns effect is the tendency to generalize a specific notable trait or accomplishment as representative of success in any endeavor, no matter how unrelated.[1] For example, the fact that a candidate was a successful professional football player may be interpreted by some interviewers as an indication that this same individual would be an excellent sales manager or a successful development officer.

This effect can be either positive (halo) or negative (horns), and it might well be the most pervasive error in any evaluative situation, such as an interview or a performance evaluation session. Research shows that it is a very difficult tendency to correct. It is most prevalent in situations where a given trait is not easily observable, clearly defined, or subjective in nature (honesty, conceptual thinking, creativity, etc.).[2]

Primacy effect—In interviews, first impressions carry a lot of weight. The initial impact of the candidate, positive or negative, tends to color the rest of the interview and the resulting decisions. Research has consistently demonstrated that negative information carries more weight than positive information. One writer notes that "just one unfavorable impression was followed by a reject decision 90% of the time. Positive information was given much less weight in the final decision. . . . The interview," he concludes, "is primarily a search for negative information."[3]

The impact of these effects can significantly erode the quality of the interview. One of the most important findings by researchers is that interviewers tend to develop their own stereotype of the ideal candidate and then begin the search for the person who most closely matches that picture. Studies also show that candidates with good eye contact, smiles, and attentive posture receive higher ratings. Similarly, attractive candidates are preferred over unattractive candidates. They may be good interviewees, but they are not necessarily qualified for the job.[4]

There's one more effect that bears mentioning. Let me call it the recency effect. Several studies have found that if an interviewer evaluates a candidate who is just average after seeing three to four unfavorable candidates in a row, the "average" candidate tends to receive high ratings (by comparison)—and the job![5] When we interview more than one candidate at a time, we tend to compare the candidates to each other rather than to the criteria.

So how do we avoid these traps? Let me suggest that you:

Be aware of them. These tendencies are found to one degree or another in all of us, and only when we acknowledge this vulnerability can we correct these tendencies. Socrates challenged us "to know thyself." Along the same vein, Psalm 51 notes that God desires truth in the innermost part of the man.

Use multiple interviews. Seeing the same person several times gives you a chance to validate a particular quality or observation. Often you'll find that concerns that loomed so large in the previous meeting were a product of the moment, rather than of some intrinsic, ongoing problem. It's important to remember that you aren't trying to validate only the problems, but unconfirmed strengths as well.

Use multiple interviewers. Gaining several different perspectives on the candidate gives you insights that are not available to you with your preconceived notions.

Confront your hypothesis. When you find yourself feeling uncomfortable about someone or something in the interview, confront it. Take a moment to ask yourself why you might be uneasy, and then consciously move against this issue in the interview. The majority of the time, I've found that the cause of my lack of peace with a candidate was well founded, but there have been several dramatic instances where withholding judgment and objectively trying to prove my hypothesis found my "feelings" unfounded and saved me (and my client) from losing an excellent candidate.

Stick to well-defined criteria. Being clear about what you are looking for, when coupled with well-designed questions to elicit critical information, is an excellent way to avoid the tendency to generalize. Most important is the discipline to stay "in process" and to ask the questions even though you may have already concluded that this is or is not the person.

THE INTERVIEWER IS NOT THE ONLY BIASED PERSON IN THE MEETING

As you develop and ask your questions, remember that you are not the only person in the room with a well-established set of biases and blind spots. Interview time is preciously short, so focus on questions best answered in the interview and not by another information source. For example, references are the best source of information about the candidate's character. How would you expect any candidate who badly wanted a job to respond to the question, "Would you consider yourself a responsible person?" It's unlikely anyone would answer in the negative, regardless of the truth.

One of the most frequent interview requests is to ask the person to describe his or her strengths and weaknesses. It's used so much that an interview is not thought of as "official" without it. "Unfortunately, the correlation between self-assessment of abilities and actual tested abilities is so small as to have no practical significance."[6] To make matters worse, the answer takes forever, as the candidate creatively attempts to explain why he or she can't think of any weaknesses and sound sincere at the same time. This question is better answered by referencing and testing.

HOW MANY INTERVIEWS?

The number of interviews is entirely dependent on the level and importance of the position, the risks of being wrong, the costs involved in the interview process (transportation, time of the interviewing managers, etc.), and the length and detail incorporated into each interview.

Typically, even for a secretarial or clerical position at our firm, I try to have two interviews. The costs are minimal and it allows the candidate and me to validate first impressions.

Generally we focus on skills and chemistry in the first interview. If these are positive, the second visit emphasizes value systems and work styles (from both of our perspectives). It's during the second interview that we expose the candidate to the rest of our staff as well.

For executive positions we suggest a minimum of two, and generally more, depending on the specific circumstances. One of the best means of evaluation is to see the candidates in multiple settings, thus providing an opportunity to see poise, versatility, and consistency.

One law firm with whom we are acquainted has a tradition of asking themselves if they'd like to spend a day fishing with the candidate under consideration. They call it the "boat test." If the answer is no, it's unlikely the candidate will get the offer. Now, neither the fishing ability nor the social acumen of the candidates "in the boat" has a lot to do with their ability to practice law. Nor do they actually take the candidates fishing. The tradition springs from the firm's early roots when they really did go fishing. At that time, every lawyer was viewed as a potential partner, and the founding partner was convinced that he couldn't team up with someone who couldn't pass the "boat test."

HOW MANY INTERVIEWERS?

Multiple interviewers have been shown to consistently provide higher validity ratings than those attained by a single interviewer. When several different interviewers are in agreement about their observations, predictive results regarding the candidate's success in the job are significantly higher. We can only assume that the no decisions were of a similarly high quality as well.

As to who the other interviewers should be, that varies with the situation. Often for CEO positions in both corporate and parachurch settings, the board of directors deputizes a formal search committee. The search committee seems to be the primary vehicle for pastoral searches as well.[7] For other positions, the makeup of the interviewers seems to be less structured. I suggest that for the typical executive in either a ministry or a corporate setting you consider the following, each chosen because of either the perspective or the needed support he or she brings to the decision:

- Your immediate supervisor (if you're the hiring manager). Although this is often required, it's a good idea even when it isn't. He or she brings a unique perspective and, in the event of later problems, ensures a willing hand of help as well.
- At least one of your peers, particularly if he or she interacts with or depends on this position in some manner.
- At least one peer of the position for which the candidate is being interviewed. Can this person see himself or herself working with the candidate?
- I always try to find at least one relatively high-level person who has been with the organization a while, who knows the culture, the philosophy of management, the management team, and particularly the hiring manager. However, this person should not have a vested interest in the position and therefore brings a more objective perspective about the candidate's ability to fit in.

Certainly there can be others, but the above should be employed when possible. Regardless of whom you put on the list, all should have the following qualities: demonstrated judgment, knowledge of the position and your selection criteria, training as an interviewer, interview preparation (study of the résumé, selection criteria, and key issues), and a serious attitude about the task.

When you use multiple interviewers, it's advisable to give each an area of emphasis (technical proficiency, interpersonal skills, career aspirations, etc.), generally one to which each brings a unique insight. This isn't to say they can't probe other areas, but it helps ensure that you cover the key issues, and it also gives your colleagues a sense of direction and priority most find helpful.

How many should be present at one time? I've never been an advocate of committee interviews except for the very highest level positions and, even then, only as a final interview for the final candidate following interviews with individual members of the committee. In this setting, initial hurdles have been passed and the atmosphere tends to be relaxed and positive. Like any interview, there should be a well-defined objective with role assignments for the respective committee members.

I do encourage team interviews with two individuals. This not only allows the one not questioning to observe more attentively, but it gives the team members a means to validate their perceptions and conclusions. Generally, I've not found a team interview format to be too intimidating to the candidate if the principles of rapport discussed earlier are followed. There is one caution, however; sit in such a way that it is easy for the candidate to maintain eye contact with both interviewers at the same time.

What about subordinates interviewing their future supervisor? I am often asked if subordinates should be able to interview the candidates for management positions. Generally I recommend no. It too often conveys the impression that they are voting on the next leader, and if their vote isn't honored they might have a problem accepting leadership. I'm a strong advocate of servant leadership and empowered staff. However, one role of leadership is to take us where we haven't been before—out past our comfort zones. Although some of us have been blessed with a sense of adventure, most of us find the areas of growth beyond the current status quo to be somewhat turbulent and uncomfortable. Thus we're seldom going to endorse someone who's going to push us out there.

There have been times when I have violated my own counsel in this situation. Several times when the subordinates have been very mature and high level (for example, vice presidents), and when their input was very important to the success of the decision, we felt that such meetings were important. There have been several instances when the candidate wanted to meet future subordinates as well. In both cases these meetings came well toward the end of the process and with candidates who were well qualified and interested in the position.

Who's making the decision? Whenever there are multiple interviewers, it's critically important that you are clear about what you want from them. Who's making the decision, me or we? A consultive decision is one where I make the decision but would like your input (I may not take it, but regardless, it is helpful as I make up my mind). A consensus decision is one we make. It basically says that I feel heard and, although I might not have gone that way if left to my own devices, the process was fair and I can actively support this decision.

I mention this here because whichever approach you take (and either is appropriate in the right circumstances), it has a significant influence in how the interviewers will approach their task and feed back their observations. Subordinate interviews are invariably consultive decisions and need to be conveyed as such.

EVALUATING THE INTERVIEW RESULTS

In a later chapter I will address how to integrate and evaluate the information we gather from the various sources in the process of making our final decision. However, we need to close the books on our interview conclusions immediately after the interview, while our impressions are still fresh. It is here that you will shift from facts to causes and assign meaning to what you have seen and heard.

It's unlikely that a candidate who did not fare well in the interview will be a serious contender later. The emotional impact of the face-to-face encounter of the interview is seldom offset by contrary data on the résumé or references. Thus in many instances, if the interview results are poor, the final decision is being made at this point. Regardless, record your observations and conclusions quickly and carefully. This advice is most often ignored if the candidate was either very poor (he's out, no sense in going further) or very good (we've found our person, no sense in going further). Assume that, in either case, you will have to justify your conclusions later, and the key to that is good notes.

Summarizing your notes is particularly important for the candidates who demonstrated both strengths and weaknesses in the interview and when information from our sources as well as possible additional interviews are needed to make a final decision. Your notes will provide the list of questions that need to be emphasized in subsequent evaluation, particularly in referencing, which is the focus of the next chapter.

CHAPTER FIFTEEN

In Reference to . . .

IN ACTS 6 the Church was feeling the strain of dramatic growth. Support systems were overloaded and breaking down, as were the tempers of some of the parishioners. Therefore, the twelve apostles decided to reorganize and strengthen their administrative capabilities. Luke writes, "Select from among you, brethren, seven men of good reputation, full of Spirit and of wisdom, whom we may put in charge of the task" (Acts 6:3, NASB). "Men of good reputation." How were they going to verify that? As candidates surfaced, do you suppose they might have checked with others in the community to see what they thought of these men? "What do you think about Nicanor and Stephen? . . . Timon's so committed. . . . Do you think Nicolas is for real?" In listing the qualifications for elders and deacons in 1 Timothy 3, Paul notes that they too must have a good reputation, particularly with those outside the Church. How would they validate this if not through referencing?

THE PURPOSE OF THE REFERENCE

Perhaps the most critical concept in this book is that the best predictor of future behavior is past behavior. The reference is a primary source of information in our selection process; our only window into past behavior outside the reports given by the candidates themselves. The interview is a self-report, but few of us have a really accurate, objective picture of the skills, behaviors, and contributions we bring to the work setting. So we *need* the outside validation the reference provides.

Additionally, the reference gives us access to information that can't be collected by any other means. As we have already observed, when God asks men to choose other men for a specific task (Exodus 18:21, Acts 6:3, 1 Timothy 3:1-13, Titus 1:6-9), He provides the selection criteria so that we might better recognize qualified candidates. For the most part these criteria deal with character. Prudence, temperance, dependability, gentleness, and many other important character issues are best found through referencing. Finally, the reference is a good place to confirm or clarify information gained in the candidate interview.

WHY REFERENCING ISN'T DONE MORE OFTEN

There are several barriers to referencing. One common perception is that people won't respond or won't be honest in their feedback. I often hear that more and more organizations are refusing to provide reference information beyond verifying dates of employment because of the fear of possible litigation. However, in over ten years of executive search, I can only remember being turned down twice. In one, the reason was "company policy." In the other, the former supervisor quickly said, "I just don't want to discuss her," but her manner and tone told me a lot.

We find that people do respond—they like to share their insights and opinions. Have you ever been called by a public opinion survey company researching people's feelings about one subject or another? Did you respond? If you're like me you probably did. As we'll see in a moment, the way you introduce and position the reference is key in helping the reference open up.

Another assumption is that reference information is too subjective, distorted, or superficial to be helpful. Many people feel that any reference, particularly those suggested by the candidates themselves, isn't going to be objective. I'm not naive. Of course candidates are going to put their best references forward. I would! However, with the help of good questions and the proper approach, most people are willing and able to provide a balanced picture of both strengths and weaknesses.

REFERENCE METHODS

There are three channels for soliciting reference information: mail, in-person interviews, and telephone. Although mail is still fairly popular, particularly with search committees and personnel departments, I firmly believe it is the poorest method of obtaining meaningful reference information. It takes an inordinate amount of time both for the reference and the referencer. Second, if it is difficult to get a reference to reveal the shortcomings of the candidate in a phone conversation or in person, it is doubly difficult to get the reference to put it in writing. In this litigious society of ours, people are very cautious about taking risks and committing themselves on "hard copy." Additionally, mail references do not provide the dynamic of either in-person or phone references. There is no way to follow up a response or to catch the tone or emphasis of a significant point. Finally, in this time-short, video culture of ours, few people have the time or the skills to communicate a clear and complete picture of another person in writing. Generally you will receive, if anything, a few safe, surface observations that contribute little to the evaluation process.

Without a doubt, in-person references have the potential to yield the highest quality results. In chapter 13, I noted that only 7 percent of communication is found in the words themselves, while 93 percent of meaning in any communication comes in expression, gestures, tone, and body language.[1] In-person references provide access to the "total" communication. They provide an opportunity to establish rapport and trust with the reference that might increase his or her willingness to be more open and candid.

Several years ago I conducted a phone interview with the past supervisor of a candidate for an important management position. During the reference session I sensed a hesitancy on the part of this person to answer some of my questions about his former subordinate. There were too many pauses, ah's, and generalizations. After nearly an hour, I was convinced he wasn't going to open up on the phone and asked him if we could schedule a meeting. Without expressing my frustration with his responses to this point, I explained how important this position was to my client and, since he was in town, possibly he'd be willing to spend an additional thirty minutes in person. He agreed and as we met several days later the quality and candor of his responses were considerably different. Meeting in person not only demonstrated how important we thought the position was, it also allowed me to establish enough trust so that he was willing to take, what he considered, a risk. He explained that this candidate could not work effectively with stress or pressure. In fact, he became almost dysfunctional when confronted with big problems. This was critical information because the position for which I was recruiting was a turnaround situation that had already beaten two top-flight managers.

As good as in-person references are, time and cost make them impractical in most instances. However, in high-level and/or risk situations, such as the case above, it is sometimes worth it.

The most popular reference method is the telephone. It's immediate, cost-effective, and allows some (although limited) rapport to be established. If we work hard to be perceptive listeners—listening for the subtle nuances of tone and meaning—we can glean many of the benefits available in the in-person setting. But be careful, don't misinterpret a thoughtful pause or other perceived variations of tone or emphasis as a concern. If in doubt, ask, "Mr. Smith, you seem to hesitate on this answer. Is this reflection or are we confronting a sensitive issue?"

WHOM TO REFERENCE

To some extent, whom you reference depends on the criteria you are validating and who is in the best position to comment on these issues. Generally, you should always include former supervisors, for they carried the burden of evaluating performance on a day-to-day basis. Coworkers (peers) provide insight into topics like teamwork and reputation. If pertinent, subordinates are an excellent source of information about management ability, leadership style, and the ability to get work done through others. In some instances we also talk to informed outsiders and suppliers like CPAs, consultants, vendors, and others who might help us gain deeper insight into technical competence and thinking ability.

The best predictor of future behavior is past behavior, but not all past behavior is equal. The more recent the behavior, the better the indicator of what we can expect to see in the near future under similar circumstances. Therefore, current references are more valuable than older ones. References from similar job or work settings are better than those from dissimilar situations. For this reason, I tend to steer away from old teachers, former athletic coaches, and personal references (neighbors, friends from church, etc.) unless they have insight into a specific criterion in which I am interested.

The order in which you approach your references may be important. I recommend that you do not start with your best (most informed, candid, etc.) reference, but rather practice on a few of the more marginal ones first. Often issues and information from the initial references can strengthen the latter ones. "Mr. Smith, several references mentioned that. . . ."

As to how many, that depends. The level of the position, the degree of risk, the consequences of being wrong, and the responses flowing out of the interviews and previous references all influence the scope of your reference efforts.

I remember, as a child, when my dad became infatuated with a new type of creative endeavor, paint-by-numbers art. I was fascinated as the picture slowly took shape, becoming more complete as each color was added. Ultimately the final number was covered and the picture was finished. At some point in the reference process someone will supply the missing ingredient (that is, the color) necessary to complete the picture, a balanced picture, of the candidate. Paint until the picture is complete.

SECONDARY REFERENCES

It's seldom that we don't check at least one secondary reference and, more often, several. A secondary reference is one suggested by the original (primary) references given to us by the candidate. We insist that our consultants reference a candidate until they have a fairly balanced list of both strengths and weaknesses. If we are unable to get the reference to provide a balanced perspective, then we capture what useful information we can and attempt to identify secondary references. "Mr. Smith, are there other employees who might be able to give us further insight to Susan's qualifications for this job?"

One important note of caution. If you are referencing a candidate who is currently employed and confidentially exploring your position, you must exercise extreme care in using secondary references. Often, in this situation, the candidate has given you references who can be trusted to maintain confidentiality. The secondary reference may not have the same commitment or even know that such discretion is necessary. We make it a policy when working with employed candidates to ask their permission before using secondary references. "Susan, we've not been able to get as balanced a picture of your abilities as we feel necessary from your references. Several have suggested that we also speak to (name of the reference). I'd like your permission to talk to him or her."

It's probably a good policy to give advance notice to the candidate about any reference you desire to approach. If there is resistance, probe into its causes. You might gain a valuable insight about your candidate. Recently I notified a candidate that I wanted to talk to a former supervisor who, surprisingly, was not on his original list of references. He became very agitated and quickly responded, "I don't want you to talk to her!" As I pushed for the reasons behind his resistance, it finally surfaced that she had fired him (wrongly, he felt). After some discussion, he finally agreed that I could proceed with the reference. Watching him respond to my request provided new and valuable information about this candidate. Without going into details, he didn't handle this situation well, and this information (coupled with other evidence) later played a part in our decision not to proceed with his candidacy.

As an aside, when you run into resistance from the candidate about talking with secondary references, you should handle it the same way you would with a reference who was hesitant to provide any possible shortcomings about the candidate. In most cases it's a matter of trust. The candidate doesn't trust that you can hear bad news and still keep him or her in the running. I can appreciate that—most people aren't able to do that. However, I find that most candidates will respond positively if you patiently and firmly explain the rationale of needing a complete and balanced picture to seriously consider them as candidates. I suggest a way to frame this conversation in "The Reference Interview," which begins on the next page.

WHO SHOULD DO THE REFERENCE?

I firmly believe that the hiring manager should do some of the referencing, at least with the final candidate. This gives the manager access to some of the intangibles such as tone, energy level, and other nuances that allow him or her to see a more complete and colorful picture of the candidate. Although in completing a search for a client we talk to all references, we generally recommend at least one of these to the hiring manager for follow up. This would be a reference we found particularly insightful, objective, or able to bring a unique perspective that would help our client in his or her decision or in subsequent management of the candidate if hired.

Notice that I said the hiring manager should do some of the referencing. The press of time generally doesn't allow the manager to do the whole job. This, and the pervading hesitancy to do references in the first place, motivates a lot of managers to delegate the task. But this is too important to delegate to an untrained or uncommitted person. Either use your search consultant if you have retained one (some consultants are available for just this type of work), or a human resource professional from your own organization. The nuggets will be found in the pauses, nuances, and tones of the reference. The follow-up questions often provide better insight than the original question. The referencer needs to be a consummate listener—alert, courageous enough to push, and diplomatic enough to get away with it.

THE REFERENCE INTERVIEW

Depending on the level of the position and the complexity of the issues a complete reference will take a minimum of twenty to forty-five minutes. One of the most frustrating experiences is to get cut off ten to fifteen minutes into the reference with "I'm sorry, I have a meeting in two minutes," or "I really must go now." Equally damaging is to have the reference rush through his or her responses or to respond superficially because of time constraints. I always start a reference by introducing myself, stating the purpose of my call, and asking if this is a convenient time. If not, I schedule a more appropriate time.

In many respects the quality and completeness of the responses from your reference will be determined by the level of rapport and trust you are able to establish with this individual. However, unlike the candidate interview, this conversation will most likely be over the phone and under some time constraint. The needed trust will be a product of a warm but poised, professional manner rather than an extended period of small talk, as is the case in an in-person interview. It's important that you come across relaxed and low-key but not laid-back. If you're too casual you'll convey an unprofessional demeanor. If you're tense the reference will sense it and mirror it back. In either case the reference will be hesitant to share risky information.

I strongly recommend that you script out your introduction, including a brief overview of the position and the primary selection criteria. It not only brings the perspective of your reference into alignment with the task, it moves you into the core of the conversation more quickly. Additionally, I recommend you prepare a reference form, similar to the interview form, with your key questions and leave space for the responses. This not only allows you to move through the interview in an efficient manner, but it ensures that crucial issues are covered in a consistent manner for all candidates.

As to the structure of the conversation, start on a safe, neutral note. For example, establish the relationship of the reference to the candidate. Many references have a personal, as well as a professional, relationship with the candidate. It's important that you know this, for the reference interview is like getting a video record of your candidate on his or her previous job. The eyes and perspectives of your reference serve as the camera lens; therefore, it's critical that you identify any bias (positive or negative) of the reference that would distort the picture.

Another safe, front-end issue would be to verify dates of employment and other factual elements of the previous position. One well-known professional referencer notes that he always begins his reference interview with the statement, "We're thinking about hiring Mary Adams, and I'd like to verify a few facts with you."[2] Verifying a few facts is a lot less threatening than, "Tell me all about Mary." These types of questions on the front end of your conversation not only help you position the relationship between the reference and your candidate, but allow the interview to build momentum safely as well.

Next, deal with the basics of the job, the primary qualifications of this individual against the criteria being referenced. Save the sensitive issues till last. During a typical reference session, you build trust and rapport with the reference as you move through the interview, and he or she may become more willing to take a risk with you on the more sensitive issues later in the conversation. This might mean that, if he or she alludes to a potential problem early on in the reference, you (depending on your assessment of the level of rapport) sit on a tack for a while and come back to it later—"Bill, earlier in our discussion, you noted that . . . can you expand on that (or why do you think that she . . .)?"

Trust and rapport are necessary but not sufficient for a high-quality reference. They merely provide the climate for your questions. Ultimately, the questions themselves make the reference—salty, pithy questions that elicit the interest of your reference and get him or her engaged in the process. Again, the questions must be tied to your selection criteria, particularly those criteria that don't lend themselves to self-evaluation by the candidate—for example, character issues like faithfulness, reliability, work ethic, integrity, and courage under fire. Additionally, this is an excellent time to validate or clarify important issues from the candidate interview.

Typical requests from a former supervisor might include:

■ Listing the candidate's strengths and weaknesses. To help the reference feel more open about sharing shortcomings about the candidate, we often provide a short overview of management philosophy. "Mr. Smith, in business all of us have discovered that people with strong strengths tend to have counterbalancing weaknesses. In fact, author and business consultant Peter Drucker observes that if we don't want a person with weaknesses then we'd better be prepared to accept mediocrity. You've described Susan as an exceptional sales manager for someone her age. Can you also identify some of the areas in which she might need to develop?"

■ Comparison of the work style and/or results of your candidate to other employees.

■ Teamwork, that is, how your candidate worked with his or her associates.

■ The best management style to use with this person.

■ The candidate's ability to achieve results and assigned objectives. Here is an excellent opportunity to validate the responses you've already received from your candidate.

■ Response to feedback about performance, that is, teachability.

■ Best type of work environment—structured versus unstructured, people interaction versus individual tasks, pressure versus lack of pressure, etc.

■ Criteria-oriented questions—ability to handle pressure, conceptual thinking ability, attention to detail, etc.

There is one question you should always ask a past supervisor, generally toward the end of the reference—"If given the opportunity, would you rehire this person?" If the answer is a direct no, ask why not. Often the answer, even if negative, is not so direct. Listen carefully for pauses. If you sense any hesitancy, put it on the table: "Mr. Smith, I sense a little hesitancy. Do you have any reservations? If so, what might they be?" Related questions might be, "Mr. Smith, given how I've described the job, how well do you sense it fits Mary's aptitudes and abilities?" "In what areas do you believe she might experience difficulties?" "Would you recommend her for this job?"

There is also a question I always ask last of every reference. Several years ago I was having lunch with the president of a client organization for whom my firm did extensive search work. This individual felt that selecting good people was just about the most important thing he could do for his company. He loved the selection process, and we'd often share war stories of selection successes and failures and the lessons contained in each. He told me of a recent reference call he'd received concerning a former employee who had left at his own initiative but who would definitely not be hired back. In my client's description of the incident, the person taking the reference did a terrible job. It was perfunctory at best, and although my friend was forthright in his answers, he didn't take any initiative to move into areas not addressed by the referencer. There was one specific issue with the candidate that made that person less than ideal for this new position, and although it was alluded to by my client the referencer never picked up on it. There was little listening, no follow-up questions to some very carefully crafted hints by my client, and as a result the issue was never surfaced. "MacMillan," my friend exclaimed, "I couldn't believe that this person didn't ask the right questions! I gave him hint after hint but felt uncomfortable being any more direct than I was." As a result of that lesson, I have made it a policy at our firm that we close every reference with this question: "Mr. Smith, is there a question I should have asked you but didn't?" Over the years this question has brought a wealth of information we'd have left on the table without it.

With coworkers we ask questions dealing with teamwork, interpersonal relationships, initiative in helping others, reputation, and others from our criteria list that might best be known by a peer. Former subordinates provide good insight into management style, ability to delegate, and creating a climate for growth.

Invariably a reference will jump into a general description of the candidate before you've even asked your first question. Listen carefully. These comments, although somewhat unstructured, often contain valuable information. Additionally, many of the principles we discussed in the previous chapter on interviewing are also applicable as you interact with the reference. For example:

- Don't "lead the witness" with leading questions.
- Refrain from completing a sentence as the reference pauses looking for just the right word.
- Always ask for examples and specific instances to substantiate the reference's remarks.
- Press for clarification and definition of ambiguous or general terms and descriptions.

Clarifying ambiguity may be one of the biggest challenges in getting an accurate, clear reference. Too often, when the reference has negative experiences concerning the candidate, the reference veils his or her true feelings in ambiguity. Sometimes this is motivated by a concern for legal repercussions. But often, particularly with Christians, the reference desires not to be negative or unedifying in his or her remarks about anyone. However, when shortcomings are present but covered over, the subsequent pain and cost of dealing with these issues would be much greater than a momentary burst of candor on the part of the reference. Shortcomings can be expressed in positive, edifying terms, and sometimes we need to help the reference "position" such comments in an acceptable, safe manner.

Robert Thornton, a professor of economics at Lehigh University, designed a lexicon for ambiguous recommendations. He intended to provide tongue-in-cheek illustrations of how one might convey negative information about a candidate in a safe, innocuous manner. I found the following six recommendations particularly creative:[3]

- To describe a candidate who is woefully inept: "I most enthusiastically recommend this candidate with no qualifications whatsoever."
- To describe a candidate who is not particularly industrious: "In my opinion you will be very fortunate to get this person to work for you."
- To describe a candidate who is not worth further consideration: "I would urge you to waste no time in making this candidate an offer of employment."
- To describe a candidate with lackluster credentials: "All in all, I cannot say enough good things about this candidate or recommend him too highly."
- To describe an ex-employee who had difficulty getting along with fellow workers: "I am pleased to say that this candidate is a former colleague of mine."
- To describe a candidate who is so unproductive the position would be better left unfilled: "I can assure you that no person would be better for this job."

Although I am sure you will appreciate his humor and creativity, these types of comments are found too often in the context of a reference. Thus, the challenge to press for clarification and definition.

Finally, in parting, I always ask the reference's permission to call back if I later find the need for further information or detail.

WHEN TO REFERENCE

Because a major purpose of the reference is to confirm and clarify information gained in the candidate interview, the reference generally comes toward the end of the selection process. Additionally, because referencing is difficult and time-consuming, you will want to expend the major part of your effort only on the final few candidates. However, when you must fly candidates in for interviews, we suggest that you conduct some preliminary references to ensure that such an expenditure is merited. In this instance, your focus is on the major, knockout type of issues that, if known, would save you the cost of airfare or further evaluation of the candidate.

There are instances when you can't reference. We've often encountered situations where the candidate was employed and referencing would endanger his or her present job. Many of these individuals have worked for their present employer for so long that references from previous positions that might provide the needed information may not even exist. In these circumstances, proceed as best you can, but if an offer is extended it should be done with the provision that final approval is contingent on acceptable references. Such a proviso will certainly motivate the candidate to be very clear and candid in his or her interview sessions.

CREDIT CHECKS, HEALTH EXAMS, AND ACADEMIC RECORDS

If the financial reliability and credit worthiness of the candidate is an issue as to qualification for the job (for example, handling money), then a credit check may have merit. There are technical aspects to this type of reference that make it best left to experts. These reports are available from local or national credit-reporting agencies. However, the Fair Credit Reporting Act of 1971 requires that you inform the candidate that such reference will be taken. Many companies have a release statement (signed by the candidate) on their application forms that serves both as notification and a record of permission from the candidate. Although I suggest that you have any such statement approved by your attorney, it might read along the following lines: "Because of the nature of the work, our selection process will involve obtaining references as to the credit standing, character, and reputation of applicants. . . ."

The reporting agency must also notify the candidate that you have requested such a report and that he or she may review any information obtained in the investigation, if desired. Should the candidate choose to do so and disagree with some of the findings, the candidate can provide his or her own explanation of the information contained in the report. You have the prerogative to choose either version.

As for medical information and exams, they are most often viewed as a test to be passed rather than a piece of needed information about the qualifications of the candidate. In most cases this is a proper perspective, with the issue being insurance coverage and the need to identify preexisting conditions. There are some tasks that require specific information dealing with the physical capabilities of the candidates (some manual labor positions, high stress situations, etc.). Remember, a number of laws constrain the hiring organization as to the specific medical information they can collect. It must have demonstrated relevancy to the job requirements. Of particular concern would be individuals in certain legal "protected classes." For example, people with diabetes or a terminal illness cannot be turned down for the job (only for that reason) unless a professionally given medical exam proves they are incapable of doing that particular job. I provide more detail on the legal aspects of referencing, credit and character investigations, and medical exams in chapter 6.

As for academic records, they should always be verified.

Unless you need a copy of the grade transcripts, a phone call to the college registrar's office will be sufficient. Remember that the presence of a degree does not guarantee that the candidate can do the job; we are merely verifying that the candidate has the degree he or she claimed.

WHAT IF YOU GET AN UNFAVORABLE REFERENCE?

Don't "die in a pile" if you receive a negative report. Anyone willing to put forth the negatives is willing to explain them. In most instances, a single bad report shouldn't sink the candidate. It just raises a yellow flag that motivates you to dig deeper. If you discover a pattern, that's another matter.

In a previous chapter I noted that research shows that in an interview, candidates are turned down 90 percent of the time when the interviewer was confronted with negative information. The same instincts prevail with the reference, and therefore you must fight your first instincts and not jump to conclusions until such information is validated.

Remember, people with strong attributes will tend to have a balanced portfolio of strengths and weaknesses. It would be unlikely that a thoroughly and properly done reference would not reveal a candidate with some shortcomings. I've already mentioned that our search consultants are required to develop a fairly balanced list of strengths and weaknesses. A list of only positive qualities doesn't mean there aren't weaknesses; it just means you don't know what they are. Testing, our last evaluation tool, may help you get a firmer grasp on an accurate profile of your candidates.

CHAPTER SIXTEEN

First, Let Them Be Tested

SOME YEARS AGO my firm was retained to assist a ministry in finding a new marketing manager. When our representative presented the ministry with several good candidates, the client CEO asked us to first have them tested with a particular test before the ministry interviewed them. "We never see a candidate unless he or she has received a good score on this particular test," he explained. "It's never proven to be wrong, and the one time I ignored the results we found later we had made a terrible mistake." This particular test required the participant to fill out a questionnaire, which was then mailed to the testing bureau for interpretation. The results, in the form of a written report, were then mailed back to the organization. If the test results indicated material shortcomings on the part of the candidate, he or she was rejected out of hand.

Because this procedure violated policies by which our firm operated, as well as a number of the principles of good selection in general, our search executive asked me to intervene with this CEO, an individual, I might add, who was also a good friend. In spite of my eloquent appeal, he wouldn't budge from his position. "I thought you approved of testing," he responded. I assured him that I believed, in the right circumstances and when done in the proper manner, testing was a useful and valid source of input when evaluating candidates. However, the process used with this instrument didn't appear to meet these criteria: There was no interview with a psychologist who could help us interpret the results; the results didn't take into account the position requirements; and there was no confirming evidence that the instrument accurately measured what it was reputed to evaluate.

To evaluate the reliability of the testing service, I suggested that we resubmit test responses, which were previously given by another candidate for a different position nearly a year earlier. This person had been, based on the test results, turned down by the client. The evaluation of the testing service paid off. Using the same answers, the results were markedly different. In fact, based on the new report, this was a very hireable candidate. My friend was confused and frustrated, for I had just eliminated what he had believed was a reliable shortcut to good people decisions.

Of the four sources of candidate information—résumé, interviews, referencing, and testing—testing is by far the most controversial. No other evaluation tool depends on the interpretation of its users as does testing. Some hiring executives see tests as a panacea, a magic means to short cut what promises to be a complex, arduous process. In one fell swoop we can cut to the chase and get back a clear, straightforward yes or no supported by a pile of technical jargon. Others fear them, perceiving tests as inaccurate, unreliable instruments used by the impatient, or by those who do not have the skills to pull the salient facts out of the interview and references. Still others see tests as merely expensive alternatives to their own intuition and gut instinct.

In reality, psychological tests used to evaluate people are none of these things. As I observed with my client above, the right tests in the right situations, used in an appropriate manner, can greatly enhance our people decisions. But tests are double-edged tools and, if used improperly, can cut the decision process to ribbons.

The purpose of this chapter is to draw the boundaries of testing in selection decisions and to identify some of the principles and pitfalls involved with its use. Again, as with many of the topics in this book, our purpose is not to provide an in-depth treatise on the subject of testing, but merely to present an overview and to position testing in the overall process of decision making.

PURPOSE AND USE OF TESTS

Psychological testing is a relatively new area of social science, first appearing late in the last century. Tests emanated, to a large extent, from the efforts of pioneering psychologists attempting to differentiate and measure the levels of intelligence among individuals.[1] Today, psychologists can avail themselves of over a thousand accepted tests that measure virtually the entire array of human traits with varying degrees of reliability and validity.

People are different, and effective people decisions require relevant insight into that individuality. Basically, the purpose of psychological tests is to measure those differences, not only between individuals but also between the same individual in different circumstances.[2] Measurement—that's exactly what we need. We have already seen that any people decision is filled with an almost overwhelming amount of subjectivity and many more unknowns than knowns. Into this environment, we introduce an instrument that presents the first hint of objectivity and rationale. It presents its conclusions in a straightforward, concise manner, often to the point of using numbers to describe the degree to which the individual does or doesn't meet a given criterion. Some of us, overwhelmed by mounds of confusing and even conflicting subjective data about the candidates, race to embrace the conclusions of the test, even at the expense of more compelling information from our other sources.

Measurement in itself is not sufficient. Tests vary in their precision. Do the results merely put the test-taker into broad categories (e.g., slow learners, fast learners, etc.), or can they provide more precise indications of magnitude (e.g., IQ of 93 versus that of 120)? Can we compute mean scores, percentile ranks, and norms that allow even more sophisticated comparison of individual differences? And, is this test (or tests) actually measuring what it purports to measure? Is it dependable, that is, will it deliver consistent results over time and in different circumstances?

As laypeople we can easily appreciate the importance of accuracy in any test. One testing expert makes this observation:

> The main purpose of psychological measurement is to make decisions about individuals, but if measurement procedures are to have utility, they must produce dependable scores. The typical selection situation is unlike the situation at a shooting gallery where the marksman gets 25 shots for a quarter; if he misses his target on the first shot, he still has 24 tries left. In the case of a job applicant, however, he or she usually only gets one shot. It's important, therefore, to make that shot count, to present the "truest" picture of one's abilities or personal characteristics. Yet potentially there are numerous sources of error that can distort that "true" picture.[3]

Psychologists use several different measurements to evaluate the overall accuracy of different psychological tests, but the most fundamental elements of test effectiveness are validity and reliability. Validity is at the very core of what the test is about, for it concerns the degree that the test can actually measure what it claims to measure. For example, if a certain test was designed to measure students' aptitude for math, and actual results of their subsequent math scores agreed with the test predictions (i.e., those whom the test predicted to have strong aptitude received good scores in contrast to those predicted to have low aptitude), then the test would appear to be valid.

The following diagram shows the concept of validity graphically. The vertical axis shows test scores. The horizontal axis represents actual results (e.g., math grades). The diagonal line reflects the degree of validity. Any scores on or close to this line (shaded area C) demonstrate a high correlation (i.e., validity) between the test predictions and actual results. Scores in the shaded area A reflect a situation in which the test scores predicted higher actual performance than was achieved. In area B, students actually performed better than predicted by the test. In both cases (A and B) the correlation (validity) between what was predicted by the test and the actual results was low.

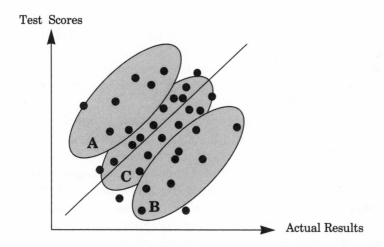

The second important measure of test effectiveness is reliability, that is, consistency. Will the test deliver the same results over time? One author describes test reliability as being the consistency of scores obtained by the same persons when retested with the identical (or equivalent) test form.[4] If on a certain test my IQ score were 132 and a month later using the same instrument in similar circumstances my results were 98, we could conclude that this test did not appear to be very reliable.

Reputable tests must be *both* valid and reliable, as a test could be highly reliable but not valid. Standardized tests have been thoroughly evaluated as to both their reliability and validity using objective, independent means. It's important to note that both measurements are relative concepts. Individual tests are not simply valid or invalid (reliable or unreliable), but rather are described as having a certain "degree" of validity. The "acceptable" degree of either dimension depends on the type of test, the risk or importance of the decision, the specific criteria being measured, the correlation of other tests and information, and many additional influencing factors.

WHAT ARE WE MEASURING ANYWAY?

There are literally thousands of acceptable tests available to test for virtually every possible psychological trait—intelligence, creativity, tendencies to trust, to be defensive, to be extroverted or introverted, to conform or rebel, to affiliate or be alone, etc. The list is nearly endless.

We can organize tests into broad groupings based on what they are designed to measure. A few such categories would include intelligence tests, aptitude or ability tests, personality tests, educational tests, and interest tests. In each of these groups there might be hundreds of specific tests created to measure a specific aspect in that category of interest.[5] For example, there are many components in the testing of intelligence. Some tests are designed to look at it from a predictive perspective (aptitude tests); others measure what has been learned (achievement tests). Many intelligence tests are designed for particular age groups; others focus on specific dimensions of intelligence, such as verbal skills or quantitative ability.

Because of the complexity and the richness God has woven into the human mind—we are "fearfully and wonderfully made" (Psalm 139:14)—no one test is able to address the entire spectrum of criteria that might be of interest in a people decision. The complexity and diversity required in the design of such an instrument introduces too great a potential for error. Therefore, whereas most tests can provide an acceptable level of insight into a specific or selected portion of our overall interest, it generally takes several different tests looking at our criteria from several different perspectives to gain a complete picture. Psychologists call a group of different tests used to predict performance in a given area(s) a test battery. The selection of such a battery can be very complex. The psychologist must choose tests that validly predict against the specific criteria, and that do so efficiently with a minimum of duplication and cost. Additionally, the individual tests will probably be scored in different ways and the results based on different norms. The total results need to be integrated into a comprehensive, understandable recommendation. All of this takes considerable technical ability as well as judgment based on past experience. It's not a job for an untrained layperson. And this brings us to an important point.

TESTING IS CREDIBLE BUT COMPLEX

For all of the power psychological tests bring to the selection process, there are also considerable complexities in the choice of the proper instruments, as well as in their administration and interpretation. Lack of understanding regarding the nature and purpose of testing and misinterpretation or inappropriate use of the results, including violating confidentialities, underlie much of the criticism and fear of testing in the selection process.

Over the years a number of safeguards have been instituted to ensure that tests are used in an appropriate and ethical manner. Most test publishers require certain qualifications for the administration of their instruments. This might be a master's degree in psychology or counseling, its equivalent, or the completion of a specified training course. Psychologists and the various test publishers have adopted ethical standards that govern the use of tests as well. Guidelines include the assurance that test results are handled in a legal, professional, and confidential manner.

Because of these precautions, access and use of most psychological tests are restricted to some degree in an attempt to ensure that they are used with an acceptable level of competence. However, not all such testing instruments are so "protected." Many are specifically designed to be used in less restricted, educational settings with a minimum of professional oversight. (Team Resources publishes one such instrument, The Personal DISCernment Inventory™. For more information refer to pages 263-265.) These instruments are specially designed to provide personal insights to the participants about themselves and others. Most instruments of this type focus on the broader, more visible aspects of the individual's personality or temperament. Although they can surface clues about what might motivate me or how to best communicate with me, they do not provide, in themselves, a satisfactory means of identifying potential success in a given position. They merely supply insight into the work style an individual would use to achieve success. Because of their availability, these types of instruments are most often used inappropriately in selection decisions. The validity and reliability of such instruments (although adequate for their intended use as educational tools) are not sufficient to be relied on as a predictor of job success.

The results of such a test are used after the selection decision to provide information about how to shape work tasks and environments for specific individuals and to help work teams gain insight about each other's temperaments as they relate in the work setting. If you desire to use such an instrument in your selection process, I recommend that you have your consulting psychologist include it in his or her test battery. Integrating the results of the other tests into the interpretation of this instrument will certainly leverage its impact.

TESTS ARE AN EXCELLENT EVALUATION TOOL FOR SOME KEY CRITERIA

If you were hesitant to use tests before, I have confirmed your worst fears with these introductory comments regarding the technical and ethical dimensions of testing. But don't draw your conclusions too quickly. I advocate testing because there are certain critical aspects of people decisions for which tests are best suited.

For example, the closer the nature of the work is to the interests of an individual, the greater the potential for high motivation and productivity. Although interests are a critical factor of selection and placement, Michael Nash points out, "It is not always possible to correctly identify interests by asking people what they are interested in, nor is it always possible to identify and interpret your own interests."[6] An individual's ability to assess his or her interests is an accurate reading of self-awareness and experience. Tests provide an excellent mirror against which to reflect those interests. The Strong-Campbell Interest Inventory is one of the most popular instruments used in helping people catalog their interests.

Intelligence or cognitive ability is also an important success predictor that is best determined through testing. Intelligence is particularly important in executives. Managers generally score in the top 10 percent of intelligence norms, and many managers of all levels would score above average intelligence against the general population.[7]

A brief review of research literature would tell us that interest in the job, cognitive ability, and the need to achieve are core factors that correlate with productivity.[8] Although we can gain insight into the presence of these qualities from interviewing and referencing, testing might be an important, if not the best, source of information.

LEGAL IMPLICATIONS

Contrary to popular belief, testing is legal. In its Guideline in Employee Selection Procedures (Title 29), the Equal Employment Opportunity Commission observes that its guidelines are based on the belief that properly validated and standardized employee selection procedures (i.e., psychological tests) can significantly contribute to the overall development and maintenance of an efficient workforce. However, it does require that such tests and testing procedures not discriminate against any "protected" class. Such tests must have objective, empirical data that demonstrate significant correlation to important work behavior and selection criteria. Much of this concern is directed to the protection of women, ethnic minorities, the elderly, and other designated work groups in Title VII of the 1964 Civil Rights Act.

The legal implications are another reason to rely on a qualified, licensed industrial/organizational psychologist in the administration of these tests. Such an individual should be able to counsel you on the legal aspects of your screening process, as well as manage the actual administration and interpretation of the test results.

WHEN AND WHEN NOT TO USE TESTS

I've already acknowledged that I am a proponent of testing when administered in a proper manner, in the appropriate situations. And that's the key—not every situation is suitable for the use of tests. Because testing is both time-consuming and expensive, I recommend you be selective in their use, and use them in the following situations:

- In high-level, expensive, important positions where the cost of being wrong is high.
- In risky situations where the cost of a mistake would fall emotionally and financially on the shoulders of the candidate and his or her family. For example, missionary couples being sent to assignments overseas.
- In situations in which we sense good potential in a candidate but yellow flags have surfaced from other sources of information (i.e., references and interviews).

As to the use of psychologists, I've shown my hand here as well. I'm a strong advocate of incorporating a competent industrial/organizational psychologist into your selection team. Such input works best when this person is familiar with not only the selection criteria for the position in question but with your organizational culture, values, philosophy, and leadership style of key managers as well. Such insight is best gained through an ongoing relationship with a competent psychologist who shares your value system and with whom you have good interpersonal chemistry. Such an individual can not only implement and interpret the test battery, if and when required, but he or she can provide additional objective insight into the interview process as well, even when tests aren't used.

In using tests it's best to view them as rifles rather than shotguns. Use them to assess specific issues or criteria rather than casting about in some random fashion and seeing what floats to the top. To this end, when you send the assignment to the testing psychologist, include the selection criteria, as well as a specific list of issues or concerns.

Testing can be a stressful experience for your candidates. Therefore it's important to set their expectations and try to make this a positive, growing experience. Explain what you are doing, why, and for what you are testing (in broad, general terms). I highly recommend that you build in the cost of a psychologist-candidate feedback session—even with candidates who didn't get the job. This not only relieves anxiety about what the tests may or may not have shown, but it's an excellent opportunity for increased self-awareness as well.

ARE THEY BIBLICAL?

A psychologist with whom I work closely has been frequently challenged by Christians as to whether tests are biblical. I've never had anyone challenge the biblical soundness of interviews, résumés, or references, but the mystery and technology of psychological testing causes some to pose the question.

In 1 Timothy 3:10, the Apostle Paul suggests that potential deacons should first be tested. Unlike my friend, the psychologist mentioned above, Paul was not referring to psychological tests or formal examination of any type. Rather, Paul was speaking about the general understanding and opinion of the Christian community as to the qualifications of the individuals against the criteria for church leadership set forth by him.

Like so many "things" we have available today, tests weren't a part of the culture of New Testament times. Therefore, we must navigate on the basis of principle rather than with the specifics of chapter and verse. And, as with so many tools (technology, systems, etc.) available to us in business or ministry today, I believe that our motives, not the process itself, are what might get us crossways with God's desire. If a specific situation warrants the use of testing, and the motive is to choose the very best person against our criteria versus screening out qualified people who don't appeal to us for other reasons, then by all means, use testing.

Legislation governing the use of testing is almost all devoted to preventing its use in situations in which the potential employer is intentionally, or unintentionally, biasing the selection process to the detriment of a particular group or type of candidates. Additionally, the instruments must be used in a professional manner that not only serves the decision process but proves edifying to the candidate as well.

Using several highly reliable personality tests, one psychologist researched whether he could find discernable differences between Christians and nonChristians in certain areas of their test results. He could not. He could find "no important differences in either maladaptive or in normal, positive behaviors between Christians and non-Christians."9 If a nonChristian has a problem in being able to trust others, he or she would most likely have that problem as a Christian, too. The behavioral impact appears to be the same regardless of whether the individual is a Christian or not. The difference is that Christians can avail themselves of God's help and spiritual resources in confronting the problem.

Finally, remember that tests aren't appropriate or needed in every situation. Even in circumstances in which testing makes a needed and positive contribution, it is only one of several sources of information. Never let test results become the sole source, or even the primary source, of information in your decision. Over the years there have been many instances in which I have been confronted with negative test information but still chose the candidate because of what I considered stronger and offsetting data from references and interviews. However, there have been a considerable number of times when the test results alerted us to oversights in these other sources. When the test results appear to disagree with the other sources, we do our best to revisit and deepen the interview and reference information. Often, with the hints provided by the tests, we are able to find confirmation of the same issues in our other sources.

It might appear from the above that tests mainly provide negative information, but that isn't the case. I remember one instance in particular in which reference information on a certain candidate indicated a problem with stress. We indicated this concern to our consulting psychologist when we sent the candidate in for testing. He, in both his interview and test results, found plenty of evidence to the contrary. We revisited the reference and found that, in this one instance, the comments were founded on philosophical disagreements between this candidate and the reference, a former superior. We were able to confirm with additional referencing that this individual categorized all of his subordinates who didn't agree with the work style he desired (an unhealthy one, I might add) as not being able to "handle the pressure."

Now, can you see why I was perturbed with my friend's approach to testing at the beginning of this chapter? The test had not been proven valid to the task at hand; it was a single instrument attempting to do what most professionals claim would take a battery; there was no qualified "professional" to administer and interpret the results; and, in some respects, it was the only source of information about the candidate used to decide if the client would even see this individual.

Can you imagine the results if such a testing process had been used in the selection of the apostles? One person did imagine it, and I think his conclusions do an excellent job in confirming the thoughts I've shared above.

SOMETHING TO THINK ABOUT[10]

TO: Jesus, Son of Joseph
        Woodcrafter's Carpenter Shop
        Nazareth 25922

FROM: Jordan Management Consultants
        (Via Dr. Bryan Crenshaw,
        Greenville, SC, USA)
        Jerusalem 26544

Dear Sir:

Thank you for submitting the résumés of the twelve (12) men you have picked for managerial positions in your new organization. All of them have now taken our battery of tests . . . and we have not only run the results through our computer, but also arranged personal interviews for each of them with our psychologists and vocational aptitude consultant.

It is the staff opinion that most of your nominees are lacking in the background, education and vocational aptitude for the type of enterprise you are undertaking. They do not have the team concept. We would recommend that you continue your search for persons of experience in managerial ability and proven capability.

Simon Peter is emotionally unstable and given to fits of temper. Andrew has absolutely no qualities of leadership. The two brothers, James and John, the sons of Zebedee, place personal interest above company loyalty. Thomas demonstrates a questioning attitude that would tend to undermine morale. We feel that it is our duty to tell you that Matthew has been black-listed by the Greater Jerusalem Better Business Bureau. James, the son of Alphaeus, and Thaddaeus definitely have radical leanings, and they both registered a high score on the manic-depressive scale.

One of the candidates, however, shows great potential. He is a man of ability and resourcefulness, meets people well, has a keen business mind and has contacts in high places. He is highly motivated, ambitious and responsible. We recommend Judas Iscariot as your comptroller and right-hand man. All of the other profiles are self-explanatory.

We wish you every success in your new venture.

Sincerely yours,

CHAPTER SEVENTEEN

Making the Decision

YOU HAVE INTERVIEWED, referenced, tested, pried, and probed, and your final candidates all appear to be qualified for the job. Many have been eliminated, but the remaining few all meet the must-have criteria and many of the want-to-haves as well. But there is only one opening, so which person do you choose? These are not apples and oranges. They're people—real, complex, confusing, unique, and seemingly incomparable people. Candidate A is strong in a key area in which candidate B is weak. But then candidate B is stronger than A in a number of areas and very much stronger than candidate C in a few important criteria. The very fact that you have used the criteria-based process we've suggested has, in some respects, gotten you into this dilemma. Remember the old days when you had only one qualified candidate? Well, not qualified exactly, but he or she was the only candidate and had a lot of the things you were looking for. Anyway, beggars can't be choosers. Then again, the beauty of that system was that you didn't have to choose, you just went with the one person you had. Those kinds of decisions sure were simpler, but then they had to be because you were so busy dealing with the problems you had with the last person you hired.

Take heart, it's not as complex as it looks. We anticipated this problem when we first profiled the position, defining and prioritizing our selection criteria. These criteria have played a number of significant roles throughout the process, telling us what to look for, helping us screen out irrelevant information, and now they will provide the structure for comparison among the candidates. Even with the screening and organization, the use of criteria brings to the remainder of the decision process a large amount of information, and we need some means of organizing our thoughts as we compare the candidates.

FIGURE 17.1

Selection Criteria	Priority
Demonstrated "sales" ability—must be able to take a "consultative" sales approach versus hard sell	Must-have
Minimum of two to three years in bank/financial marketing—knowledge of the financial services industry, the problems confronting it, etc.	Must-have
Self-starter, able to work without direct or close supervision	9
Excellent verbal communication skills	10
Goal-oriented—able to set and achieve goals	8
Good written communication skills (e.g., follow-up correspondence, proposals, etc.)	6
Corporate image and poise creditable to vice president of bank as "peer" versus merely a vendor	5
Able to develop and maintain long-term relationships with clients	6
Degree in marketing/advertising	3
Sales management potential	5

Let's look in on a manager who is just about ready to confront the task of making the final decision of an important selection. The hiring executive is Mary Wells, a regional sales manager for a fast-growing bank newsletter service. Her company sells customized newsletters to banks, who, in turn, send them to current and potential clients. Mary has just lost an excellent salesperson. This is one of her best territories with some of her biggest customers, and therefore she has been particularly careful in her selection process. Because of the fast growth in her region, she's been spread very thin and needs a replacement who can hit the ground running without a lot of training and supervision. Using her own experience, input from her boss, and her model salespeople as examples, she identified and prioritized her selection criteria (figure 17.1).

She'll use a decision matrix, a spreadsheet of sorts, that will help her organize and compare the information she's collected throughout the evaluation process (figure 17.2). Down the left column, she has listed the selection criteria. Notice that she has followed our process, identifying the must-have, or required, criteria and the want-to-have items with assigned priorities. Now she is ready to evaluate the candidates against the criteria and, through that, to each other.

After screening many possible candidates, Mary was able to identify four final ones. Actually, there were only three; the fourth candidate, Jack Peterson, did not have the requisite experience and knowledge in banking. She had liked him a lot because of the sales skills and high energy he would bring to the position. As a result, she found herself rationalizing and leaving him in the "keep" pile each time she cut the pile of résumés and interview notes for serious consideration.

However, in the end, she decided to stick with the process and eliminate Jack from further consideration. *A must-have is a must-have,* she thought to herself as she sighed and put the résumé and attached notes aside. She knew that she had been right in making banking/financial marketing experience a nonnegotiable qualification. This territory was an important market with big, demanding customers who would not be patient with someone who didn't know their industry. Mary wouldn't have had the time to train him and still manage the growth in the rest of her region.

In this instance, we see the power of criteria to help us navigate through what would normally be a white-water experience as our subjective, emotional thoughts interact with the pile of data we've collected. Our list of qualities and qualifications acts as an anchor of sorts that continually pulls us back to what we really think is important as we are confronted with real, live candidates whose personalities and communication skills overshadow other skills that may be more important in this situation.

With her three remaining candidates, Mary will focus on the desired, or want-to-have, criteria. One person observed that "the MUSTS decide who gets to play, but the WANTS decide who wins."[1]

First, she will carefully review her notes from résumés, interviews, referencing, and testing and summarize how each candidate performed against a given criterion. In figure 17.3 we see her summaries. This step demands discernment and creativity. On one hand, you must select the information relevant to each criterion and present it with sufficient detail so as to prevent having to constantly sift back through the notes to remember what you really meant in summary. On the other, you don't want to duplicate the detail in your notes on the matrix.[2]

She will then compare each candidate to the others, relative to how well each person meets the criteria. And she will evaluate all the candidates in one criterion before moving on to the next. Scoring such an evaluation can be done in several ways. Some decision makers might choose the candidate they believe best meets a particular criterion, circling the winning entry and giving that criterion to that particular candidate. With this method, there is a winner but no second or third place, and in the event of a close race, these nuances might prove to be important. Look at Mary's ninth criterion, for instance, in figure 17.4, "Degree in marketing/advertising."

FIGURE 17.2

Selection Criteria	Priority	Robert Stevens	Bill James	Sandra Adams	Jack Peterson
Demonstrated "sales" ability—must be able to take a "consultative" sales approach versus hard sell	Must-have				
Minimum of two to three years in bank/financial marketing—knowledge of the financial services industry, the problems confronting it, etc.	Must-have				
Self-starter, able to work without direct or close supervision	9				
Excellent verbal communication skills	10				
Goal-oriented—able to set and achieve goals	8				
Good written communication skills (e.g., follow-up correspondence, proposals, etc.)	6				
Corporate image and poise creditable to vice president of bank as "peer" versus merely a vendor	5				
Able to develop and maintain long-term relationships with clients	6				
Degree in marketing/advertising	3				
Sales management potential	5				

FIGURE 17.3

Selection Criteria	Priority	Robert Stevens	Bill James	Sandra Adams	Jack Peterson
Demonstrated "sales" ability—must be able to take a "consultative" sales approach versus hard sell	Must-have	Yes—trained in H-M technique and did well in AP communications	Yes—IBM background; exceeded quotas three out of four years	Yes—consistently exceeded quotas at ACME Check Printing	Yes—seldom missed and was regional contact trainer with H-M
Minimum of two to three years in bank/financial marketing—knowledge of the financial services industry, the problems confronting it, etc.	Must-have	Sixteen years at Bank Services Corp. before going with AP; acceptable answers in interview	Four years with IBM Banking Systems Group; two years with First National; acceptable answers in interview	Seven years with ACME Check Printing in SE division; excellent knowledge demonstrated in interview	No—excellent sales background but no experience or knowledge in finance industry; poor interview response to questions
Self-starter, able to work without direct or close supervision	9	Headed NW division of AP (HQ in N.Y.); references very positive	References noted this was strength but need clear goals and some track	Very goal oriented and references noted she was self motivated. She says she prefers team environment and will be looking for that type of situation in L.T.	
Excellent verbal communication skills	10	Acceptable—has had Toast Master training; seemed tentative in areas in which he was new or unprepared	Excellent—lay preacher with his church; fast on his feet and is very organized in presentation	Fast, articulate but doesn't listen well—tends to start speaking before she clearly understands issue; somewhat disorganized; open to input, can be trained	
Goal-oriented—able to set and achieve goals	8	Able goal setter—references note he is not risk taking in goal setting but is "conservatively" realistic; consistently achieves sales goals	Hits or exceeds assigned quotas and constantly pushes self for goal growth	References and interview confirm she is very competitive—with others and self against goals	

ALTERNATIVES

FIGURE 17.3 (continued)

Selection Criteria	Priority	Robert Stevens	Bill James	Sandra Adams	Jack Peterson
			ALTERNATIVES		
Good written communication skills (e.g., follow-up correspondence, proposals, etc.)	6	Evaluation of written proposals: acceptable with capable, detailed secretarial support	Evaluation of written reports: acceptable—capable of doing own reports and proposals on WP if necessary	Evaluation of written proposals: excellent! Best I've seen	
Corporate image and poise creditable to vice president of bank as "peer" versus merely a vendor	5	Weak—clothing somewhat out of style, button missing from collar, shoes unshined, posture poor	Excellent—crisp, professional image; confident, relaxed, poised; neat appearance	Acceptable—very professional dress but a little matronly in style; somewhat cool and aloof. References confirm this is normal, more task oriented than people oriented	
Able to develop and maintain long-term relationships with clients	6	Very strong—Seldom loses clients; becomes personal friend; warm, people oriented	Acceptable—references possible in this criterion from First National	References say this is strength—not so much because of warm, friendly personality but because of consistent, high-quality performance	
Degree in marketing/ advertising	3	B.S. in marketing, FYU in '71—2.5 GPA	B.S. in accounting from KSU, '79—3.25 GPA; tennis scholarship	B.S. in advertising, Stanford '76; MBA with marketing emphasis in '81 from XU	
Sales management potential	5	Managed two assistants '84-'87; supervisor noted performance was acceptable; not aspiration of Robert's	No experience; but desires to learn; tests, references, and consulting psychologist noted good potential	Supervised four sales and support staff at ACME; known as tough manager, but unit was a top performer in the company; style may be a little "hard" for our culture	

This is a want-to-have issue, and using the circle approach, Sandra would have won with her undergrad degree in advertising from Stanford and an MBA with a marketing emphasis. In fact, using this approach throughout the matrix would have put Bill James clearly in the winner's circle, but as we shall see in a moment, a more detailed and discerning method turns out much different results.

A more illuminating approach might be to rate each candidate on a scale (one to ten, one to five, etc.) depending on how well he or she meets the criteria. This was Mary's approach. She used a one-to-ten scale with ten being an excellent score for a given criterion. Look at how she scored her three candidates in "corporate image and poise" (figure 17.5).

From her notes we can see that her conclusions (the numbers in parentheses) were based on her personal observations and judgment, probably in the interview, and references. Robert didn't fare well for the reasons shown, Bill received the highest marks, with Sandra on the high side in between. Sure, it's a subjective judgment call, but that's the whole point, to capture our judgments in some organized, comparative manner.

Some authors advocate giving the candidate that best meets a given criterion a ten, and then scoring the other candidates relative to that.[3] However, as you can see in figure 17.6, which shows her completed comparisons, Mary refused to give a ten to anyone she didn't believe was excellent against a particular criterion.

Now we need to take the weight or priority of the individual criterion into consideration. If a given candidate scores well against the others on several lower-priority criteria but doesn't do well on those with higher priorities, it's unlikely he or she will prove to be the best choice overall. As you see in figure 17.6, Mary multiplied the comparative score for each candidate (the number in the parentheses) with the priority for that criterion and computed a weighted score for each candidate for each criterion (the number in the brackets). These were totaled for all three candidates, and Sandra (421) achieved the highest score, finishing barely ahead of Bill (414). Robert finished a distant third with a total score of 328.

FIGURE 17.4

Selection Criteria	Priority	ALTERNATIVES			
		Robert Stevens	Bill James	Sandra Adams	Jack Peterson
Degree in marketing/advertising	3	B.S. in marketing, FYU in '71—2.5 GPA	B.S. in accounting from KSU, '79—3.25 GPA; tennis scholarship	B.S. in advertising, Stanford '76; MBA with marketing emphasis in '81 from XU	

FIGURE 17.5

| Corporate image and poise creditable to vice president of bank as "peer" versus merely a vendor | 5 | Weak—clothing somewhat out of style, button missing from collar, shoes unshined, posture poor (2) | Excellent—crisp, professional image; confident, relaxed, poised; neat appearance (10) | Acceptable—very professional dress but a little matronly in style; somewhat cool and aloof. References confirm this is normal, more task oriented than people oriented (7) | |

FIGURE 17.6

Selection Criteria	Priority	ALTERNATIVES			
		Robert Stevens	Bill James	Sandra Adams	Jack Peterson
Demonstrated "sales" ability—must be able to take a "consultative" sales approach versus hard sell	Must-have	Yes—trained in H-M technique and did well in AP communications	Yes—IBM background; exceeded quotas three out of four years	Yes—consistently exceeded quotas at ACME Check Printing	Yes—seldom missed and was regional contact trainer with H-M
Minimum of two to three years in bank/financial marketing—knowledge of the financial services industry, the problems confronting it, etc.	Must-have	Sixteen years at Bank Services Corp. before going with AP; acceptable answers in interview	Four years with IBM Banking Systems Group; two years with First National; acceptable answers in interview	Seven years with ACME Check Printing in SE division; excellent knowledge demonstrated in interview	No—excellent sales background but no experience or knowledge in finance industry; poor interview response to questions
Self-starter, able to work without direct or close supervision	9	Headed NW division of AP (HQ in N.Y.); references very positive (10) [90]	References noted this was strength but need clear goals and some track (7) [63]	Very goal oriented and references noted she was self motivated. She says she prefers team environment and will be looking for that type of situation in L.T. (8) [72]	
Excellent verbal communication skills	10	Acceptable—has had Toast Master training; seemed tentative in areas in which he was new or unprepared (6) [60]	Excellent—lay preacher with his church; fast on his feet and is very organized in presentation (10) [100]	Fast, articulate but doesn't listen well—tends to start speaking before she clearly understands issue; somewhat disorganized; open to input, can be trained (8) [80]	
Goal-oriented—able to set and achieve goals	8	Able goal setter—references note he is not risk taking in goal setting but is "conservatively" realistic; consistently achieves sales goals (5) [40]	Hits or exceeds assigned quotas and constantly pushes self for goal growth (8) [64]	References and interview confirm she is very competitive—with others and self against goals (7) [56]	

FIGURE 17.6 (continued)

Selection Criteria	Priority	Robert Stevens	Bill James	Sandra Adams	Jack Peterson
			ALTERNATIVES		
Good written communication skills (e.g., follow-up correspondence, proposals, etc.)	6	Evaluation of written proposals: acceptable with capable, detailed secretarial support (6) [36]	Evaluation of written reports: acceptable—capable of doing own reports and proposals on WP if necessary (8) [48]	Evaluation of written proposals: excellent! Best I've seen (10) [60]	
Corporate image and poise creditable to vice president of bank as "peer" versus merely a vendor	5	Weak—clothing somewhat out of style, button missing from collar, shoes unshined, posture poor (2) [10]	Excellent—crisp, professional image; confident, relaxed, poised; neat appearance (10) [50]	Acceptable—very professional dress but a little matronly in style; somewhat cool and aloof. References confirm this is normal, more task oriented than people oriented (7) [35]	
Able to develop and maintain long-term relationships with clients	6	Very strong—Seldom loses clients; becomes personal friend; warm, people oriented (9) [54]	Acceptable—references possible in this criterion from First National (7) [42]	References say this is strength—not so much because of warm, friendly personality but because of consistent, high-quality performance (8) [48]	
Degree in marketing/ advertising	3	B.S. in marketing, FYU in '71—2.5 GPA (6) [18]	B.S. in accounting from KSU, '79—3.25 GPA; tennis scholarship (4) [12]	B.S. in advertising, Stanford '76; MBA with marketing emphasis in '81 from XU (10) [30]	
Sales management potential	5	Managed two assistants '84-'87; supervisor noted performance was acceptable; not aspiration of Robert's (4) [20]	No experience; but desires to learn; tests, references, and consulting psychologist noted good potential (7) [35]	Supervised four sales and support staff at ACME; known as tough manager, but unit was a top performer in the company; style may be a little "hard" for our culture (8) [40]	
TOTAL		328	414	421	

Don't let the numbers fool you; this process is highly subjective. But can you imagine trying to do this without some type of mechanism to help you order and organize your thoughts? Without criteria, it's likely that Mary would have gone with Jack Peterson, the best salesman of the lot, whose sales skills almost sold Mary even though he didn't meet a particular must-have criterion. If left with only résumés, Sandra would have won hands down. Her experience and educational background were much superior to the other candidates. If experience alone was the issue, Robert was clearly the choice. Bill, who had the second highest score, was almost not considered because he barely had enough experience in bank marketing.

Mary sat at her desk in a reflective mood as she reviewed the matrix. *Yes,* she thought, *Sandra was definitely the strongest candidate. She must be our first choice but, if that's the case, why do I feel so uncomfortable? What about Bill? I can't believe that he scored so well; I almost didn't put him in the stack for final consideration.* Mary decided to follow her intuition and pulled the files of both candidates for one more careful review. She was looking for anything, a margin note in her interview records, a miscellaneous comment from a reference that had gone unheeded—anything that would either challenge the decision or chase the doubt away and let her proceed with confidence.

Actually, in important and closely contested decisions, it's not unusual to find some hesitancy in rushing ahead to implement our choice, and that brings us to our last step in the process, assessing the risk.

For the best alternative, ask yourself (and others involved in the decision), What's the worst thing that could go wrong on a scale of one to one hundred? How bad would that be on the same scale? What's the probability it would happen? Don't bother to add or multiply the numbers together; that's not the point. The objective of these questions is merely to get you to identify and confront any risks involved with this particular alternative. If the worst thing that could go wrong is not very bad, we'll probably proceed with our tentative choice, regardless of its probability.

However, if the consequences of being wrong are significant, we'll more than likely go to our second choice at moderate to high levels of probability. At exactly what level of probability we'll move away from the candidate with the highest score will depend on our propensity to take risks.

As Mary reviewed Sandra's file and her interview notes, she saw the faint threads of a pattern. Sandra was one tough lady. She had fantastic strengths—task orientation; an unbelievable commitment to perform, holding herself to the same tough standards to which she held her staff; a cool professional demeanor. However, as she continued to probe into her observations about Sandra, it became clear that these strengths, if overemphasized, could be a weakness as well. She might possibly be too tough, too demanding, too competitive for the climate and culture of Mary's company.

How bad would that be? thought Mary. She concluded that it could be bad. Her company was committed to engendering a cooperative spirit and team strategy as it moved into the decade of the nineties. This was an important value of both the CEO and Mary's boss, the national sales manager, as well as herself. This was one of the reasons she'd come here. *I should have put "team player" on my list of criteria*, she concluded as she moved to review Bill's file one more time.

Mary ultimately went with Bill James as her new territory salesperson. His manner and style were much more compatible with her company than were Sandra's. It was clear that the very best candidate wasn't the one with just the highest score on our matrix. The risk elements must be taken into account as well. The best candidate would be the one who had the greatest probability of successfully performing in the position with an acceptable degree of risk.

STOP! I CAN'T HANDLE THE DETAIL!

As I noted earlier in the book, some of you are not gifted with a love for detail. The decision matrix, should you have even read this far, has probably pushed you over the edge. But there's hope, so stay with me a few more minutes. Remember, when I introduced Mary and the decision she was making, I noted that this was a particularly important decision and therefore she had walked through it very carefully. Additionally, I needed the level of detail in order to lay out the entire process. I'm not a detail person either, but I find my willingness to confront the minutiae of any management process to be in direct proportion to my perceptions of the importance of the objective. Many if not most people decisions can be made with less effort—it depends on the importance of the decision.

I've made many people decisions on a yellow pad, using a rough matrix to keep my thoughts on target. Not long ago we worked with a large landscape architectural firm that was having a problem with very high turnover with its manual labor force. These were generally young men and women who did manual landscape work for minimum wage. The crew chiefs, individuals who had been there a little longer, interviewed prospective candidates and made the decision. Turnover dropped dramatically when we profiled their ideal workers and gave the crew chiefs some simple, straightforward criteria for which to look, and questions or methods to validate the presence of a particular criterion. The crew chiefs didn't use a matrix. They merely asked the questions, wrote down a brief summary of the response, and went with the individual they thought met the criteria best.

SLEEP ON IT

Peter Drucker observes that "fast personnel decisions are likely to be wrong decisions. . . . Among the effective executives I have had occasion to observe, they have been people who make decisions fast, and people who make them slowly. But without exception, they make personnel decisions slowly and they make them several times before they really commit themselves."[4]

After you have made your decision, sleep on it, if possible for several days. During this time, while you go about your other work, pray about the decision. As you envision this person working in your organization, how does that feel? Giving the decision time to age gives the Holy Spirit and your own intuition time to confirm the choice. If you have peace of mind after a few days, implement your decision.

IS A MATRIX BIBLICAL?

Did the Apostle Paul use a matrix in choosing the team for his mission journeys? Did the congregation use a matrix to choose the administrators in Acts 6? Probably not. The apostles used a selection criterion in finding candidates to replace Judas in Acts 1—"one of the men who have been with us the whole time the Lord Jesus went in and out among us" (Acts 1:21). They identified two men, Justus and Matthias, but they didn't use a matrix. Instead they prayed, "Lord, you know everyone's heart. Show us which of these two you have chosen" (Acts 1:24-25) and then drew lots. Obviously, they hadn't read my book.

Again, it's not the matrix that's the heart of the process, but rather the selection criteria. The matrix is merely a simple way to order a lot of complex information in a manner that allows comparison. The biblical part comes in understanding the information. Regardless of the process and effort we use to collect relevant information about the candidates, we are operating under a tremendous handicap. Remember God's admonition to Samuel as he attempted to discern Saul's successor in 1 Samuel 16:7. Samuel was very impressed with Jesse's eldest son, Eliab, a fine-looking young man who had the characteristics of a leader, at least in Samuel's eyes. God cut off this line of thought with a key reminder, "Do not consider his appearance or his height, for I have rejected him. The LORD does not look at the things man looks at. Man looks at the outward appearance, but the LORD looks at the heart." That's what the apostles were acknowledging in their prayer in Acts 1:24-25.

We know that we will end up with an almost-fit at best, and that we have a propensity to focus primarily on the externals. This is where prayer plays a key role. As we can see from the above example with Mary and from our own experience, every time we decide that a candidate best meets a given criterion, we're dealing with highly subjective information and we're exercising judgment. There's a lot of guesswork and intuition throughout the process. Because I'm writing to Christians, I have assumed that prayer would be an integral part of your efforts at every step. But it is here that God has the opportunity to cut a poor decision off at the pass. The matrix, if you are using one, is an excellent way to lay out the issues for prayer as you ask God for wisdom (James 1:5). The wisdom He provides, wisdom from above, is "first of all pure; then peaceloving, considerate, submissive, full of mercy and good fruit, impartial and sincere" (James 3:17). How would you like to make the final decision with that kind of insight and confidence?

DECISION PERSPECTIVES

Before moving to the next chapter, let me introduce a few perspectives that might influence our decision making.

There Are No Perfect Fits

A review of figure 17.6 on pages 214-215 will quickly reveal that none of the candidates met all of the criteria. Even the eventual "best" choice, Bill James, scored less than one of the other two candidates on five of the eight want-to-have objectives. Although he's the best fit, he's only an almost-fit. And that's what Peter Drucker reminds us when he observes that "people decisions are time consuming, for the simple reason that the Lord did not create people as resources for the organization. They do not come in the proper size or shape for the tasks to be done in the organization—and they cannot be recast for these tasks. People are almost always 'almost fits' at best. To get the job done with people (and no other resources are available) therefore requires lots of time, thought and judgment."[5]

We can best see the concept of fit graphically. On the next page I show four diagrams in which the task is represented by the box and the person by the blob attempting to relate to it.

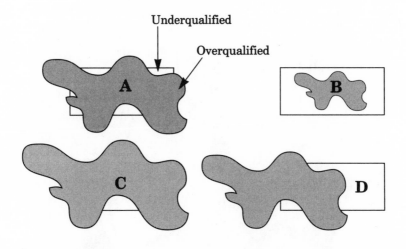

In box A we see the almost-fit described by Drucker. This could be Bill James, overqualified in few areas, underqualified in others, but overall he's a pretty good fit. In boxes B and C the individuals are under- and overqualified, respectively. Neither is very happy with his or her job. B is probably feeling a lot of stress, and C is bored and underchallenged. Box D shows an individual who has the potential to be an almost-fit, if, and that's an important if, he or she were interested in the job. In this case, the person is not, and if convinced to take the position would probably spend a great deal of creative energy and time getting you to let him or her do what he or she wants to do instead of what you need that person to do. This brings up a good point. By compromise, I don't mean forcing the point and cramming the individual into a position that clearly doesn't fit his or her skills or interests, just because you need the position filled and there doesn't appear to be any other choice available. The cartoon on page 222 provides a humorous reminder of this inclination found in most of us when confronted with the need to fill a tough position, particularly in church and ministry settings. The solution to this tendency brings me to my next point.

"We're looking for someone with a doctorate in Christian Education and five years of experience, but we'll settle for someone with a van."

There Are No Bad People

Everyone is a "ten" in the right position. The people who don't make the cut in your decision are going to be someone else's first choice. When I talk about an unqualified or mismatched person, I am doing so from the perspective of a particular position. We see in Scripture that everyone is handcrafted by God (Psalm 139:13-16, Jeremiah 1:5, Galatians 1:15). And, in the right position, each and every one of us has the potential to be excellent. A good example of this is when an athletic coach takes someone else's problem athlete and works with that person to make him or her a star.

There Are No Long-Lasting People Decisions

No other era of history has been confronted with the pace and scope of change as has this one. Change is on every front, sociologically, technologically, culturally, spiritually, and politically. Organizations of every type must see, understand, and respond to this change if they are to survive, much less succeed. Nowhere is such responsiveness more relevant than in their people decisions. The environment in which the job is done is in a constant state of flux. Such change demands constant scrutiny and adaptation.

Be careful that you don't fit the person and the task too tightly. Leave some room for growth and change. Peter Drucker has noted that in the area of staffing, things change. "The 'perfect fit' then rapidly becomes the 'misfit,'" he concludes.[6] In addition to leaving room for growth, the manager of the nineties must become like the helmsman of a sailboat, constantly adjusting the sails to take full advantage of the available wind. He or she must be alert to the small, subtle changes of climate that require adjustments in job descriptions so that the fit between the position and the people remains effective.

Focus on Strengths

As in every aspect of the Christian walk, we must exercise faith, trusting God for the highest and best. This is particularly true when it comes to people. Research is clear, the tendency in people decisions is to focus on the negative. We do not generally believe the best in people, but the worst. For example, one observation coming out of a group of studies conducted at McGill University over a ten-year period was that in interview situations, "just one unfavorable impression was followed by a reject decision (by the interviewer) 90% of the time. Positive information was given much less weight."[7] Dr. Wayne Cascio notes that in his studies "research indicates that an interviewer who begins an interview with an unfavorable expectancy (e.g. an unfavorable letter of reference) may tend to give an applicant less credit for past accomplishments, may blame the applicant more for past failures, and ultimately decide that the applicant is unacceptable."[8]

As we ponder the results we find on our decision matrix, it's quite likely that we are also confronted with such tendencies. In this case the focus is much more on disqualifying than on qualifying the candidates. Many Bible commentators have alerted us to the ability and the inclination of our Lord to see the potential in people. Could any of us have seen the potential in those rough, uneducated Galilean fishermen? There wasn't a master of divinity in the bunch.

Peter Drucker believes that "the effective executive makes strengths productive." He observes that "these strengths are true opportunities. To make strength productive is the unique purpose of the organization. It cannot, of course, overcome the weaknesses with which each of us is abundantly endowed. But it can make them irrelevant. Its task is to use the strength of each man as a building block for joint performance." Drucker concludes, "The area in which the executive first encounters the challenge of strength is in staffing. The effective executive fills positions and promotes on the basis of what a man can do. He does not make staffing decisions to minimize weaknesses but to maximize strengths. . . . Whoever tries to place a man or to staff an organization to avoid weakness will end up at best with mediocrity."[9]

As you wrestle with your decision, be careful of the tendency to run from bad news and avoid weakness. The strongest people on your matrix will have correspondingly strong weaknesses. They come as one package. The challenge is to match strengths against the situation, against your selection criteria.

PART FOUR

THE ONGOING PROCESS OF STAFFING AND RECRUITING

CHAPTER EIGHTEEN

The Chase
and the Challenge

A CRITICAL STEP in your overall selection process is to ensure that you have a pool of qualified candidates from which to choose. Both quantity and quality are important factors.

Not many years ago I was contacted by the national sales manager of an international paper products company. He was pretty frustrated by the fact that his West Coast sales manager had just spent ten hours interviewing twelve unqualified candidates. He had plenty of quantity but no quality. On the other hand, in Christian ministries, quality aside, we frequently see a pronounced shortage of candidates, and the decision is often made with only a single individual under consideration. This is called a "binary trap." In decision-making theory, a binary trap is a yes or no answer to a single alternative. And it's just that, a trap! The quality of your decision can be no better that the best alternative on your list. If you have only one candidate, you'd better pray that that person is the best candidate, and very often he or she is not.

The Lord was familiar with binary traps. In the eighth chapter of John, the Pharisees brought Him a woman caught in adultery, confronting Him with the fact that the law said to stone such a woman. Their basic question was, Should we stone her or not? A single alternative, yes or no. In Matthew 22:16-17, the Pharisees again "laid plans to trap him." In this case the issue was taxes: "Tell us then, what is your opinion? Is it right to pay taxes to Caesar or not?" In both cases the Lord got out of those traps by finding creative alternatives.

Because of the complex, subjective nature of people decisions, it's important that you have multiple, qualified candidates, forcing you to examine the details and ask the hard questions. The contrasts between your alternatives will help you to more clearly see and evaluate their strengths and weaknesses. Although making a yes or no decision regarding a single candidate appears to be easier than wading through the process of evaluating and comparing several, it's considerably more dangerous.

So where do you find this pool of candidates? You have several possible sources.

IN-HOUSE CANDIDATES

The first and best place to look is in your own organization. I believe that starting any people decision with an evaluation of in-house candidates ought to be a matter of organizational policy. Any time a current staff person gets a promotion to a new position, you get a tremendous boost in morale throughout the organization. Additionally, you save a significant amount of time and money. Such an individual is already familiar with your organization and will generally hit the ground running the first day on the new job.

There are two pitfalls associated with in-house promotions and transfers. The first is that often, because the person is already "on board," we see no need to work through the process steps to qualify the candidate with the same level of energy that we would apply to an external candidate. We assume that because the candidate was excellent in the previous position, he or she will be good in the new one as well. We also assume the we don't need to do a thorough job checking references (with supervisor, peers, and subordinates), either. After all, we know this person!

Both assumptions can be wrong. Good performance in one position is no guarantee of similar work in a different position. As for referencing, I can't tell you how many staff members I've seen who were transferred or promoted, only to experience significant problems with people from their old position. Fellow employees, peers, and subordinates will seldom rock the boat and take the initiative to provide critical information to management in such a case without being asked. They're just happy the problem went somewhere else.

A second potential pitfall is dealing with employees who were considered and didn't get the job. This is of particular concern when the successful candidate comes from an outside source. The rejected candidates must be handled with great sensitivity and diplomacy. A key to this is the process itself. Before you even begin to evaluate in-house candidates, set their expectations. Explain the process to them, stressing its objectivity and completeness. The process makes the decision outcome less personal, even though a person must ultimately make the decision. Unlike external candidates, they're here, observable, and you know a lot about them. In order not to unsettle their emotions unduly, quietly, confidentially attempt to contrast their strengths against the criteria. If possible, work with their supervisor or someone you trust who knows them in the work setting. Only after you are pretty sure they really are in the running for the position should you approach them directly.

ADVERTISING

Where to Advertise

There are few of us who haven't, at least once in our lives, responded to an advertisement in attempting to find a job. It is probably the most popular recruiting tool used. In finding candidates my firm has used a variety of advertising vehicles. Although local newspapers usually get the lion's share of such ads, I have found the more specialized publications a much better source. Virtually every trade, profession, and industry (e.g., banking, engineering, the oil and gas industry, financial planning, media, etc.) has its version of a magazine or newsletter. These specialized publications screen out many of the seemingly thousands of unqualified responses you get from the local paper. Some of the larger, more sophisticated publications, like *The Wall Street Journal,* even give you the option of advertising in specific geographic regions of the country.

Christian nonprofit organizations have their own sources as well—denominational newsletters and magazines, Christian magazines like *Christianity Today,* and association newsletters (Christian Management Association, Fellowship of Companies for Christ, etc.).

If you use a newspaper, my experience suggests Sunday's edition to be the most productive source of responses. In fact, if you don't word your ad carefully, you will be buried in responses, the vast majority of which will be from unqualified people. The economy of the nineties promises a continuation of corporate "downsizing." This trend will swell the already large numbers of people who respond to newspaper ads. Although the newspaper appears to be a fast, economical way to generate a large number of names, the cost of responding to and screening the applicants can make it a very time-consuming, expensive source of unqualified leads. I generally recommend it as the source of last resort. Attempt first to find a trade publication that speaks directly to your target audience.

What to Say
Several years ago I was consulting with a client to develop a city-wide evangelistic campaign in Barcelona, Spain. All of the evangelical churches in the city banded together, trained their people, and prepared to advertise in the newspapers and other media for people who would like to know more about Christianity. One of my jobs was to design the advertising and, in the process of doing so, I tested several ads, each with different messages and amounts of information. As expected, those ads with the least amount of copy

and explanation generated the largest response. However, when the respondents found out the reason behind the ads, they were often frustrated and felt misled—not the best attitude for sharing the gospel. Responses went down correspondingly as we increased the amount of copy and explanation in the ad, but the quality of the responses went up. These responders knew exactly what the issue was and were sincerely interested in knowing more. This illustration is a long way of making a significant point: The wording of your ads is very important.

Like every other aspect of the process, your ad must sell and screen at the same time. The best headline is the title of the position (e.g., National Sales Manager, Vice President of Development, etc.). The body of the ad must cover the nature of the job, the type of organization, location, compensation, and any other significant benefits. Be careful not to oversell with clichés and hollow adjectives like "fantastic opportunity." The best source of good ideas as to specific wording and approach to the ad is other ads. Get a *Wall Street Journal* and review the way its employment ads are written. I specifically suggest the *Journal* because its ads are very expensive and therefore advertisers tend to put more thought into the wording of their messages. The more wording, the more screening. You might pay a little more for the ad, but you'll more than recoup the cost in processing the responses. As you write your ad, keep in mind that your objective is to increase the number of qualified responses and to decrease the number of unqualified applicants. Choose every word carefully to that end.

What about blind ads? Although I see a lot of "send your résumé to PO Box 123" sorts of appeals, most experts in the field of recruiting would advise against blind ads. Robert Half observes that research has shown that blind ads rarely draw responses from people currently employed (confidentiality is too big a risk) and that people, overall, are mistrustful of them. Half points out that three types of people generally respond to blind ads: people who are unemployed, people who think they will be unemployed shortly, and those who are indiscreet enough to sent a résumé to a blind box number.[1] I recommend a blind ad only if you are looking for external candidates and do not want individuals currently in your organization to know you're looking.

There are legal constraints here as in other parts of our process. If you are a for-profit firm, you can't specifically ask for a Christian. Generally, the publication will challenge this. But even if they don't catch it, it's still illegal. Robert Half points out that "it is no longer acceptable to advertise for a 'Gal Friday'" or for someone thirty to forty years old. You can, however, specify forty or above because the law protects people between the ages of forty and seventy.[2] Aside from the obviously illegal aspects, be careful that you can deliver what you promise, and one of the things you can't ensure is a "permanent career" or "guaranteed promotion opportunities."

PERSONAL CONTACTS

Working through you own network of personal acquaintances may be the single best source of candidates. These are people in whom you have confidence. But be careful. Not everyone is a good judge of people in the job setting. I have found this to be particularly true with some Christian acquaintances who are in, or come out of, a ministry setting. They tend to give me people who are really "nice" (but not necessarily competent in this kind of work), or those who really need the job. Additionally, there is a hesitancy on the part of some to name the shortcomings of their suggested candidates. Even though such weaknesses on the part of the candidate may not disqualify him or her from consideration, the people suggesting the candidate may be hesitant to let "anything unedifying proceed from their mouths." Over the years I've learned who and who not to call. Still, overall, friends and acquaintances have always been my most fruitful source of candidates.

There are several things you can do to make this source more productive. First, I attempt to send a copy of my position profile and selection criteria to my list of contacts ahead of time with a note that tells them I'll call for any suggestions in the very near future. This gives them a clear picture of what I'm looking for and, as we discuss possible candidates over the phone, we can use the criteria as a point of reference. And *I* always call, never relying on them to take the initiative to call or write me with their suggestions.

Several years ago, I was retained by the search committee of a large ministry that was in the process of deciding on their next CEO. They wanted me to help them assess several in-house candidates. In passing, they noted that they had sent out letters with their selection criteria to over one hundred people in the Christian community for possible suggestions. They had received virtually no response. Several months earlier I had done a similar mailing to a slightly shorter list of people. I received almost fifty possible candidates from this group. The difference? I called everyone on the list. Some of the best candidates came from individuals who initially told me they couldn't think of anyone, but with a little probing and brainstorming, God brought creative suggestions to their minds. The person who heads our search efforts for Christian ministries sends out his letters and then prays for these sources a week before calling, asking God to give them names from among their acquaintances.

When contacts do suggest possible candidates, I don't take things at face value. I probe into why they think these people are qualified. This is why it helps them to have the criteria ahead of time. I ask them which criteria best describe the candidate and in which they think the candidate might be lacking. This gives me an excellent sense of whether or not to follow up with the candidate.

SEARCH FIRMS

For many organizations, for-profit as well as nonprofit, executive search firms have become a primary source of candidates, particularly for management and technical staff. This is often the case even for firms with their own human resource departments. It is estimated that roughly 20 percent of all available positions with salaries of more than $100,000 in the Fortune 1,000 companies are filled by outside search firms.[3] A search firm can bring several things to the recruiting process. Often it can supply technical expertise as to the process and techniques to use in finding and qualifying good candidates. In this case the services are essentially consulting. We spend a lot of time with search committees of Christian ministries, outlining the process of how to profile the position, find good candidates, and evaluate them. The search committee does the work; the ministries merely need a little technical help to get them headed in the right direction.

Often the organization has the expertise to conduct the search, but not the time or resources. The search firm provides the extra manpower to get the job done. Finally, search firms can often go where the client organization cannot in order to find good candidates. The most qualified people are generally gainfully and happily employed, and it's difficult for an organization to identify and access individuals working for a competitor.[4]

Most firms are hesitant to use search firms because of the cost. It is expensive. But in most cases, the cost would be comparable if the organization computed the full cost of doing the search itself. In the corporate world, for the more reputable search firms, search fees can range from 25 percent to 33 percent of the first year's salary for the position being filled. Most would add expenses to that figure.

If you choose to use a search firm, find one that has been in business for a few years. Many people enter the field because the costs of getting started are so low and the returns appear to be so high. However, they soon find out it's more difficult than it appeared, and they are soon gone. Additionally, experience—and the skills and knowledge it brings—counts a lot in the search business.

Second, reference the firm with some of its recent clients. Talk to organizations that have used its services. Did it produce good candidates? Did client organizations receive value for their fee? Would they use the firm again? Ask how many qualified candidates they were presented. One of my observations over the years is that some search people find one person and then start selling and stop searching. You should require multiple candidates.

Finally, interview the search executive who will actually do the search. The chemistry between you and this person is critical. In many respects he or she is your surrogate, acting on your behalf in the community. Obtaining qualified candidates at the price of the reputation of your organization is not worth it. Will the executive represent your organization to candidates and sources of candidates with poise, courtesy, and professionalism? How skilled and experienced is this person? How would you assess his or her judgment, integrity, and competency? How well does he or she know your industry? How will he or she do this search? What sources will the executive use? How will he or she find the most qualified candidates? Remember, although you may be retaining a firm, the search will be no better than the skills and judgment of the particular search executive who performs the search. Make sure both of you are clear about who will do what and how much it will cost, and then put it in writing.

THE VERY BEST RECRUITING STRATEGY

The very best recruiting strategy is anticipation. Someone once asked Wayne Gretsky how he became such a good hockey player. He responded that it was because he skated to where the puck was going to be instead of where it was at. Although you might not know when or who, you do know you will have to replace a key person in your organization at some point, maybe even yourself. Now is the time to start preparing for it. Assuming your organization is big enough, the ideal situation would be to identify individuals with the right kind of potential and begin to implement a development strategy that would prepare them for the position when the time came. Such a strategy is called succession planning, and as good as it sounds, few companies or nonprofit ministries have successfully implemented it. Those who have done the best job in this area are the companies like IBM and Procter & Gamble who have a nonnegotiable policy of promotion from within.

However, most organizations are not big enough to effectively implement such a strategy. In many cases, individuals who are ready and strong enough to move to the higher position often, for a variety of reasons, aren't willing to wait around if the move isn't going to happen in the immediate future. Frequently, small- to medium-sized organizations can't afford to maintain the needed bench strength of management to be prepared for such contingencies. So what are the alternatives?

I recommend that you are always in the process of shopping. In the early years of our marriage, my wife and I enjoyed going out shopping. During those years, first in the army, then serving with a parachurch ministry, we didn't have much money and couldn't afford to buy anything. But that didn't stop us from shopping. Even though we bought very little, we shopped for thousands of dollars of merchandise every month.

Some of the most effective executives I know in both the ministry and the corporate world are like that. They are always on the lookout for top talent. They have a short list of criteria in their heads, criteria not specific to any particular position but rather the more general qualities they look for in any executive. They keep records of the top people, even establish and cultivate relationships with them. They find them in the paper, at trade association meetings, through vendors and mutual friends, anywhere. They are always shopping. And when the opportunity or need opens up, they know just whom they would like to talk to and where to find them.

THE CHALLENGE

It would seem that this would be the proper place to discuss how to make a compelling offer. I could discuss how to negotiate salary, benefits, responsibilities. However, I seldom see lack of response on the part of an interested candidate for lack of information in one of those areas. There are exceptions. Sometimes the parties arrive at the end of the process and the organization's offer is so far from the candidate's expectations that things fall apart. Then I wonder how they got so far into the process without at least establishing the boundary lines. I noted in chapter 7 ("Describing the Person") that it is important to get salary ranges and expectations on the table early in the process.

It's been my experience that the very best candidates in both corporate and ministry arenas seldom respond to new opportunities because of compensation or title. Invariably, it is a challenge to do something significant with their lives. These are people with a sense of calling and personal purpose. They want to make a difference. In the next chapter I share the story of how Steve Jobs recruited John Scully from Pepsico when everyone else failed. Jobs asked, "Do you want to spend the rest of your life selling sugared water or do you want a chance to change the world?"[5] This was a secular man responding to a secular opportunity, but . . . a challenging one! During the past two years I have seen three men take leadership positions with three separate Christian ministries for salaries that were at best 25 percent of their corporate salary. They willingly traded salary for challenge and the opportunity to make their lives count for God. I've stayed in close touch with these men as well as the many others we helped challenge to staff the work of the Kingdom. They wouldn't change jobs for the world, not when they have the opportunity to change the world in their new jobs instead.

A successful challenge is an exercise of leadership at the highest plane. You are challenging people to leave their comfort zones and move to new territories, territories with little in the way of maps. In the next chapter I focus on the recruiting challenges that confront Christian ministries in today's world and identify possible strategies for effective recruiting. You will find that many, if not most, of the principles are adaptable to the corporate setting as well.

CHAPTER NINETEEN

Staffing the Kingdom: Recruiting for Ministries and Missions

FOR OVER FIFTEEN years of consulting with Christian ministries in the areas of strategy and structure, I have consistently seen that their greatest need continues to be people—enough people and the right kinds of people. But during this same period, I've also seen the recruiting effectiveness of many ministries decline.

Whenever I speak to groups of executives of nonprofit ministries I take the opportunity to elicit their current challenges. Invariably, it is money and manpower. And if you had to choose one, I ask, which would it be? Manpower, they respond. What's the problem? I ask. Without fail they suggest it's the modern culture in which we live—secularization seeping into the Church and eroding the sense of sacrifice and commitment of the people they seek to recruit. Certainly, this is a valid issue, but I think the problem is bigger than that. I believe that many of the ministries have drifted into a kind of malaise as they have seen old ways become ineffective, and have been perplexed with how to recruit in a changing world. The world is changing rapidly, and ministry strategies of every type must change accordingly.

To answer the question, What must we do differently? we first need to look at some of our current practices. Having studied the current recruiting methods of various ministries, I have categorized my observations into six broad areas.

Waiting Like Spiders in a Web

My first concern is that the recruiting efforts of many ministries are, for the most part, passive and as a result reactive. "Oh, no," the chorus responds, "we have all kinds of recruiting strategies—brochures, direct-mailing kits to graduating seniors, and speakers for church mission conferences. We even place ads in periodicals."

However, as I look at the initiative taken by Christ to seek out His disciples and challenge them to ministry, I find many of our modern recruiting strategies listless by comparison. Like spiders in their webs, we sit ready to respond should someone stumble in and inquire, but we sorely lack aggressiveness.

Harvesting Without Cultivating

As we should, we pick only the ripe fruit, but we seldom participate actively in the cultivation process. This lack of active cultivation may be another dimension of the passivity that often characterizes our recruiting methods. Because many ministries seldom become involved in the building and discipling process, we are constrained to wait on the fringes and take what's available or left over. On the other hand, those churches and ministries that cultivate and disciple often have first call on the commitments of their followers.

For example, church and parachurch campus ministries have a direct advantage because one of their primary ministries is often the discipleship of young college students and early career adults. These organizations actively minister to the potential recruits and have the resources (time, opportunity, and manpower) to cultivate the relationships. The competition for talented, committed people is stiff, and ministries need to use the cultivation process to the fullest.

Harboring a "Poor-man's" Attitude

I've often seen a "poor-man's" attitude in Christian organizations' recruitment and selection processes. Many groups become convinced that no really qualified person would want to join their ministry, or that Christian young people today are too caught up in the world to consider a life of service with its inherent sacrifices. Such an attitude not only makes these organizations tentative in their efforts to recruit the very best, but it also makes them more willing to abandon all of their selection criteria except that of "availability." The consequences of this approach are often worse than if the position had remained vacant until a qualified candidate was found.

Setting Unrealistic Requirements

A fourth tendency, which is really the opposite of the poor-man's attitude, is to establish unrealistic qualifications and commitment requirements. I have already observed in an earlier chapter that if the apostles had been required to meet the qualifications and commitment currently demanded by some Christian ministries, the Great Commission would never have been launched.

Perhaps some ministries have not analyzed the tasks properly and, as a result, have an unrealistic or inappropriate set of selection criteria. For example, many mission agencies require a Bible degree for individuals who are not going to be in a Bible-teaching role (that is, support staff, mechanics, printers, teachers, or nurses). Adopting this policy can significantly narrow the supply of available candidates.

Ministries may also require an unrealistic level of commitment, which can prematurely eliminate candidates who may, over time, decide to make the long-term commitment to those ministries. One of the most innovative ministries I've heard of is Youth with a Mission (YWAM). Floyd McClung, their chief operating officer, noted recently that they will send nearly one hundred thousand people out during the summer for two-week stints at their mission sites. He also observed that one of the biggest challenges of their ministry is to struggle with their own tendencies to make the threshold of participation too high.

Losing Touch with the Context and Culture in Which We Recruit

Another barrier to recruiting the young career person or recent college graduate is that many ministries have become disconnected from the value systems and the thinking process of today's youth. North America is undergoing profound cultural changes. The most pronounced theme is secularism, a worldview that casts doubt upon the relevancy of God and the spiritual dimension of life. Science, education, social enlightenment and policy, technology, economics, and other human agencies and efforts contend for our society's hope and loyalty. These cultural forces are so persuasive that they do more than just impact the environment in which we minister. Secularization affects even the Christian, most particularly the youth and young adults from whom we acquire most of our recruits. They are riddled with the effects of this pervasive influence.

As recruiters, we need to understand the context and culture that shape the people we hope to recruit. The "currency" of recruiting is communication, audience-sensitive communication that breaks through the cultural preconceptions and filters. James Davison Hunter notes, in his book *Evangelists: The Coming Generation,* that the driving motivations of young Christians are changing. They are not as rigid theologically; they are more concerned about self-actualization than self-sacrifice; they demand a more participative management style than did their parents; their wives have been influenced to one degree or another by feminism (which may prove a challenge to the more conservative mission agencies); and they are looking for "relevance"—they want to be a part of something significant.[1]

Many ministries, either unaware of the trends or choosing to ignore them, wonder at the same time why so few respond to their call. We may not like these developments, but they greatly influence our ability to recruit the next generation.

Sending Dusty Messages

Many feel that better, more up-to-date communication techniques will increase our recruiting effectiveness. And certainly the use of substandard or outdated media for mission education and recruiting conveys in a subtle but powerful way that the cause we are representing is itself substandard and not worth the effort.

Although I agree that more up-to-date communication methods would contribute to our effectiveness, they are secondary in our communication efforts. It's not the medium that needs dusting off, it's the message! We are not communicating God's plan and the work to which He has called us in an exciting and compelling manner.

HOW MUST WE CHANGE OUR RECRUITING METHODS?

Recognizing areas of weakness moves us only one step toward solving the problem, however. I need to put clear, positive suggestions on the table, rather than merely pointing out possible shortcomings and leaving the remedies to chance. Accordingly, I recommend five specific steps to effective recruiting.

We Must Develop a Clear Vision

In some respects, vision can be defined as a "picture of purpose." When vision is communicated clearly and lived convincingly, it can become the most powerful recruiting force at our disposal. Vision becomes the source of confidence and conviction to us and to those we lead and recruit.

Warren Bennis, in his classic book *Leaders*, explains that "a vision articulates a view of a realistic, credible, attractive future for the organization. . . . A vision is a target that beckons." He points out that "great leaders often inspire their followers to high levels of achievement by showing them how their work contributes to worthwhile ends. It is an emotional appeal to some of the most fundamental of human needs—the need to be important, to make a difference, to feel useful, to be a part of a worthwhile, successful enterprise."[2]

A modern corporate recruiting story reflects this ability to communicate a simple, compelling vision. Part of John Scully's attraction to the Apple Computer Corporation was the challenge put to him by Steven Jobs. John Scully had become Pepsi's youngest president at thirty-eight. He was the mastermind behind the "Pepsi Generation," the campaign that put Pepsi-Cola in front of Coke for the first time. He had turned down numerous opportunities to explore top positions with other Fortune 500 companies.

Steve Jobs, the young chairman of Apple, had been persistent in his pursuit of Scully, but to no avail. In their final meeting Jobs asked once more, "Are you going to come to Apple?"

Scully relates the story:

> "Steve," I said, "I'd love to be an adviser to you, to help you in any way. Any time you're in New York, I'd love to spend time with you. But I don't think I can come to Apple."
>
> Steve's head dropped as he stared at the pavement. After a weighty, uncomfortable pause, he issued a challenge that would haunt me for days: "Do you want to spend the rest of your life selling sugared water or do you want a chance to change the world?"
>
> It was as if someone reached up and delivered a stiff blow to my stomach. I had been worried about giving up my future at Pepsi, losing pensions and deferred compensation, violating the code of loyalty to Kendall, my ability to adjust in California—the pragmatic stuff that preoccupies the middle-aged. I was overly concerned with what would happen next week and the week after next. Steve was telling me my entire life was at a critical crossroads. The question was a monstrous one; one for which I had no answer. It simply knocked the wind out of me.[3]

Bill Bright, president and founder of Campus Crusade for Christ, has challenged almost eighteen thousand staff members to come "help change the world." It's a compelling call to people (of any age) who want to put their lives to the highest and best use.

A vision, clearly and compellingly communicated, acts like a magnet drawing people to fulfill the purposes to which God has called them. However, I sense that with too many of us in full-time Christian endeavors, the windshields of our vision need to be washed. Bennis and Names note that "the visions of many organizations are out of focus and lack coherence."[4]

Lack of vision for our ministry and who God is and what He can do through it saps our confidence, making us tentative and hesitant to express boldly the needs of our ministry and the demands we must make to meet them. Without such conviction we issue small demands. Such demands lack challenge and perceived relevance and are seldom grasped by those looking to make a significant difference.

A clear vision is the source of the level of conviction that allows us to issue significant challenges.

We Must Issue a Clear, Challenging Call

In 1900 an unusual ad was run in the London newspapers: "Men wanted for hazardous journey. Small wages, bitter cold, long months of complete darkness, constant danger, safe return doubtful. Honor and recognition in case of success."

The ad was placed by explorer Ernest Shackleton, who was seeking volunteers for his South Pole expedition. Who would be foolish enough to respond to an ad that assured those chosen of pain and danger? It turned out that many people were. Commenting on the results of the ad, Shackleton said, "It would seem as though all of Great Britain was to accompany me."

Shackleton is not the only one who has learned the drawing power of a strong challenge. One of the most intriguing insights into challenge and its role in the recruiting process is found in the book *Dedication and Leadership* by Douglas Hyde. Hyde was a top member of the Communist party in Great Britain for nearly twenty years until he was reached for Christ by the Catholic Church. He shares that the communists have become some of the most effective recruiters in the world by applying principles sorely needed but often ignored by the Christians. He observes: "The communists' appeal to idealism is direct and audacious. They say if you make mean little demands upon people, you will get a mean little response which is all you deserve. But if you make big demands on them then you will get a heroic response."[5]

Indeed, the communist philosopher Friedrich Engels closed his great manifesto with the words, "The philosophers have only tried to explain the world, but the job, however, is to change it." Hyde points out that for 120 years communists around the world have made "change the world" their party slogan. Hyde continues with a real indictment against some Christians' commitment. "To the Christian there is an element of sheer tragedy in this: That people with such potentialities should give so much energy, zeal, and dedication to such a cause, whilst those who believe they have the best cause on earth give so little to it. And their leaders are so often afraid to ask for more than the merest minimum. . . . They speak with a muted voice when they speak at all."[6]

Indeed, the Apostle Paul asks us, "If the trumpet does not sound a clear call, who will get ready for battle?" (1 Corinthians 14:8).

The communists' vision fueled their conviction and confidence and allowed them to issue strong, clear challenges. The recruits responded with enthusiasm. The perceived purpose and its relevance is such that people were willing to make any sacrifice to achieve it. The cost of service built into the challenge reinforces this perception, for anything that is costly in commitment and dedication must be valuable indeed.

The Lord made sure His disciples understood the cost of following Him (Matthew 8:18-22, Luke 14:26-33). But cost also determines value (John 6:66-68), and He matched the cost with the significance of His challenge: "Come, follow me . . . and I will make you fishers of men" (Matthew 4:19).

If we are to see the world changed for Christ, we must be able to issue such aggressive challenges. Individuals looking for significant opportunities to make their lives count will not pour out those lives for insignificant gains and small ends.

We Must Develop a Relational Recruiting Strategy

I recently spent some time with the president of a large financial planning firm. This unique organization emphasizes helping clients to integrate biblical principles into the management of their finances and to maximize the resources available for Kingdom work. He pointed out that fund raisers discovered long ago that, in general, people who make significant financial gifts to organizations have four qualities:

- A vision for what that organization is doing.
- A relationship with that organization.
- The means to give.
- A plan that governs their giving strategy.

Many organizations focus on only the means to give and are disappointed with the lack of response after making an eloquent appeal. I see many parallels between the giving of money and the giving of lives. Ministries, particularly nondenominational ones, are often put in the position of attempting to recruit those who have the means (i.e., they are prepared and desiring to serve) but have no relationship with those ministries and no vision for their work. Building such a relationship requires time, resources, and strategy, but the effort is essential if organizations are to do a better job of cultivating and protecting their supply lines.

Two major tenets should guide the typical ministry and mission agency in developing a more effective relational approach to its recruiting efforts.

Coming to grips with the time it takes to recruit an individual—This past year I've been working with a couple of U.S.–based ministries to develop training in lifestyle evangelism. Early in the research process I recognized that the key to effective evangelism in a secular society is a relationship. The messenger must be accepted before the message will be considered. It is often the same in the recruiting process. We must know and trust the messenger before we accept the message and join the ministry. When these conditions exist, we are recruiting within an existing relationship. I suspect that the Lord enlisted His disciples in this manner.

In Matthew 4:18-22 we find the disciples responding to Jesus' call to follow Him and become "fishers of men." Matthew writes, "They *immediately* left the nets, and followed Him" (Matthew 4:20, NASB; emphasis added).

But did it really happen that fast? The disciples' response certainly was instantaneous once the call was issued, but the relationship had been established some time before. Johnston Cheney, in his book *The Life of Christ in Stereo*, observes that in the Matthew passage Simon was already "called" Peter. When the Lord first met Simon, He observed, "You shall be called Cephas (which translated means Peter)" (John 1:42, NASB). In the intervening time these men had spent time with the Lord, they had followed Him around and had become familiar with His message before they responded to His call to leave everything and follow Him (Luke 5:11).[7]

Understanding the decision process—A decision to embark on a missions or ministry career is not a spontaneous event. It's the end product of a relatively lengthy and complex journey that reaches into the core of who we are and why we are here.

Several years ago, I was asked by the Inter-Varsity Missions Department to work with them in developing a better understanding of the path that takes a person from "ground zero" to a meaningful involvement in missions. After exploring a number of possibilities, we concluded that, in very simple terms, the journey could be broken down into four distinct phases:

1. *Becoming aware of God's plan*—This first phase involves learning more about God's purpose and plan for our world and coming to terms with the magnitude, complexity, and urgency of the task. Here we begin to develop an understanding of the role of missions in this plan.

2. *Recognizing our role*—In the second phase we begin to

personalize the concept. The focus in the first phase was God-awareness; here, it is self-awareness. This stage is where we begin to wrestle with the issue of individual purpose and start to explore our spiritual gifts, skills, and goals. We begin asking how we fit into God's plan, and those questions may lead us into missions involvement.

3. *Considering our options*—Now we begin to look at specific avenues of service, moving from general directions to specific possibilities. Here we sort out geographical, functional, and cultural preferences, attempting to match them to specific opportunities for service. The question becomes, "What organization, place, or type of service best matches me?"

4. *Making the decision*—Finally we arrive at the point of decision—moving from intention to actual implementation.

I acknowledge that this is a simplistic model of a highly complex process. However, the model allows us to discuss the process on a conceptual level and possibly develop strategies and structures that might assist those making the journey. A diagram follows that shows how the four phases fit together.

A better understanding of the decision process for ministry involvement can benefit your overall recruiting effectiveness in several ways. An understanding of the process will allow you to profile and screen applicants, better ensuring that they are making an informed, high-quality decision. Also, it will help you better respond to inquiries and pleas for help from those on the way.

In addition, you can become known as a resource in helping people work through these issues, offering training, tools, and encouragement as well as providing opportunities, direction, and strategies.

Creative possibilities for involvement in this process are endless. If a ministry can develop a reputation as a credible resource to those working through this process, it will have plenty of people with whom to talk about positions in these people's organization as well.

Ministries that are open to the longer-range, more complex, relational approach to recruiting can come alongside individuals working through this decision and act as guides and counselors. This kind of help represents discipleship at its highest level.

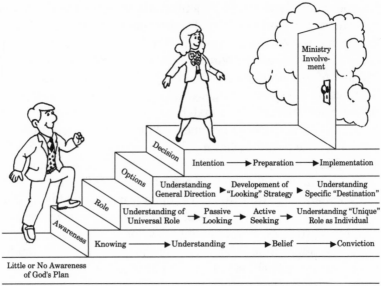

	Intention ———▶ Preparation ———▶ Implementation		
	Understanding General Direction	Developement of "Looking" Strategy	Understanding Specific "Destination"
	Understanding of Universal Role ➜	Passive Looking ➜	Active Seeking ➜ Understanding "Unique" Role as Individual
Knowing ———————▶ Understanding ————————▶ Belief ————————▶ Conviction			

Little or No Awareness
of God's Plan

We Must Provide for Long-Term, Professional Recruiting Staff

Providing a reliable supply of qualified candidates must be considered a key result area of any ministry. If that is the case, this area needs a champion, someone who will devote his or her entire time and energy to seeing this effort succeed. Recruiting demands special skills, gifts, and aptitudes to be successful, and, as we've seen, it also takes time. The highest form of recruiting is discipleship.

Many of the recruiting staff for missions aren't trained or even necessarily gifted for the job. And rotating the recruiting staff makes a relational, long-term approach to recruiting nearly impossible. About the time relationships begin to develop, the recruiter is rotated, slowing and perhaps even blocking the process.

Organizations would clearly benefit from retaining highly qualified, long-term recruiters who not only meet a list of tough selection criteria, but also see recruiting as a discipling process and a meaningful ministry. You may be surprised to learn that those who do best at this task also tend to be the star performers in the field. Excellent corporate recruiting strategies often stress the use of top-line officers. Procter & Gamble, IBM, and other successful companies frequently ask their top leadership to put in quality (and expensive!) time on campuses attempting to persuade candidates to come on board.

We Must Build Short-Time Staff into a Long-Term Strategy

Corporate America is, and will continue to be for the next ten years, in the throes of a major structural upheaval. The lack of built-in profits from a high inflation rate coupled with stiff foreign competition will force major cuts in the middle-management sector. Profits will be hard to come by, and even now companies are exploring every avenue for cost cutting.

One creative trend in management—using temporary help—takes advantage of the large number of displaced persons, and addresses the need to minimize fixed overhead. Not only is the "temp" effective in the secretarial and clerical ranks, but the hottest trend is the "temp" executive vice president or chief financial officer.

Similarly, the fastest growing sector in foreign mission service is that of short-termers. A few years ago foreign mission service meant a two-year stint. Today it would probably include stays of two to eight weeks. My own church, which has about 750 members, sends over 100 people on such assignments every year.

As I've worked with agencies and churches that use shorter-term assignments, I've found many to be concerned about the tensions that may occur between the "visitor" and the "resident." Much of this tension can be attributed to the lack of, or ineffective training for, the summer intern. However, some amount of the blame may be placed on the fact that this "visitor" is a fish out of water in the overall scheme of things.

What would happen if the local strategy were specifically designed to take full advantage of a periodic influx of short-termers and less-than-fully-trained people? Might it not make the short-termers more effective and, as a consequence, more positive and open about long-term service? Would it be possible to see faster progress of the local strategy because this extra resource was built into the plan? Perhaps we could learn something from our corporate cousins in this area and make a significant contribution to our recruiting and overall ministry goal as well.

A FINAL WORD

Recruiting top young people for the ministry must include setting clear goals, pursuing a well-formulated strategy, and introducing innovative concepts. No longer can we employ our old methods to staffing viable programs. Our vision must be clear; our call must be creative and challenging. Our approach must be relational, flexible, and strategically sound. We must commit our best efforts to attracting the best candidates for the all-important work of spreading the gospel in the twenty-first century.

CHAPTER TWENTY

The Most Important People Decision

The focus of this book has been how you and I can make good people decisions. In this chapter I would like to explore how God chooses people, particularly in what I consider to be the most important people decision.

Throughout the book I've stressed that one of the best indicators of what a person will do is what they have done. Basically, I've advocated a performance-based selection process. Our strategy has been to develop a list of selection criteria that describe the ideal candidate. Ideal in the sense that few individuals are able to meet all of the criteria on this demanding list. As we have seen, in the end we compromise, settling for an "almost fit"—the best candidate among our alternatives. The difference between a qualified candidate and these ideal criteria can be creatively addressed in a number of ways—training, structure, and staffing.

When it comes to determining admittance to Heaven, God doesn't use that kind of selection criteria. He loves us and desires that every person have eternal life with Him in Heaven. His criteria are very strict and He is impartial in His evaluation (Romans 2:11, 1 Timothy 2:4, 2 Peter 3:9). He also knows that not everyone will respond to His initiative of reconciliation (Matthew

7:13-14,21; 13:18-23). For all practical purposes, His selection criteria are summarized in His law. God's law, in simple terms, is His standard, the plumb line against which He will measure the life and deeds of every person when they stand before His throne (Romans 2:6, Revelation 20:11-15).

The Bible explains that everyone's deeds, their life résumé and references, are entered into books kept in Heaven (Revelation 20:12-13). When we stand before God—and we all will—He will open these books and judge us according our deeds. The standard of performance is His law and He demands perfect obedience. God will not accept "almost fits" into Heaven, not even a 99.99 percent fit.

The Bible teaches that our sin keeps us from meeting God's standards. The word *sin* comes from a Greek root meaning "missing the mark." I have heard that when an ancient Greek archer was practicing his craft, a slave stood next to the target and shouted the result after each attempt. When the archer missed, the slave would shout "sin," alerting the archer that his results were less than acceptable. (It occurred to me when I heard this illustration, that if the slave didn't yell, it meant one of two things.)

Sin is not clearly understood in our modern, secularized culture. A secular perspective disregards or rejects any aspect of God in deliberations and decisions of daily life. God, His Word, religious faith, and worship are seen as irrelevant.

Such a perspective frees men from the clear absolutes of God's Word. Things become more "relative," and instead of measuring ourselves against God's standards, we compare ourselves to each other. Our society sees truth as a personal and relative concept. Any guilt that does seep through the rationalization ("rational-lies") is assuaged by a society whose highest value is tolerance, encouraging its members to "do their own thing."

In the early 1960s a scientific philosopher, Thomas Kuhn, dusted off an old term, using it to explain why scientists had trouble seeing and accepting data that ran counter to their expectations. The term was *paradigm*. Kuhn defined a paradigm as an accepted model or pattern. Other definitions are frame of reference, worldview, conceptual framework, or assumptions.

Our paradigms act as filters, deflecting information that doesn't agree with our assumptions and letting supporting data through. Paradigms aren't wrong unless they don't accurately reflect reality. A wrong paradigm is like a mental map that doesn't correctly reflect the terrain. Modern culture has convinced many to adopt a new paradigm, a secular one that doesn't acknowledge God's standards. The problem is that even though many of us have changed paradigms (i.e., assumptions or worldviews), God and His standards don't change. Even though the world looks different through the lens of society's perspective, it isn't an accurate picture. We're looking at life through the wrong paradigm!

God's Word in Scripture, reflecting His selection criteria, makes it clear that all of us have "missed the mark" (Romans 3:23). No one has ever "performed" their way into Heaven. When it comes to this particular people decision, the best indicator that we will not get into Heaven is our past performance!

It appears that we have a significant theological dilemma. On one hand God is not willing that any should perish; on the other, no one can meet His criteria. Although God loves each one of us to an extent that we cannot imagine, He is also holy and just and demands payment for our sin. This payment is spiritual death, eternal separation from God. The Bible clearly teaches that all of us will exist for eternity. The issue is where: Heaven, or hell?

God the Father provided a substitute payment for this penalty, however. This substitute must be a person who is perfect, without blemish (i.e., without sin). This substitute must meet all of God's selection criteria . . . perfectly! God's solution to this seemingly irresolvable dilemma is His Son, Jesus, whose name means "God saves."[1]

Only the Holy God can meet His standards, but He says, "Without the shedding of blood there can be no forgiveness of sin" (Hebrews 9:22). God sent His Son, Jesus Christ, to earth in the form of a man (2 Corinthians 4:4, Philippians 2:6-8, Colossians 1:15-20). Being God Himself, Jesus met the criteria; being man,

He was an acceptable substitute for the penalty of our sin (Galatians 3:13).

The Bible makes it very clear that Jesus is not *a way* we can be reconciled to God but *the only way* (John 14:6, Acts 4:12). It's critically important to understand that Christianity is not a philosophy or even a way of life but rather a relationship with a living person, Jesus Christ.[2] He is, at the same time, fully God and fully man (John 5:18, 10:10-30; Philippians 2:6-7).

The place of payment was the cross. Although death on the cross was terrible and agonizing, this is not the main point of His sacrifice. Remember, Jesus came to earth from Heaven. He had spent all of time to that point in the presence of God the Father. He had no doubt in His mind that there was life after physical death. He knew that dying, as fearful as it was to men, was like stepping through a veil or curtain into a different place.

Jesus went willingly to the cross on our behalf, but He didn't go willfully. We see this in His prayer the night before His death: "My Father, if it is possible, may this cup be taken from me. Yet not as I will, but as you will" (Matthew 26:39). Why, since He knew that His death on the cross would be a painful but brief transition back to Heaven, was He hesitant? It was because there was a more critical dimension to His experience on the cross. There Jesus shouldered the burden of the sin of the world—each and every sin of every person, past, present, and future, who would accept His sacrifice as the gift of grace that it is. He paid the price for every instance that I did not meet the standards outlined in His Word—the Ten Commandments, the Sermon on the Mount, and all of the other commands expressed throughout the Bible.

Never having had to pay those penalties, it's often difficult for us, as humans, to comprehend the weight and worth of this act. Let me take a moment to frame the context of Jesus' love gift to us. In doing so I draw heavily on the work of Dr. R. C. Sproul, a theologian who has made clear the practical elements of theology. In his book *Following Jesus*, Dr. Sproul explains that blessing, from a biblical perspective, is to behold the face of God.[3] The closer one is to God, the greater the blessing. In the Garden of Eden,

Adam was truly blessed for he had direct, face-to-face contact with God, but after he sinned—what we refer to as the Fall—things changed. No one is allowed to look into the face of God (Exodus 33:20). The traumatic result of Adam's sin in the garden was to be removed from intimate fellowship with God, his Creator.

Curse, on the other hand, is the exact opposite of blessing. Dr. Sproul says that in the Old Testament, curse refers to the negative judgment of God and that the curse of God involved being removed from His presence altogether. "To be cursed was to enter into the place of absolute darkness outside the presence of God," Sproul concludes.

God gave the Old Testament nation of Israel a ceremony to illustrate this concept. Each year the Israelites celebrated the Day of Atonement as a reminder that the day-to-day burnt offerings were not sufficient to make amends (i.e., to atone) for sin (Leviticus 16).

To prepare for this ceremony, the high priest sacrificed a young bull for his own sins and those of his family. He then took two goats for sacrifice. One was slaughtered for the sins of the people.

The second goat was called "scapegoat." The high priest would "lay both hands on the head of the live goat and confess over it all the wickedness and rebellion of the Israelites—all their sins—and put them on the goat's head. He shall send the goat away into the desert" (Leviticus 16:21). The goat was driven to a barren, solitary place outside the camp, away from the presence of God who dwelt in the Tabernacle among His people. The goat was cursed.

On the cross, at that moment when Jesus took on the sin of the world, He became the scapegoat for us. He was cursed, cut off from the presence of the living God with whom He had spent eternity. Fulfilling the picture of the Old Testament sacrament of the Day of Atonement, the cross was "outside the camp" on a hill beyond the city limits of Jerusalem.

As painful as the nails through Jesus' limbs must have been, there was a greater, unimaginable pain. Dr. Sproul points out that "only one man has ever felt the pain of the fullness of the unmitigated curse of God upon him. When he felt it, he cried out, 'My God, my God, why have you forsaken me?' (Mark 15:34). That is the whole point of atonement. Without forsakenness, there is no curse. God, at that moment in space and time, turned his back on his Son."[4]

We've seen that none of us meets God's selection criteria, and the consequences are terrible. But God's Son paid the penalty for our transgressions. According to the Bible, the blood Christ shed on the cross covers our sin, and when God looks at us He sees the perfection of His Son (Ephesians 1:7, 1 Peter 1:19, 1 John 1:7, Revelation 1:5). But we're not home free yet, for God's initiative demands a response from us. We must make a decision.

It is important to understand the spiritual dynamic under-girding this most important decision. The primary decision is God's as He determines whom He will call to Himself (Romans 1:6-7, 8:28-30; 1 Corinthians 1:24; Hebrews 9:15). The initiative lies with Him. In chapter 9 we noted that call comes in several levels. First and foremost is the call to faith and repentance. The Puritans described this as "general" or effectual call. This is what we are now discussing.

However, even though God calls, we are not in a position to respond. In a number of passages throughout the New Testament God paints a graphic picture of the state of the nonChristian. They are described as being in the dark, blind, in prison, unable to hear and comprehend God's call, and even dead (Romans 7:23, 11:8; 2 Corinthians 3:14, 4:4; Galatians 3:22; Ephesians 2:1-4; Colossians 1:13).

In such a state the nonChristian cannot hear, understand, or respond to God's call. God's Spirit must penetrate these barriers with the light of His message of reconciliation (2 Corinthians 5:19, 1 Peter 2:9). In my mind's eye, I picture the typical nonChristian as being held captive in a small, dark underground cell with thick bars. That person is blindfolded and his or her ears are muffled to prevent hearing. The person is drugged so that his mind cannot make sense of nor comprehend God's message.

Humanly speaking it's an impossible situation. But God has

a threefold strategy; it's a team effort. His Holy Spirit opens the doors of the heart and the mind of the nonChristian so that they are able to hear and comprehend the message. This same Spirit pricks the heart of the unbeliever with conviction of guilt in regard to sin and righteousness and judgment (John 16:8). God's Word brings the message of reconciliation, often through the other member of the team, the evangelist. In many respects evangelism can be construed as a spiritual jailbreak. God rescues Christians from this dominion of darkness and spirits us away into the Kingdom of His Son (Colossians 1:13).

The initiative and the power are God's. Salvation is a gift of grace. Our only recourse is to respond, accepting His gift, acknowledging our need, repenting of our sin, and accepting Jesus Christ as Lord and Savior.

As I said previously, the Bible clearly states that Jesus is *the only way* to God: Jesus said, "I am the way and the truth and the life. No one comes to the Father except through me" (John 14:6). A certain philosophy, a good life, even religious zeal will not bridge the gap sin created between God and man. Only Jesus Christ can do that.

God also says that we must individually receive Jesus as Savior and as Lord: "Yet to all who received him, to those who believed in his name, he gave the right to become the children of God" (John 1:12). Notice the verse doesn't say *earn* or *perform* but rather *receive*. Eternal life is a gift from God. As with any gift, you can accept and receive it, but you cannot earn it or work for it. God's Word explains, "For it is by grace you have been saved, through faith—and this not from yourselves, it is the gift of God—not by works, so that no one can boast" (Ephesians 2:8). By *grace* the Bible means "unmerited favor"—even though we don't deserve it, God offers it.

To receive Jesus we must do two things: First, we must agree with God that we have failed His standards, that is, we have sinned. That's what the word *confession* means: to acknowledge or to agree with God. When we confess to God that we are sinners, we're not telling Him anything He doesn't already know. We're merely telling Him that we know it too. Second, we must turn from our ways to God's ways.

Basically, the person who is not a Christian is in rebellion to God. To change this condition, we must surrender, come out with our hands up, asking for mercy. Before we can experience the peace of God we must make peace with Him. This is what the word *repentance* means, "to turn from."

To make a good decision in any significant matter we must involve and balance all three dimensions of our personality: our *will, intellect,* and *emotions.* A major decision made through only one of these elements at the expense of the others will seldom last long. Establishing a relationship with anyone is an emotional experience. But it involves more than the emotions.

When we accept Him, we are agreeing intellectually that Jesus is the Son of God and that He died on the cross for our sin. We accept Christ as our Lord and Savior by an act of the will. Receiving Christ is an act of faith. By faith we are taking God at His word. Faith means we are "fully persuaded that God had the power to do what he had promised" (Romans 4:21).

This entire transaction takes place in the heart but can be expressed in prayer, a quiet declaration in your mind from you to God. When I accepted Jesus my prayer was something like this: "Lord Jesus, I acknowledge that I have missed the mark in every area of my life. I need You. Thank You for dying on the cross on my behalf. Thank You for forgiving my sins and giving me eternal life. Please come into my life as Lord and help me to become the kind of person You want me to be. Thank You."

As I concluded my prayer, in the solitude of my study on a rainy March day some twenty years ago in Seattle, I didn't hear trumpets blowing (although Jesus says there "will be more rejoicing in heaven over the one sinner who repents than over the ninety-nine righteous persons who do not need to repent," Luke 15:7). I still had the mild headache that had been with me all that day. And, as it does in Seattle, the rain continued. But over the next days, months, and years I saw change in me.

Jim Petersen, author of *Living Proof,* asks, "Can it be possible for the Creator of all that exists, the one who possesses all power and wisdom, to slip into a life and remain there unnoticed?"[5] The answer is clearly no. Having made peace with God, I began to experience God's peace. Over time, He began to put the various areas of my life in order. Looking back on the past twenty years, I can say truthfully that God saved my life. He traded what would have been a life of mediocrity and futility for one of meaning and fulfillment—not a life without problems, but a life of peace and purpose.

I was selected not because of my performance but because of Jesus' performance. Responding to God's initiative on my behalf—acknowledging my sins, turning from my ways to God's, and accepting Jesus' sinless sacrifice as a gift from God—was the most important people decision I ever made.

A CLOSING THOUGHT

I hope that every person reading this book who has not already responded to God's call to salvation might make this most important decision and respond. As you make people decisions regarding others, do so in the manner you would desire others to make such decisions about you.

Throughout this book I've stressed a criteria-driven process—an objective, logical process of making people decisions in the area of selection and placement. The importance and complexity of such decisions demands some type of process. My prayer is that you use this process with the attitude reflected in Philippians 2:3-4: "Do nothing out of selfish ambition or vain conceit, but in humility consider others better than yourselves. Each of you should look not only to your own interests but also to the interests of others." Use this process with the wisdom characterized in Jesus in Philippians 3:17: "Join with others in following my example, brothers, and take note of those who live according to the pattern we gave you." Use this process with compassion—focusing on the potential and promise of people.

Personality Inventories

Knowing how people will react and relate to tasks, other people, and circumstances is of immeasurable value as we attempt to work with, serve, and communicate with others.

Behavior is influenced by a number of complex factors in our basic personality or temperament, our current emotional and physical state, our skills, experiences, IQ, and motivational needs. These and many other factors play both direct and indirect roles in shaping our responses.

Many of us have discovered that the more we know about ourselves and others, the better we can anticipate behavior in certain situations and, therefore, better serve and relate. Both of the personality inventories presented below (DISC and MBTI) allow people to gain good insight into their personalities as well as those of others. Both instruments are educational in purpose and not, in themselves, suitable for making placement decisions. However, when coupled with other test instruments, they add a valuable dimension to assessing potential job fit.

DISC

The DISC system was originally developed by Dr. William M. Martson, a Columbia University psychologist in the 1920s and

1930s. He focused his research on the emotions and behavior of normal people and developed a theoretical model that provided the foundation for future test instruments.

Today, I estimate there are twenty-five to thirty-five different versions of DISC instruments. Major vendors would include the "Predictive Index" by Arnold & Associates, "The Personal Profile System" by Performax Systems International, and "The Personal Concept" by Jack Mohler & Associates. The newest version of such instruments is the "Personal DISCernment Inventory"™ (PDI) published by my firm, Team Resources, Inc. Building on the base of its predecessors, we invested over two years in developing this very unique instrument.

A number of features make the PDI unique:

- The PDI is self-contained, providing all necessary explanatory and interpretive information in the instrument itself.
- The PDI confronts the issue of strengths and weaknesses in a clear, positive, straightforward manner.
- The PDI shows the implications and dynamics of behavioral styles in different settings.
- The PDI incorporates a series of application modules to assist individuals in applying insights regarding their personality to situations and subjects such as team, time, task, and sales.

All DISC instruments provide insight on four key elements that influence behavioral styles:

Dominance: The drive to overcome and achieve. The basic intent is to conquer.

Influence: The drive to influence, to express and be heard. The basic intent is to persuade.

Steadiness: The drive to be steady and systematic. The basic intent is to support.

Competent: The drive to be right, sure, and safe. The basic intent is to avoid trouble.

Although all of us have threads of all four elements woven into our basic temperament to one degree or another, most of us find that one or two of these elements express themselves more strongly in our behavioral style.

An excellent book on personalities based on the DISC concepts is *People Smart* by Tony Alessandra, Ph.D., and Michael J. O'Connor, Ph.D., with Janice Alessandra (La Jolla, CA: Keynote Publishing Company, 1990).

For more information on the DISC concept in general and the "Personal DISCernment Inventory"™ contact:

Team Resources, Inc.
5500 Interstate North Parkway, Suite 425
Atlanta, GA 30328
(404) 956-0985

MBTI

The purpose of the Myers-Briggs Type Indicator (MBTI) is to make the theory of psychological types, as first described by Carl G. Jung (1921–1971), understandable and useful in people's lives. The manual used for the MBTI, *A Guide to the Development and Use of the Myers-Briggs Type Indicator* by Isabel Briggs Myers and Mary H. McCaulley, notes,

The essence of the theory is that much seemingly random variation in behavior is actually quite orderly and consistent, being due to the basic differences in the way individuals prefer to use their perception and judgment.

Perception involves all of the ways of becoming aware of things, people, happenings, or ideas. Judgment involves all the ways of coming to conclusions about what has been perceived. If people differ systematically in what they perceive and in how they reach conclusions, then it is only reasonable for them to differ correspondingly in their reactions, interest, values, motivations, skills and interest.

The MBTI is based on Jung's idea about perception and judgment, and the attitudes in which these are used in different types of people. The aim of the MBTI is to identify, from self report of easily recognized reactions, the basic preferences of people in regard to perception and judgment.[1]

Use of the MBTI requires a trained, certified facilitator. It is proven to be a popular, very creditable instrument in teaching people about themselves and others.

Several excellent books describe the people types identified in the MBTI and explore the implications on how we relate to the people in the world around us.

- Briggs Myers, Isabel. *Gifts Differing*. Palo Alto, CA: Consulting Psychologist Press, 1980.
- Kroeger, Otto, and Thuesen, Janet M. *Type Talk*. New York: Delacorte Press, 1988.
- Lawrence, Gordon. *People Types and Tiger Stripes, A Practical Guide to Learning Styles*, second edition. Gainesville, FL: Center for Applications of Psychological Type, 1979.

For more information about the MBTI contact:

Center For Applications of Psychological Type
2720 Northwest 6th Street
Gainesville, FL 32609
(800) 777-CAPT

POSITION PROFILE

The purpose of this profile is to assist you in accurately defining a specific position and in identifying the qualities that describe an individual who has the greatest potential to succeed in that position. Not every item in this profile is relevant to every company or position, but rather this is a general guideline or checklist of key questions. You will realize from the terminology that this profile was designed specifically for use with for-profit corporations. Using this form as a guide, those in the non-profit sector can adapt it for their specific needs.

Client firm _____   Today's date _____

Firm address _____   Date needed _____

City _____ State_____ Zip_____   Phone (_____)_____

Position title _____

Hiring manager _____   Title _____

Notes:

Note: Most organizations have existing collateral material, prepared in advance, that replaces sections of this profile. When available, attach such information after you are sure that it is complete and current. Typical items include:
- ☐ Job description and standards of performance
- ☐ Organization chart
- ☐ Summary of fact sheet describing the company
- ☐ Policy sheets covering life and health insurance, vacations, etc.

I. DESCRIPTION OF COMPANY/ORGANIZATION

A. Type of company or organization—Product lines/services (attach promotional and product literature if available). If sales, production, or profit contribution breakdowns by product are relevant, include such information in this section. _____
_____
_____

B. Brief description of competitive position (for example, comparisons of the number of employees, sales, profit, market share, etc.). _____
_____
_____

C. What are the *competitive advantages* or distinctives of this company (for example, price, service, quality, etc.)? Why would a person want to work here in contrast to another company in this industry? _____
_____
_____

267

D. Who are the major competitors? What are their distinctives? From which ones (if any) can we recruit? _____

_____

_____

E. Is there a short history, fact sheet, or brief overview of this company (for example, brochure, article, press release, etc.)? If so, attach to this profile. _____

_____

_____

F. How would informed outsiders describe your company, using the word pairings below?

	Very	Some-what	Neutral	Some-what	Very	
Innovative	☐	☐	☐	☐	☐	Conservative
Growing	☐	☐	☐	☐	☐	Stable
Playing it safe	☐	☐	☐	☐	☐	Risk-taking
Relatively unknown	☐	☐	☐	☐	☐	Well known
Formal	☐	☐	☐	☐	☐	Informal
Young	☐	☐	☐	☐	☐	Mature
Experienced	☐	☐	☐	☐	☐	Inexperienced
Organized	☐	☐	☐	☐	☐	Unorganized
Sets the pace	☐	☐	☐	☐	☐	Follows the pack
Profitable	☐	☐	☐	☐	☐	Unprofitable

G. What other words not included in question F could be used to describe this organization?

_____

_____

H. Corporate priorities or value system
   Rank the top three values in order of priority (1=high).

   _____ Profit   _____ People
   _____ Integrity   _____ Service
   _____ Competency   _____ Corporate growth
   _____ Product quality   _____ Innovation

I. Work climate—Just like people, organizations themselves have distinct personalities that differentiate them from similar firms in the same industry. This "corporate personality" is a subjective, intangible blend of the individuals, strategies, values, purpose, and leadership style of the organization. How would you describe the climate in your company, using the word pairings below?

	Very	Some-what	Neutral	Some-what	Very	
Changing	☐	☐	☐	☐	☐	Unchanging
Relaxed	☐	☐	☐	☐	☐	Tense
Laid back	☐	☐	☐	☐	☐	Fast paced
People oriented	☐	☐	☐	☐	☐	Task oriented
Friendly	☐	☐	☐	☐	☐	Unfriendly

	Very	**Some-what**	**Neutral**	**Some-what**	**Very**	
High morale	☐	☐	☐	☐	☐	Low morale
Team players	☐	☐	☐	☐	☐	Individualists
Confident	☐	☐	☐	☐	☐	Tentative
Formal	☐	☐	☐	☐	☐	Informal
Warm	☐	☐	☐	☐	☐	Cool
Rigid	☐	☐	☐	☐	☐	Flexible
Sensitive	☐	☐	☐	☐	☐	Insensitive
Faces problems	☐	☐	☐	☐	☐	Avoids problems

II. BASIC TASK

Note: If job description is available, merely attach it to this profile. If no description is available, write details in space provided below.

A. Briefly describe the overall responsibilities of this position.

_____
_____
_____

B. Working relationships (attach organization chart if available).

1. Reports to _____ Title _____
2. People reporting to this position: (If space is not sufficient, use separate sheet.)
   Name _____ Title _____ Time in position _____
   Name _____ Title _____ Time in position _____
   Name _____ Title _____ Time in position _____
3. Works closely with: (peers)
   Name _____ Title _____ Time in position _____
   Name _____ Title _____ Time in position _____
   Name _____ Title _____ Time in position _____
4. Are there any existing problems in subordinate or peer relationships (for example, peer politics, subordinate aspirations for position, etc.)? _____
   _____
   _____
   _____

C. Specific responsibilities and standards of performance (What are the major goals to be achieved in this position over the next twelve months? How is performance for each major responsibility measured; how will this person be evaluated?)

1. _____
   _____
2. _____
   _____

3. _____

_____

4. _____

_____

5. _____

_____

6. _____

_____

D. Concerns/issues (What are the immediate risks, threats, problems, opportunities, needs, etc., both internal and external?) _____

_____

_____

E. Is this a new position? ☐ Yes   ☐ No
If this is an established position, what was the disposition of the previous incumbent (transferred, promoted, fired)? _____

_____

_____

In what specific ways did that individual succeed or fail? _____

_____

_____

If a new position, what factors or events influenced the decision to create this position? _____

_____

_____

Are any employees in this department or elsewhere in the company potential candidates for this position? _____

_____

_____

If other employees aspire to the position, what are the sensitive interpersonal considerations for new leadership? _____

_____

_____

F. Promotion path (Describe the "potential" promotional steps from this position.) _____

_____

G. General comments/observations _____

_____

_____

III. CANDIDATE SELECTION CRITERIA

This section is designed to help you identify specific selection criteria that will help you recognize candidates who have the greatest potential for success in this position. You will be looking for specific qualities in four major categories:

- **Competencies**—Specific skills required for the position (written communication skills, ability to motivate people, etc.)
- **Chemistry/Climate** (fit with the company)—This area deals with qualities that allow a person to "fit" into the philosophies, strategies, and climate of a given firm. For example, some individuals are more productive in a more "structured" environment while others prefer an unstructured climate. Some may prefer a "soft-sell," consultive marketing strategy, others a more direct, "hard-sell" approach.
- **Compatibility** (fit with the job)—Here it is a match between the personality and the specific task. These issues are similar to those above (chemistry) but are *task* related versus *company* related. For example, in a specific task someone may have to stay in one place, such as a desk or booth. Therefore, personality with a high degree of "sitability" is required. Some jobs, like sales, provide clear, fast feedback on results, while others, such as teaching, do not.
- **Character**—These qualities involve personal values and priorities. If an individual's personal values or priorities conflict with those of the company, it is unlikely that the association will endure. For example, an individual who has a strong commitment to his or her family and works in a company that demands long hours and extensive travel will have difficulty being effective long-term.

The previous sections of this profile have described the company, the present climate, and the task. Your objective here is to review these sections and develop a specific list of qualities or selection criteria that describe a qualified candidate.

A. General Criteria
1. Education/certification/licenses required if any _____

_____

2. Specific experiences required, if any, and time in experience (for example, three to five years of direct management experience) _____

_____

B. Competencies/Skills—Areas of consideration should include:
- People skills required (management, motivation, training, etc.)—For example, will this person have the authority to:
  ☐ hire?   ☐ promote?   ☐ fire?
- Process skills required (planning, decision-making, problem-solving, etc.)
- Technical knowledge required (specific product knowledge, law, accounting, processes, industries, etc.)

_____
_____
_____

C. Chemistry (fit with company)—What specific qualities must this person possess to effectively "fit" with this company? _____
_____
_____

D. **Compatibility** (fit with the job)—What specific qualities or characteristics are demanded by this task (for example, decisiveness, flexibility, etc.)? _____

_____

_____

_____

E. **Character**—We believe that basic character, from the perspective of integrity, is nonnegotiable. Here we are using "character" to mean the area of values, priorities, etc. These do vary in type and degree from individual to individual. For this position, what are special issues in the area of character? _____

_____

_____

_____

IV. CANDIDATE EVALUATION

A. Who will interview potential candidates?

Name _____ Title _____ Phone _____

Name _____ Title _____ Phone _____

Name _____ Title _____ Phone _____

B. Who is responsible for technical evaluation (if needed)? _____

C. Will final candidates be interviewed by an in-house or a consulting psychologist? _____

D. Will psychological, personality, or aptitude tests be used in evaluation? _____

E. Is a physical required? ☐ Yes   ☐ No

V. COMPENSATION & BENEFITS

A. Salary range _____

B. Bonus _____ Basis for computation _____

C. Stock option or purchase plan _____

_____

Limits and qualifications _____

D. Indirect compensation (car, car allowance, clubs, etc.) _____

_____

E. Medical and life insurance, other insurance, if available (for example, dental, salary protection, etc.). Note basic points of coverage, including amount paid by firm. (For example, what are the deductible amounts? Is the employee's family covered by the firm or by deductions from the employee's salary?) Is a brochure available? _____

F. Vacation and sick leave policy _____

_____

G. Educational assistance and training (tuition assistance, time off, company-paid seminars, etc.)

_____

H. Relocation expenses (Is there housing or interest assistance, for example, loan subsidy, etc.?)

_____

I. Retirement/pension plan (Explain type, benefits, vesting provisions, eligibility requirements, etc.) _____

_____

J. Profit sharing plan (type of benefits, eligibility requirements, computation, etc.) _____

_____

K. General comments about benefits and compensation _____

_____

_____

_____

ADDITIONAL NOTES/OBSERVATIONS

_____

_____

_____

_____

_____

_____

_____

_____

INTERVIEW EVALUATION GUIDE

Candidate_____   Interviewer _____
Client _____   Date _____
Position _____

• Remember there are two sides to the desk. Candidates are going to put their best foot forward; you must do the same as you represent the company and your open position.

• Spend the first few minutes establishing rapport, but be sensitive to EEOC considerations (non-job-related subjects that could be construed by the candidate as disqualifiers).

• Explain that you will be taking notes in order to retain important facts.

• Remember! *The best predictor of what a person will do is what he or she has done.*

I. SUMMARY OF OBSERVATIONS

	Unsuitable		Acceptable		Excellent
Personality	1	2	3	4	5
Appearance	1	2	3	4	5
Eye contact	1	2	3	4	5
Energy/enthusiasm	1	2	3	4	5
Poise/confidence	1	2	3	4	5
Verbal communication	1	2	3	4	5

II. RÉSUMÉ

Job history, education, and experience (attach résumé with notes)
Walk through résumé from past to present, recording salary history and reason for leaving each position. Look for specific activities, responsibilities, and skills that relate to your selection criteria. Beware of words like *coordinated, implemented, organized,* etc. Counter with, "Specifically, what did you . . . ?" Make notes on the résumé itself.

A. **Education**
Degree _____ School _____ Date_____
Degree _____ School _____ Date_____
Degree _____ School _____ Date_____

B. **Work Experience**
Company _____ Dates_____
Position _____ Salary _____
Responsibilities_____

Reason for leaving _____

274

Company _____   Dates_____
Position _____   Salary _____
Responsibilities_____
_____

Reason for leaving _____

Company _____   Dates_____
Position _____   Salary _____
Responsibilities_____
_____

Reason for leaving _____

C. **Interests, Accomplishments**_____
_____
_____
_____
_____

III. EVALUATION

From the selection criteria (skills, experience, etc.), list those you hope to identify during this interview. Accompany each one with questions designed to reveal evidence of that specific characteristic or qualification. Use résumé as point of reference.

Criteria/Questions   **Candidate Response**

A. Criterion_____
_____
Questions _____
_____
_____
_____
_____

Summary conclusions for this area:

☐ unacceptable   ☐ marginal   ☐ acceptable   ☐ exceptional
Comments_____

B. Criterion_____
_____
Questions _____
_____
_____
_____
_____

Summary conclusions for this area:

☐ unacceptable   ☐ marginal   ☐ acceptable   ☐ exceptional
Comments_____

Criteria/Questions	**Candidate Response**
C. Criterion _____	
Questions _____	
_____	
_____	
_____	
_____	

Summary conclusions for this area:

☐ unacceptable   ☐ marginal   ☐ acceptable   ☐ exceptional

Comments _____

D. Criterion _____	
Questions _____	
_____	
_____	
_____	
_____	

Summary conclusions for this area:

☐ unacceptable   ☐ marginal   ☐ acceptable   ☐ exceptional

Comments _____

IV. INTERVIEW SUMMARY

Overall assessment of this candidate:

A. **Competencies/Skills** (experience needed to perform this job)

☐ unacceptable   ☐ marginal   ☐ acceptable   ☐ exceptional

_____
_____

B. **Compatibility** (fit with job)—Do you feel this candidate's personality matches the demands of this position (for example, ability to be detailed, to work under pressure, to juggle several balls at one time, etc.)? Supporting comments:

_____
_____

C. **Chemistry** (fit with company)—Do you feel the candidate will "fit" well within the company (be accepted and work well with other staff, accept our way of doing things, etc.)? Supporting comments:

_____
_____

D. **Character**—Do you feel this person's value system, morals, ethics, and commitment are compatible with our corporate purpose and values? Supporting comments:

_____

_____

_____

V. CONCLUSIONS

_____

_____

_____

_____

_____

_____

_____

VI. REFERENCES

A. Name _____ Phone (____) _____ (h)
Professional relationship_____ (____) _____ (o)

Title/Company _____

B. Name _____ Phone (____) _____ (h)
Professional relationship_____ (____) _____ (o)

Title/Company _____

C. Name _____ Phone (____) _____ (h)
Professional relationship_____ (____) _____ (o)

Title/Company _____

D. Name _____ Phone (____) _____ (h)
Professional relationship_____ (____) _____ (o)

Title/Company _____

Specific issues for references

_____

_____

_____

_____

_____

_____

Notes

Chapter One—Who Hired This Person, Anyway?
1. Peter F. Drucker, *The Effective Executive* (New York: Harper & Row, 1966), page 113.
2. Leroy Eims, *The Lost Art of Disciple Making* (Colorado Springs, CO: NavPress, 1978), page 38.

Chapter Two—Counting the Cost
1. Peter F. Drucker, *The Effective Executive* (New York: Harper & Row, 1966), page 33.
2. Bradford D. Smart, *Selection Interviewing* (New York: John Wiley & Sons, 1983), page 4.
3. Peter F. Drucker, *Adventures of a Bystander* (New York: Harper & Row, 1978), page 280.
4. Charles A. Garfield, *Peak Performers* (New York: William Morrow & Company, 1986), page 194.
5. Doug Sherman and William Hendricks, *Your Work Matters to God* (Colorado Springs, CO: NavPress, 1987), page 87.
6. Sherman and Hendricks, page 131.

Chapter Three—It's Worth the Walk
1. Ron Zemke and Dick Schaaf, *The Service Edge* (New York: New American Library, 1989), page 118.
2. Pricilla Hayes Petty, "Behind the Lines at Procter and Gamble," *Harvard Business Review*, November-December 1985, page 78.
3. Harvard Business School Case Study, 9-382-092, Rev. June 1982.

Chapter Four—Six Steps to Staffing Excellence
1. Adapted from Wayne F. Cascio, *Applied Psychology in Personnel Management*, 2d ed. (Reston, VA: Reston Publishing Co., 1982), page 217.
2. Peter F. Drucker, *The Effective Executive* (New York: Harper & Row, 1966), page 144.
3. As cited in Peter M. Senge, *The Fifth Discipline* (New York: Doubleday/Currency, 1990), page 168.
4. Senge, page 168.
5. Drucker, page 89.

Chapter Five—Caution: Handle with Prayer
1. E. M. Bounds, *Power Through Prayer* (Grand Rapids, MI: Baker, 1972), page 5.

Chapter Six—Preliminary Caution:
Those Loathsome Legal Issues
1. *USA Today*, January 7, 1992. A fifty-three-year-old woman who had worked for the airline twenty-seven years claimed she wasn't considered for a promotion because of previous open-heart surgery. She was later fired in a reorganization. She sued the company and won, including a fine of $125,000 against the chairman of the board.
2. Like most professions, the legal community is highly specialized. If your organizational attorney is not well versed in labor law, then I recommend that you build a relationship with one who is grounded technically in this field.
3. *Griggs v. Duke Power Company*, U.S. Reports, U.S. Government Printing Office, volume 401, pages 424-432 (1971).
4. Wendell Bird, *Exempt Organizations and Discrimination*, volume 1 (Englewood Cliffs, NJ: Research Institute of America, 1986), page 3299.
5. Martin Bowers, a former managing director of McKinsey & Company and author of *The Will to Manage*, as quoted in Terence E. Deal and Allen A. Kennedy, *Corporate Cultures* (Reading, MA: Addison-Wesley, 1982), page 4.

Chapter Seven—Defining the Task
1. Sun Tzu, *The Art of War*, ed. James Clavell (New York: Delacorte Press, 1983), page 32.
2. Peter Drucker, *The Effective Executive* (New York: Harper & Row, 1966), pages 78-79.
3. Robert Half, *On Hiring* (New York: Plume, 1985), page 9.

Chapter Eight—Describing the Person
1. Robert E. Coleman, *The Master Plan of Evangelism* (Old Tappan, NJ: Revell, 1987), page 79.

2. For those who would like to explore the topic of spiritual gifts in more detail I recommend any of the following books: D. A. Carson, *Showing the Spirit* (Grand Rapids, MI: Baker House Books, 1987); Richard B. Gaffin, Jr., *Perspective on Pentecost* (Phillipsburg, NJ: Presbyterian & Reformed, 1979); J. I. Packer, *Keep in Step with the Spirit* (Terrytown, NY: Chosen Books, 1984).

Chapter Nine—Call: Conviction, Confusion, and Controversy

1. Gary Friesen, *Decision Making and the Will of God* (Portland, OR: Multnomah, 1980), page 313.
2. Friesen, page 314.
3. Martin Clark, "The Christian's Decision Manual," in *Choosing Your Career* (Phillipsburg, NJ: Presbyterian & Reformed, 1981), page 92.
4. Introduction, "Treatise on Good Works," in *Works of Martin Luther* (Philadelphia, 1915), I, 179, as excerpted from Robert Michaelsen, "Changes in the Puritan Concept of Calling or Vocation," *The New England Quarterly*, page 315.
5. Michaelsen, page 317.
6. Michaelsen, page 318.
7. Michaelsen, page 319.
8. Michaelsen, pages 319-324.
9. Os Guinness, "Dreamers of the Day—The Recovery of the Dynamic of Calling," address given in 1989. Used with permission.
10. Guinness, "Dreamers of the Day."
11. Oswald Chambers, *So Send I You* (Fort Washington, PA: Christian Literature Crusade, 1964), page 12.
12. Michaelsen, page 326.
13. God may call some but not necessarily all. The rest of us must depend on what Os Guinness would call "enterprise." For example, we have no record that those individuals in the parable of the talents (Matthew 25:14-30) were told what to do. Each had to rely on enterprise—his own good judgment, skills, and knowledge of his master's expectations.
14. Chambers, pages 12-13.
15. Some counseled me not to mix the terms *call* and *calling* with *purpose*. In their eyes the terms are practically synonymous. I agree, if not synonymous, then they are first cousins. However, others use both terms depending on the context or subject of their effort. When talking about ministry, jobs, or occupation, most seem to use call; when dealing with personal priorities and direction, the term *purpose* tends to be more prevalent. As I define purpose here, universal purpose might be equivalent to the "general calling." Unique purpose might equate to the "particular call" espoused by the Puritans.
16. Patrick M. Morley, *The Man in the Mirror* (Brentwood, TN: Wolgemuth & Hyatt), page 59.
17. Doug Sherman and William Hendricks, *Your Work Matters to God*

(Colorado Springs, CO: NavPress, 1987), page 143.
18. Pat Morley presents an excellent step-by-step process for discerning your life purpose in *The Man in the Mirror*. Another book that deals well with the subject from a secular perspective is *The Seven Habits of an Effective Person* by Steven Covey.
19. Sherman and Hendricks, pages 142-143.
20. Friesen, page 88.

Chapter Ten—What I Look For in a Candidate
1. J. Oswald Sanders, *Spiritual Leadership*, (Chicago: Moody, 1967), page 20. This book is an excellent reference for lists of the spiritual qualities we should look for in Christian leaders in any endeavor.
2. Paul J. Brouwer, "The Power to See Ourselves," *Harvard Business Review*, November-December 1964, as cited in *Executive Development: Part I* published by *Harvard Business Review*, page 127. This is an excellent article for anyone interested in personal growth and is available from the *Review* in reprint form, number 64602.
3. Brouwer, page 127.
4. Sanders, page 26.
5. Michael Nash, *Making People Productive* (San Francisco, CA: Jossey-Bass Publishers, 1985), page 105.
6. As cited in Nash, pages 40-41.
7. John P. Kotter, *A Force for Change* (New York: Free Press, 1990), page 111.

Chapter Eleven—Evaluating the Candidates—The Process Overview
1. Chapters 18 and 19 will cover the topic of how to find and recruit candidates in some detail.
2. Arthur H. Bell, *The Complete Manager's Guide to Interviewing* (Homewood, IL: Dow Jones-Irwin, 1989), page 1.
3. John D. Drake, *Effective Interviewing* (New York: Anacom, 1982), page 9.

Chapter Thirteen—"Inter" Viewing: The Art of Inner Viewing
1. John D. Drake, *Effective Interviewing* (New York: Amacom, 1982), pages 9-10.
2. Bradford D. Smart, *Selection Interviewing* (New York: Wiley & Sons, 1983), pages 64-65.
3. Jerry A. Dibble and Beverly Y. Langford, *Communication Skills and Strategies* (Atlanta, GA: Dibble & Langford, 1990), page 14.
4. Arthur H. Bell, *The Complete Manager's Guide to Interviewing* (Homewood, IL: Dow Jones-Irwin, 1989), page 23.
5. Note: The legal considerations will vary as we move from the nonprofit organization with a religious charter to the corporation. We covered the legal issues of people decisions in some detail in

chapter 6.
6. Bell, page 81.
7. Wayne F. Cascio, *Applied Psychology in Personnel Management*, 2d ed. (Reston, VA: Reston Publishing Co., 1982), page 197.
8. Smart, page 8.
9. Smart, page 96.
10. Cascio, page 204.
11. Michael Nash, *Making People Productive* (San Francisco, CA: Jossey-Bass Publishers, 1985), pages 46-47.

Chapter Fourteen—No One from New York Could Do This Job
1. Richard F. Olson, *Managing the Interview* (New York: Wiley, 1980), page 135.
2. Wayne F. Cascio, *Applied Psychology in Personnel Management*, 2d ed. (Reston, VA: Reston Publishing Company, 1982), page 318.
3. Cascio, page 198.
4. Cascio, page 198.
5. Cascio, page 198.
6. A. D. DeNisi and T. B. Shaw, "Investigations of the Uses of Self-Report of Abilities," *Journal of Applied Psychology* (1977), pages 62, 641-644. As cited in Michael Nash, *Making People Productive* (San Francisco, CA: Jossey-Bass Publishers, 1985), page 40.
7. For some very practical help in a church/search-committee setting see Robert W. Dingman, *The Complete Search Committee Guidebook* (Ventura, CA: Regal, 1989). Bob is a committed Christian and an experienced search executive.

Chapter Fifteen—In Reference to . . .
1. Jerry A. Dibble and Beverly Y. Langford, *Communication Skills and Strategies* (Atlanta, GA: Dibble & Langford, 1990), page 14.
2. Robert Half, *On Hiring* (New York: Plume, 1985), page 153.
3. Robert J. Thornton, "I Can't Recommend This Candidate Too Highly," *Chronicle of Higher Education* (1987). Used with permission. Refer also to his book *Lexicon of Intentionally Ambiguous Recommendations* (Deephaven, MN: Meadowbrook Publishers, 1988).

Chapter Sixteen—First, Let Them Be Tested
1. For a straightforward, readable summary of the beginnings of psychological testing see Ann Anastasi, *Psychological Testing*, 4th ed. (New York: Macmillan, 1976).
2. Anastasi, page 3.
3. Wayne F. Cascio, *Applied Psychology in Personnel Management*, 2d ed. (Reston, VA: Reston Publishing Co., 1982), page 130.
4. Anastasi, page 27.
5. One of the most comprehensive classification systems for psychological tests is found in the *Mental Measurements Yearbook*. This

volume, published yearly for professionals in the field of testing, organizes tests used in industry, education, and psychology into fifteen categories.

6. P. J. Atarian, "Early Recollections: Predictors of Vocational Choice," *Journal of Individual Psychology* (1978), B4(1), pages 56-62. As cited in Michael Nash, *Making People Productive* (San Francisco, CA: Jossey-Bass Publishers, 1985), page 38.

7. Nash, pages 54-55.

8. Nash, page 41.

9. Paul A. Mauger, "Specialized Personality Inventories for Christians?" This paper appeared in William J. Donaldson, *Research in Mental Health & Religious Behavior: Introduction to Research in the Integration of Christianity and the Behavioral Sciences* (Atlanta: The Psychological Studies Institute, 1976), page 420.

Dr. Mauger used the MMPI and PRF instruments in his research. He observed, "On the basis of these results, it is reasonable to conclude that secular personality inventories can be used with Christian people. The norms for the MMPI and PRF are appropriate for Christian populations."

10. This letter was written by Dr. Bryan Crenshaw of Greenville, SC. Used with permission.

Chapter Seventeen—Making the Decision

1. Charles H. Kepner and Benjamin B. Tregoe, *The New Rational Manager* (Princeton, NJ: Princeton Research Press, 1981), page 88.

2. Although I've attempted to make this illustration as real as possible, it is still only an illustration and will be lacking in detail and even consistency under close scrutiny. The purpose, as in most examples used throughout the book, is to present the concept in principle, allowing you to practice the level of detail your particular situation warrants.

3. This chapter uses an approach (i.e., a matrix for decision making) that's been described in a lot of different books over the years. But none have done it better than Charles H. Kepner and Benjamin B Tregoe, *The New Rational Manager* (Princeton, NJ: Princeton Research Press, 1981). I highly recommend this book to anyone confronted with important decisions. They would advocate giving a ten to the best alternative for any given criterion.

4. Peter F. Drucker, *The Effective Executive* (New York: Harper & Row, 1966), page 32.

5. Drucker, page 33.

6. Drucker, page 81.

7. Wayne F. Cascio, *Applied Psychology in Personnel Management*, 2d ed. (Reston, VA: Reston Publishing Co., 1982), page 198.

8. Cascio, page 200.

9. Drucker, pages 71-72.

Chapter Eighteen—The Chase and the Challenge

1. Robert Half, *On Hiring* (New York: Plume, 1985), page 49. Half's book is short, readable, and comprehensive and covers the entire hiring process. I highly recommend it.
2. Half, page 57.
3. John A. Byrne, *The Headhunters* (New York: Macmillan, 1986), page 2.
4. Because I'm writing to executives in both the corporate and ministry arenas, I think some explanation may be needed here. Team Resources was one of the pioneers in developing search services for Christian ministries. In order to minimize cost to the ministry, we perform this service on a consulting basis rather than for a fixed fee. I do not believe ministries have competitors. We're all involved in God's Great Commission. To that end, we view our search efforts as spiritual; we attempt to serve the client ministry in finding God's person for that position. We do not try to get people to move from one ministry to another. If we see individuals who match the criteria and for whom the new position may be a growth opportunity, we usually get permission from the CEO of that ministry to approach the candidate. I've never had one say no. Often, even when a candidate calls us to express interest in a position, we ask the candidate to contact his or her manager before proceeding.
5. John Scully, *Odyssey* (New York: Harper and Row, 1987), page 90.

Chapter Nineteen—Staffing the Kingdom:
Recruiting for Ministries and Missions

1. James Davison Hunter, *Evangelicalism: The Coming Generation* (Chicago: University of Chicago Press, 1987).
2. Warren Bennis and Burt Names, *Leaders* (New York: Harper & Row, 1985), pages 89-93.
3. John Scully, *Odyssey* (New York: Harper & Row, 1987), page 90.
4. Bennis and Names, page 93.
5. Douglas Hyde, *Dedication and Leadership* (Notre Dame, IN: University of Notre Dame Press, 1966), page 18.
6. Hyde, page 32.
7. Johnston M. Cheney, *The Life of Christ in Stereo* (Portland, OR: Western Baptist Press, 1969), pages 242-243.

Chapter Twenty—The Most Important People Decision

1. Footnote to Matthew 1:21 in *NIV Study Bible*: "*Jesus* is the Greek form of *Joshua*, which means *the LORD saves.*"
2. Paul Little, *How to Give Away Your Faith* (Downers Grove, IL: Inter-Varsity Press, 1966), page 56.
3. R. C. Sproul, *Following Christ* (Wheaton, IL: Tyndale House Publishers, Inc., 1991), pages 78-88.

4. Sproul, page 87.

5. Jim Petersen, *Living Proof* (Colorado Springs, CO: NavPress, 1989), page 173.

Personality Inventories
1. Isabel Briggs Myers and Mary H. McCaulley, *A Guide to the Development and Use of the Myers-Briggs Type Indicator* (Palo Alto, CA: Consulting Psychologists Press, 1985), page 1.

Additional Sources on Interviewing

Bell, Arthur H., Ph.D. *The Complete Manager's Guide to Interviewing*. Homewood, IL: Down Jones-Irwin, 1989.

This book is a solid "basics" reference to interviewing. It reads easily and integrates a lot of the issues surrounding the interview. For example, I found the section outlining the different roles the interviewer plays over the course of the interview to be particularly interesting. Another section on evaluating the nonverbal signals from the interviewee is very relevant as well.

Drake, John D. *Effective Interviewing*. New York: ANACOM, 1982.

This book introduces a number of helpful concepts in interviewing. Drake suggests the use of the "hypothesis method," a system of interpretation that assists the interviewer in understanding the underlying meaning of what he or she heard in the interview.

Smart, Bradford D. *Selection Interviewing*. New York: John Wiley & Sons, 1983.

Dr. Smart, a management psychologist, integrates solid principles with a lot of practical help and examples. The book is a rich resource of reference material and examples you can easily adapt to your specific situation. Smart includes a number of helpful appendixes. One section lists over a hundred selection criteria to assist anyone in defining and articulating the qualities sought in candidates.

Smart, Bradford D. *The Smart Interviewer.* New York: John Wiley & Sons, 1989.

This is a newer, more condensed version of the above book. It focuses to a great extent on the "how to's" of selection interviewing.

Author

Pat MacMillan is president of Team Resources, a consulting firm for team and organizational development. Founded in 1980, Team Resources has offices in Atlanta and Colorado Springs and serves clients in both the corporate and not-for-profit sectors.

Pat has authored numerous articles on management topics and serves as an adjunct Professor of Management at Reformed Theological Seminary in Jackson, Mississippi. He resides in Atlanta with his wife, Jill, and three children: Becki, Jennifer, and Matthew.